CINDERELLA IS A MAN

A Picaresque
Passage
To Serenity

An autobiography by
R. Eric Gustafson

I have tried to be accurate in telling my story,
but names have been changed on a few occasions
to protect the closets of some participants.

Published by W A M Press,
P.O. Box 16, Peapack, NJ 07977

©1998 R. Eric Gustafson

ISBN 0-9668396-1-7

Library of Congress Catalog card number 98-90891

Designed and typeset by
AAH Graphics, Inc., Fort Valley, VA 22652

Cover designed by Stephen R. Hunter

Printed in Canada

DEDICATION

For all the fairy godmothers of both sexes who have
enriched my life with magic and loving care, especially
Lila, Ysabel, Dorothy, Nina, Eloise, and O.M. Miller
affectionally known as "Uncle Monkey."

ACKNOWLEDGMENTS

Sincerest gratitude to Nathalie Marshall, Lotte Lichtblau, Frank Daykin, Susan Boyton, Carol Easton, Jimmy McCourt, Ginny Dustin, Bruce Whitacre, David Eddleman, and Marion Filler for their encouragement and advice; Barbara Palfy for her astute copyediting; Stephen and Ann Hunter at AAH Graphics for their insightful, tasteful attentions; and to the many personalities that helped catalyze events in my perigrinations.

CONTENTS

ILLUSTRATIONS

PROLOGUE

The dazzling morning sunshine stung my eyes, adding to the general discomfort I felt from my "last fling" the night before. Boarding the small plane in Los Angeles, I tried to summon courage. I was about to commit myself to the Betty Ford Center near Palm Desert. Telling myself that many people had done this before me, I felt enormous apprehension grip me. Elizabeth Taylor's words, "Get your ass over to Betty Ford's," gave me some reassurance. I needed something more than the alcohol I was used to medicating myself with, and I needed a rest from the treadmill of alcohol abuse.

Swollen from decades of excessive drinking and inflamed by the previous night's indulgences, I fingered the silver flask full of Stolichnaya that was safely tucked in my inside jacket pocket. Once the plane took off, I would have a quick final slug—and, if I could sneak it, another in the airport men's room at Palm Desert before being whisked off by the Betty Ford attendant to who knows what fate.

When I was born in the mid-1930s, America was emerging from the depths of the Great Depression. The Time of Radio colored my early days. I grew up listening to *The Shadow*, *The Green Hornet* and *The Lone Ranger*. One of the most popular radio serials was *Our Gal Sunday*. How I related to that program. It began with a man's voice intoning, "Can a young girl from a small mining town in Colorado find happiness as the wife of a wealthy and titled Englishman?" followed by a crescendo of music from Tchaikovsky's *"Pathétique"* Symphony. My heartbeat increased as my imagination conjured up the dramatic immensity of this situation. I loved the soul-wrenching music. I identified with the heroine.

My family was not poor. However, we lived a significantly simpler life than the people I saw in the movies and on the grand streets of Manhattan, where I was taken occasionally. "Can a young boy from the northeast corner of the Bronx find happiness in the company of the rich and famous?" Could my fantasies become a reality? I knew little of the louche lowlife that swam, indistinguishable, in that pool along with them. Shoulder to fin with the very people whose images fueled my childhood fantasies, my experiences shredded that gossamer fabric that inevitably clothes such innocent dreams.

Decades of picaresque mis-adventres were to pass, leaving me bruised and confused. Once, with confidence bolstered by a champagne haze, I recklessly invited Rita Hayworth to participate in an impromptu Mickey Rooney–Judy Garland MGM floor show for the enjoyment of a celebrity-filled wedding reception. But that was not an MGM musical, and there was no miracle forthcoming. Alone on the dance floor, we were both too drunk to do more than turn and shuffle. My impetuous daydream evaporated into a singular, devastating embarrassment. And the band played on.

My mega-fantasies, played out on an international scene and fueled by alcohol, might be compiled in the annals of "Eric in search of himself." If my narrative seems like a recitation of celebrity names and places, that is what it is and what I thought I wanted. Merely being around celebrity, rubbing elbows, was sufficient for reaching my high. Often, when it was established that I was desired, that was enough. It was the chase, not the consummation that interested me. Like alcohol, the high was transient. There was need to go dipping again and again.

Years of trial and error taught me that life is like an ellipse. I often circle back to a starting point, but with a different point of view. Sometimes I do not know that I am back at the same point and have to flounder until I learn the lesson contained in it. In the peripatetic quest for self-fulfillment, I was brought back again and again to the same point: how to connect my life to my dreams. This is no small feat while living in a speeding world that has all too little time or energy for dreams.

The arts are the seashore in my dissipation and recovery, a healing, vibrant road to redemption. Bolstered by a lively sense of spirituality, I can relate my story with the fervent hope that others can benefit and blossom in the Garden of Life.

Cinderella Is a Man

Chapter 1

Once Upon a Time

Once upon a time, in a faraway land called the Bronx, a beautiful babe was born. At that time, the highest-paid film star in Hollywood was Shirley Temple, and my mother decided to turn her beautiful babe into her very own doll, made to resemble the little cinematic darling. Ebba Marie Gustafson (née Johnson) made me her object of escape, her only solace in a threatening, uncomfortable world. Combing out my "baloney" curls, dressing me in cunning outfits, Mother became a young girl playing with a doll. I sported those curls for a very long time. Shirley had nothing on me when I was dressed like the doll my mother really wanted. Thus, my earliest memories are entwined with fantasy, glamor and make-believe, and my drinking career ran the gamut from Shirley Temple to Mae West.

My parents came from Sweden, each at different times, meeting in New York, where they married. Then the Great Depression hit America. Life was difficult but they survived. Mother was disappointed in her marriage and her life, despite the distractions of the two firstborn children. Not only did they need care, but my robust father also made his demands. Too often he went elsewhere, to play in more amusing fields.

I recall my mother holding me close to her large, pendulous breasts as we snoozed in her large bed when I was two years old. I remember her warmth, which gave me a sense of security and protection. Her once fine figure evident in old photographs had

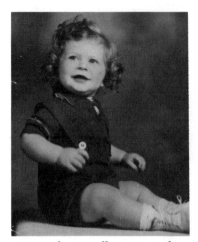

Mother's Doll at 11 months

filled out. She adopted the rigid, disapproving attitudes of her mother and her grandmother before, wielding Lutheran piety as retribution to those impious and erring in their ways. After years of ceaseless nagging, my gregarious father eventually received her righteous revenge. Lutheranism serves many functions other than the adoration of God. We children were given strict guidelines for behavior. Sunday School and church on Sundays were mandatory. Mother used religion as a stance against sex, drink and having any sort of good time. In other words, my father was to be ashamed of himself. Life was not the ribald party he enjoyed when he was not working to provide for us.

Eric Theodore Gustafson worked hard in the construction business and he let off steam by drinking with the men who worked for him. Often away from home for long periods, he found people and places to relieve him of work's pressures. When he did come home, there was spontaneous loud

Dad in Royal Swedish Cavalry

singing and rye-induced exuberance, which usually found a
cold, wet blanket of disapproval
in Mother. How long-suffering
she was! Good and seemingly
devout, she raised her children
in the fine Lutheran tradition
while helping the poor and
needy. Their payment, and her
reward, was their listening to
her problems. "Mrs. Santa
Claus" needed approbation
and adulation, even from
strangers.

Mother guided all my
early growing up. I learned to
tend my own garden around

Playhouse for Helen and me.

my playhouse in the back of our property. The tiny white cottage with red
trim had working doors and windows,
built by one of Dad's colleagues. It was
placed on a foundation in the back garden under large oak trees, a haven for
my impersonation of a busy home-
maker. What a delightful retreat for my
younger sister, Helen Marie, and me in
which to indulge our children's fantasies—imaginary tea parties with real
cookies freshly made by Mother, windows that had to be washed and holly-
hocks in profusion around our house.
On a fine day, Helen and I sometimes
packed peanut butter and jelly sand-
wiches and sat under a tree overlooking

Young Ebba

the adjacent field, where an old Italian farmer plowed with his mule. Can anyone imagine a scene like that in the Bronx today?

I learned to cook, clean, launder and be an adept housekeeper. Forget about the Boy Scouts! My place was in the home, both playhouse and big house. I remember an occasional concerned comment from both my father and my older brother, George Edward. They thought I was getting too sissyish. That made me very uneasy, and happily my mother fended off any interference with my development as her pampered creation.

What a *good* boy I was when I went to school. Although very shy with my peers, I anxiously sought approbation from the women teachers, my surrogate mothers. Being teacher's pet was my classroom goal, apple-polishing an avid art. Once, my beloved Mrs. Herman, who was pretty, charmingly spoken and very complimentary to me, announced that she was looking for a woman to take care of her house and help prepare some food. Did any of us children know of such a person? My hand went up in a heartbeat. Yes, my mother could do that. I loved the notion of a closer bond to Mrs. Herman, who was many of the things I wanted my mother to be. She had such a cultured manner and was so trim and enchanting. Surely, my mother could have kept her figure like Mrs. Herman's; she could have spent some time learning the things in which my teacher seemed so fluent.

I spent years admiring Mrs. Herman, as my mother became deeply entrenched in the Herman household. What started as a part-time helper situation became a full-time occupation. My mother, who often felt unappreciated at home, tended the Herman children and cooked terrific meals for the Doctor and his family. She took them goodies by the cart: cakes, cookies and handmade items that she sewed, crocheted or knitted for them. My jealousy was aroused, but her absence allowed Helen and me completely unsupervised free time. Mrs. Herman always held me up to her son and daughter as a role model. I had excellent posture, wore clothes with panache (thanks to my early movie play-acting), showed interest in classical music and read worthwhile books.

Years after her death, her son David confided to me that he had always daydreamed of my mother being his, as she was always so kind and sweet-tempered. "Did she ever lose her temper?" he asked me. In surprise, I mentioned how much I would have loved to have had his mother for my mother. I exposed the dark side of my mother's personality: her compulsive field-marshal authoritarianism, her willfulness and guile in gaining sympathy through her tales of long-suffering woe. Sugaring all this with mountains of delicious edibles she created for the sympathetic listener, only the hardest of curmudgeons could not empathize with the miserable woman with the heart of gold.

My favorite activity was going to the movies. World War II had started, so the newsreels were full of Nazis and Japs. Everyone hissed from their seats. Most thrilling were the adventure films, with stars like Maureen O'Hara and Yvonne de Carlo playing princesses in distress in Arabic settings and Turhan Bey or Victor Mature as their burly heroes. Indelible in my memory are the black-and-white films set either in England or on enormous estates in America (ignoring any recent reality of the Depression). I loved the marble entrance halls, the pretty clothes, manners and speech. White-gloved butlers epitomized the right way to live, in other words, the life for me. I realized a terrible mistake had been made when I went home to my family. The contrast was glaring. Even at that early age I knew where Robert Eric really belonged.

While Mother was busy tending to the Hermans, my sister and I had no one to prevent us from attending our temple of life: the Silver Screen. I remember sometimes going every day. As a result, many terrific costume dramas were reenacted on the lawn in our back garden. I made Helen play the supporting roles and the bad guys who came to steal the Princess. I rummaged through my older sister Mae Florence's closet for wardrobe or

borrowed bedspreads or curtains. I had to be the youngest transvestite actress in the Bronx during World War II!

Our early movie-going days included an 86th Street theater
in Manhattan with Mother, after her chiropractic appointment on
Lexington Avenue near 90th Street. At that movie house, vaude-
ville was featured between films: comedians, animal acts, magi-
cians and even strippers, at whom we were all shocked. Every
year around Christmas, Olga Peterson, a family friend, took
Helen and me to Radio City Music Hall for the film and stage
extravaganza that included the Rockettes and the Christmas
show. The enormity of Radio City was amazing, thrilling, as were
the live stage presentations and their awesome special effects:
angels, dancers and everything larger-than-life. I loved being
overwhelmed by the grand-scale theatrics. My imagination was
fired up with this theatrical universe that seemed endless in proportion and beauty.

Christmastime
meant playing with the
old, heavy, metal Lionel
electric train set up
under the Christmas
tree. Glögg (Swedish
wine punch spiked with
100-proof alcohol) and
other alcoholic celebra-
tions were taken by all
the grown-ups except
Mother, who naturally
did not drink. Then,
there was the midnight
service—if there had
not been too much acri-
mony over dinner. My
lovely countertenor har-

Sister Flo's confirmation:
George, Mom, Dad, and Flo (rear),
Bob and Helen (front).

Young marrieds with dog, Buck, in canoe.

monizing with the other carolers created consternation in Father. I think he believed everyone was looking at us because of my high-pitched angelic voice. Often, he did not manage to attend the service. He was left behind in a deep stupor, which relieved Mother.

Father's raucous homecomings became more and more abusive. We children knew that parental fighting was part of life. If Father came home sober and in good humor, he would enjoy himself by singing a song. One of his favorites was "If I had the wings of an angel, over these prison walls I would fly." He loved to sing, dance and drink, the songs becoming louder and more frequent in direct proportion to the amount of alcohol consumed. We were counseled by Mom that Dad would probably come home drunk again. A tirade to us about his drinking and his careless disregard for his family was a warm-up for his appearance. Sometimes, Dad came home in the nicest of humors, which was not allowed to last as Mom started the needling. Many times, he was not drunk at all, but after continuous rebuking from his wife, he would reach for the bottle. Then, the well-known battle of the wills would begin. We knew that physical violence was a result of shouting matches between the two. Many times my older brother or sister intervened when the fisticuffs began, or Mother's carving knife was drawn. I heard screams, crashing about and, eventually, silence. Sometimes Father would drive off in a rage, resulting in car accidents or disappearances for hours or days.

After my older sister (through marriage) and then my brother escaped from home, my younger sister was sometimes enlisted to join Mom in her car search for Father. Once, Helen discovered him in his car with a woman who had been a family friend for years. Even at that age, I knew that the experience was emotionally damaging for her. I could not bear the shouting, violence and total disharmony of home life. I never intervened as my brother and sisters did. Tearfully, I huddled behind closed doors or exited through a window, hiding away in quiet spots outdoors. In despair, my utter abhorrence of violence firmly established itself. The fights were usually about control. Mother felt in competition with Father. When she worked for the Hermans, she felt she was a family breadwinner as well as having a place where she was obviously appreciated. Father's construction skills were challenged by her talents. She felt obliged to use tools to fix everything herself, her expertise extended to carpentry, plumbing, even doctoring.

We spent the summer of 1942 in Elmira, New York, where Dad was building a school. One fine day, we went to a nearby farm to visit the man who had built our playhouse. His son Kenneth invited me to join a few other kids jumping from the hayloft in the barn. It was an impressive height and I tried not to show fear, especially as I admired Kenneth, who was a couple of years older. I wanted to fit in and to have him as a friend. I could not identify it then but I had a crush on him. Later, we played tag. I was "it," and had to catch someone else. A door to a tool room had been slammed shut, with a toolbox slid in front of it. I pushed open the door and tumbled over the box. The jumping and/or the fall soon gave me sharp abdominal pains. My mother, by now an expert medical practitioner, put me to bed and gave me tablespoons of blackberry brandy—her old-country cure for the grippe. Pain continued the next and a series of days, with the cure swallowed dutifully. Not until I turned green and started to urinate blood did Mother call a physician. I remember the handsome young doctor and his alarming rudeness to Mother. He laid into her for taking such a foolish chance with my life. The doctor claimed I could have died days earlier, as he telephoned the hospital to prepare an emergency operation. Then he carried me, bundled into a blanket, into his green coupe (with rumble seat) and sped away, Mother following in her car. A burst appendix had tied around my intestines, calling for fast action, not blackberry brandy. That may have marked the beginning of my drinking career. To my great annoyance, tubes were shoved up my nose. I tore them out shouting obscenities to the doctor. I remember Mother's mortification on hearing her darling son use such expletives! She claimed innocence as to where I might have heard such words.

Another memory from my "summer of '42" is of sitting in the wheelchair in the garden of my parents' home in Elmira, knitting in the sun. A stray dog wandered by and lifted his leg on my blanket. My sense of propriety was sullied. Why should a sweet child engaged in the charming occupation of knitting be treated in this manner? Certainly, my mother would never have tolerated it. The outrage remains fresh in my mind. Helpless, I suffered the indignity of being pissed on. I kept the squares I knitted that season. Decades later, Mother crocheted them into a pillow cover and gave them to me. They are a reminder of the maternal tutelage in my youth.

Life at P.S. 78 continued with a few outstanding memories. One morning I heard on the radio, before walking to school, that President Franklin D. Roosevelt had died. I couldn't wait to share the news with the teacher. Shortly after arriving in class, I raised my hand and blurted the sad news. Teacher must have been very emotionally attached to F.D.R. Rather than thank me for sharing the information, I was scolded, made to feel stupid. I was

unaware that everyone must have already heard the news and
been affected by it. How very naive of me to imagine that I was
bringing world-gripping information. Had this been so, I would
have curried extra approbation from the teacher.

Winning the music award for creating the best model symphony orchestra was a happy achievement. It was my sixth year in
elementary school. With painstaking care, I cut from a printed
sheet a picture of each member of the orchestra holding his
instrument. With straight pins, I secured them in place on a cardboard stage. Many hours of concentrated work produced a handsome full orchestra on a stage made from a cardboard box
carefully trimmed. I still have the book of composers' lives retold
for young children, inscribed to me as a reward.

By sixth grade, I had become the butt of the school bullies'
taunts. I really was too goody-goody. I avoided certain exits from
school, or routes home that passed dangerous encounter places.
Often, I was sheltered by a knot of other kids or by my sister
Helen, who had grown into a bit of a tomboy. She and I used to
get into scrapes that were structured very much like those of our
parents. We occasionally resorted to physical abuse, but I was
bigger and stronger, so poor Helen got the worst of it. We played
out our parents' drama. Too bad we did not change the script.
Helen went on to be our mother's puppet/imitator, adopting similar habits and behaviors. There is a photo of my great-grandmother by a spinning wheel in Sweden. It is scary how much my
grandmother Thili Johnson looked like her, how much Mother
modeled herself after her humorless mother and how Helen
became trapped in the same blood memory.

I do not believe Mother was equipped to handle life in the
United States; she relied so much on her mother, whose narrow,
mean-spirited temperament reflected in turn her own mother's
grim side. Mother was fearful, clinging with determination to her
peasant mentality. Relying on conservative theology and Swedish
traditions, she was recalcitrant to change. Being Swedish, the

Great-grandmother at loom.

Three generations: Blood memory.

daylight deprivation of the country contributing to the brooding pessimism of the natives, gave her a formula for coping. No matter how much Father made or how well we could afford to live, that genetic memory running through the maternal side of her family seemed to determine the boundaries of her expectations.

Summers, Mother packed up Helen and me in her automobile for the long ride to her mother's home near Lynn, Massachusetts. That was before superhighways and urban bypasses; it took many more hours than it would today. Just having to creep through Providence, Rhode Island, was a long, hot ordeal. When we got to the large gray house on the hill outside Lynn, we were pleased to be freed from the constraints of the car. The dreaded moment was seeing our grandmother. She had a daunting habit of twisting my ear as she admonished me upon arrival never to use too much toilet paper—it would clog her plumbing. What a way to greet a grandchild! I feared her and kept a polite distance whenever possible. The great part of being there was a wonderful hill full of fruit trees and bushes that Helen and I enjoyed picking to our hearts' content. There were also lots of blueberry bushes on the other side of the road. The hill itself presented endless pleasure for rolling down or running around.

My cousin Ernie Larsen, a year older than I, was a great baseball fan. There was a ball field at the foot of my grandmother's property. With greatest reluctance I was pressured into attending, and once or twice I was even embarrassed into playing. Once, I played first base. I turned my head to look at something (probably a butterfly!), then I heard my name. I turned and received a very hard baseball squarely between the eyes. A broken nose and black eye were my rewards for pretending I could join the boys in a game of baseball. From then on, I would occasionally feign interest in attending a Yankees game with schoolmates. Clearly, active participation in team sports was to be avoided. Only individual sports interested me: skiing, figure skating, hiking and swimming. I was not one of the boys, not one of the team. I did admire some of them though, perhaps too much.

Ernie and I were always being compared by Mother and her sister Mae. Ernie was very different. He excelled in baseball but was far from being as bright or as well turned out as I was. In my favor, I had all those valuable role models from the movies and radio to draw on. I found Kenny (from hayloft jumping) and the other sons of family friends fun to be with, but I never felt comfortable with my cousin. He did not stimulate me and I had already adopted a patronizing attitude toward that side of the family. Mistrust and disdain were what my mother felt about her sister, especially as Mae lived so close to their mother. Early on, my siblings and I were warned about the deviousness of the relatives. Competition was continuous. We were to believe Mother worked harder, suffered more and was more generous than her sister. When my grandmother died, I remember Mother rushing to Lynn to hide and lay claim to as much as possible. That act was repeated by my sister Helen when Mother died, much to the hurt of George, Flo and me.

It became evident to me while growing up that the manly thing to do was to drink with one's peers. Alcohol consumption was the common denominator among grown-ups. It separated the "men from the boys" and was a bonding element, guaranteeing good times. Even though I knew Father drank too much, and I vowed I would never do that, I was eager to light up a cigarette and sip a cocktail. Everyone seemed to do that in the movies: Lauren Bacall, Joan Crawford, Robert Mitchum and that sassy Gloria Graham, for example. Smoking and drinking were adult, fun pastimes. I could fit in with others through them. I did not have to remain on the outside looking in. There were occasional Sunday School outings, often along the Hudson River. I tried to become part of the group by playing the prankster. Usually, I ended up looking silly or merely being tolerated. My social skills needed work. More to the point, my sense of self-worth needed shoring up.

Florence and Mother were not always on very good terms. Florence was in her late teens and popular with the boys. Her red hair and sunny disposition were beacons to the young men of her group. She studied stenotyping and had many friends both at school and in the Swedish circle within which our family socialized. Stormy fights erupted when Flo was asked to go to the Stork Club or some other nightspot. Mother was uneasy about such goings on. Shouts and tears ensued. Mother relented, permitting Flo to borrow a fur stole and a few other accessories to make the occasion dressy and festive. Flo's temperament did not mesh with Mother's. She bid for freedom by marrying a nice, undistinguished alcoholic whose emotional nadir was some years down the road. While Helen and I were constant playmates, Flo and I were always the closest of the siblings. She encouraged me in various endeavors and seemed uncritical of my personal flamboyance. Flo often took me to the beach and even taught me to swim as well as to waltz. We were sympathetic, but we never got into deep discussions about things. That she was there for me was evident, which helped over the ensuing years.

Dad helped George through New York University after George left the Navy, as it seemed a worthy undertaking, something he could understand. Father could not understand what direction I was taking, however. Born into a peasant family in central Sweden, my father managed to get into the Royal Cavalry before signing on board a freighter to South America. Somewhere along the line, he jumped ship and settled in the "land of opportunity." As a laborer, the energetic young Swede learned to swing a hammer and build things. He knew long hours of physical labor. His rise to a supervisory capacity came after years of struggle, responsibility and rapport with his workers that earned their respect.

When I graduated from elementary school in 1949, my parents determined that I should follow my brother's footsteps by attending Stuyvesant High School in lower Manhattan. I distinctly remember both Brother's and Father's fervent belief that going to that special school for honor students would straighten me out. I was "going through a phase"—my absorption with movie fantasy, "long-haired" music and "la-di-da" would pass. Perhaps my worthiness in my father's estimation would grow when I became more like George. I did not think I would ever achieve the high regard that George had with my father. It did not seem that I would change very much, either.

My parents bought a large Victorian house in the Hudson Valley in the northwest corner of Westchester County. With the idea of Father retiring, they were going to move there with Helen. She would finish high school nearby. I was to avail myself of the honor of attending Stuyvesant. Since it was mandatory to be a New York City resident to be a student there, I would live in an apartment within the city limits with George while he was attending NYU. Father owned the building in the Pelham Bay area of the Bronx. He converted it into three floor-through apart-

ments, George and I having the ground level. I almost never saw
my brother, as he was either at university, at his fraternity house
or somewhere with his girlfriend, Ellie (who later became his
wife). I got up in the morning, prepared my breakfast, washed
and dressed for school and took the train to Manhattan. At the
end of the school day, I returned to the empty house to prepare
dinner, wash clothes and listen to music on the phonograph. It
was a desperately lonely time for me. I took long walks in Pelham
Bay Park to Long Island Sound. When Cinderella's mother died,
nature comforted her; I found similar solace. I talked with the
squirrels in the park and thought about the music that replayed in
my head. My favorites were all the Romantics: Chopin, Tchaikovsky, Rachmaninov and their contemporaries. They became
friends, together with the authors of the many books I cherished.
I had no friends other than tenuous ones made at church or
school, no close pals or confidants to help with the many questions taunting me about life.

Sex was an elusive mystery I was terrified of exploring.
Mother had made it clear that it was bad, if not outright evil. I
wondered how we managed to get born. I did not know the things
a young boy in adolescence should know. I gazed questioningly at
the giant nude male athlete statue on the stadium in Pelham Bay
Park. My brother was not accessible for answers either, but he led
me to believe everything would be okay. We ignored the present
out of insecurity, shyness, blind faith in the future. In the mean-
time, through my confusion and ambivalence, music encouraged
tearful self-pity. As utter as the poet/musician's loneliness was my
identification with it.

My immediate world of books, radio, music and nature was
suddenly further enlivened by the introduction of opera, brought
into my life by Nancy Ogren. An attractive girl from confirmation
class, she took a shine to me and I to her. She wore her mother's
fur coat, had a page-boy haircut and used makeup. Nancy was
smart, chic, adult. She was willing to share her private-school

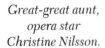

*Great-great aunt,
opera star
Christine Nilsson.*

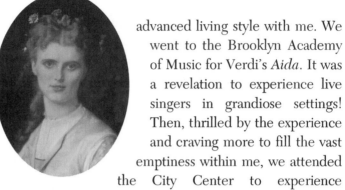

advanced living style with me. We went to the Brooklyn Academy of Music for Verdi's *Aida*. It was a revelation to experience live singers in grandiose settings! Then, thrilled by the experience and craving more to fill the vast emptiness within me, we attended the City Center to experience Gounod's *Faust*. Tales remembered from childhood about my great-great aunt Christina Nilsson came alive. She had performed Marguerite on opening night at the Metropolitan Opera House in 1883. Mother took pride in running down the young diva for her loose morals, however. In her convoluted snobbery, she was condescending to one of the great opera stars of the nineteenth century, but reveled in her being a relative.

I continued my enchantment with *Carmen* and *La Bohème*. The die was cast. Opera became an extension of my life. Yvonne de Carlo was left behind in memory. Risë Stevens's Carmen inflamed my imagination. I began to write fan letters to her, sometimes every day. The personal lives of the stars commanded my curiosity. I related to opera characters as I had to movie stars. Everything became larger than life when I indulged in those flights of fancy. When Stevens appeared on the Bell Telephone Hour, I was in the audience, then backstage afterward to ask for an autograph, although I never revealed to her that I was the guy writing all the letters.

My world further expanded with the arrival of television. From the living room I watched Arturo Toscanini conduct the NBC Symphony. Television provided live entertainment without admission charge. I attended TV shows by requesting free tickets in advance. That way, Nancy or another friend could come with me to see famous people from the theater, Hollywood films or the concert/opera stage. Memorable among them were Walter

Huston and Eve Arden. There was great inner gratification at age twelve from being exposed to and sometimes meeting those luminaries. I ached to be part of their world and made every effort to place myself in their path in New York.

Occasionally, I was brought back to the reality of the moment and my ambiguous relationship to sexuality. I was a good-looking young lad who apparently attracted the attentions of some of my peers. There were two very "fast" girls who attended Manhem, a Swedish beach club on Throgs Neck on Long Island Sound in the Bronx. They made two blatant sexual attacks on me that I thwarted, but I was shocked and panicked. The first assault was on the lawn of the beach club. We crawled under a blanket on a chilly day. The two girls proceeded to grope me with great seriousness. I never thought anyone would touch other people's private parts like that—I was a real prude. The other time, and I should have known better, they asked me to walk them home to get something. Once inside the house, I knew I had been set up for more physical investigation. With persistence, I managed to escape their concerted advances. The advances from young men in the Swedish dance club and the church group were more cautiously veiled, hence easier to ignore. What a mystery, not without enticement but so very frightening! I wanted to believe it would all work out someday, somehow. Time with Nancy was nonthreatening. We both wanted to look good, seem mature and do glamorous things. Sex was not part of the picture. So we managed to go around for a few years, comfortably living out our illusions of beauty and harmony. Sex was on the shelf, not to be considered for some time.

During the years I lived by myself in the apartment I was supposed to be sharing with my brother, I had every opportunity to run wild, or join neighborhood loafers prowling for adventure and thrills. I guess my mother knew I would not do it. My strong streak of ingrained Lutheranism kept me on the straight and narrow. I went to church regularly and truly believed that God punished sinful people. My virtue was really based on fear, ignorance and stubborn belief in what I had been taught. With no family around, my aloneness responded wholeheartedly to the romanticism I found in the arts. I could appreciate *la vie de bohème* and the soul-wrenching despair I found in Tchaikovsky. My mother's suffering was not the only kind in the world.

Walking with the doleful Romantics in my head through the park over to Long Island Sound, I began to realize that I had a heroic fate unfurling. I, too, would be an artist, sharing my sufferings, joys and insights into life's mysteries with the world. Soon, all would be revealed to me so that my destiny could be fulfilled. Probably, I would have an early and tragic death but I would have lived out a privileged mission (the exact nature of which was still ambiguous to me). Tears of valor I shed alone on those endless perambulations.

I asked Flo to speak to the president of Paramount Pictures, by whom she was employed, to request a job for me at the Paramount Theater on Times Square. The position was easily secured and further cemented when I discovered one of my classmates at Stuyvesant High School was the son of the manager of the theater. The last two years of high school were spent working after school at the lavishly decorated movie palace. I had been taught the virtues of hard work and the necessity of being self-reliant and self-supporting by my self-made father. Consequently, I was honor-bound to take work after school. It greatly appealed to me to dress up as an usher and direct people to seats and facilities, or to spout information relating to film or stage shows. As an usher after school, I could not only see lots of great, new movies but also enjoy the stage shows. Surely backstage I would meet some of the celebrities. In the milieu of Times Square types, celebrities and motley co-workers, my first brush with the underbelly of life as well as my first blackout from drinking alcohol was about to happen.

Meanwhile, in the ushers' locker room, the ritual of apply-

Paramount Days: Denise Darcel,
Billy Eckstein

ing Clearasil carefully next to nonexistent pimples or blemishes preceded appearing on the floor of the great theater in my neat uniform. A young, handsome, out-of-work actor who befriended me became my role model in this presentation ceremony. Robert was sophisticated, worldly and a bit effeminate, but that seemed part of the charisma of the sensitive actor. He regaled me with stories about summer stock and the lives of theater personalities such as Tallulah Bankhead. The ever-changing stage shows gave me firsthand exposure to many of the noted singers, musicians and actors of the time. To double my pleasure, I got to see new films over and over again. I could sing Marlene Dietrich's songs from *Rancho Notorious* ad infinitum.

I loved being given the chance to relieve the backstage elevator operator. I was thrilled to take French sex kitten Denise Darcel down to the stage door in the elevator. She handed me her key, doused in Chanel No. 5, to hang on the dressing room key board. After the mink-clad beauty swept out of the theater, I went up and down on the elevator sniffing her key and softly intoning her song, "Some girls need a penthouse to give them romance." Ella Fitzgerald was a jovial woman who enjoyed playing poker with the musicians between gigs; Ceci Robinson taught me a Charleston routine she did on stage with her husband, Budd; young, beautiful Sarah Vaughan and Rosemary Clooney were among the stars on the Paramount's stage during that time in the early 1950s.

Unforgettable was the performance of Billy Eckstein, not for his vocal technique as much as for the memory of his singing "Caravan" during one of the most outrageous experiences I was to have in my vulnerable young life. Not yet eighteen, the age required by law to be a chief usher, I was given the great responsibility of being in charge of balcony operations. No senior usher was available so the task was given to me. It was a busy Saturday night, which meant enormous crowds of people were lined up on Broadway and filling the lobby while waiting to be admitted to the vast balcony for seating. Procedure was to fill one elevator on the mezzanine while the other elevator was unloading above. *Never* were both elevators at the balcony at once. I was tired after many highly pressured hours on my feet. People were still piling in. A friendly soul was running one of the elevators and I took a moment's rest to chat with him. Both my hands were on the elevator doors, which I allowed to close gently on each side of my neck. Continuing to converse nonchalantly, I tried to push the doors back with my hands. They did not budge. I asked the elevator operator to try to open the doors so I could get my head out of the elevator. To our mutual horror, the doors would not open. There was a mechanism that required the doors to close completely, after a certain point, before they could be opened. He wanted to call on the elevator phone to the manager's office. My friendship with the manager's son and my liaison with the president of Paramount Pictures notwithstanding, I was terrified of losing my job. "No, don't report this," I blurted. Hoping something would come to mind or that I could reduce my head volume enough to squeeze miraculously out of the situation, I held out for a nonexistent solution.

As Billy Eckstein continued to croon "Caravan" on stage, the lobby was packed with impatient people wanting to know why the line was not moving. Those in the waiting elevator on the mezzanine wanted to go up to sit down. A woman on her way to the ladies' room saw my torso sticking out of the elevator. A resolution to my predicament was precipitated by her hysterical scream: "There's a man with his head caught in the elevator!" Firemen put equipment through my spread legs into the elevator. Police came. The manager and crowds of other people gathered around. To my dismay, I heard the Captain of the ushers say, "Is that Gustafson with his head in the elevator?" It was the man who entrusted the task of running the balcony to me. I had obviously disappointed him, which made my imminent firing even worse. Someone had to climb down the elevator shaft from the eighteenth floor to release a mechanism on top of the elevator. At last I was free, with black grease around my starched dickey and mortification on my face. In the manager's office, I explained plaintively that I had rested the door on my neck not knowing that the doors could not be opened without taking my head off. I made it clear that it was not the nice elevator man's fault. It was my doing (and undoing). He seemed more concerned about whether or not I was hurt. When I assured him that I was only shaken up, he gave me the rest of the night off and sent me home. The next day, there was a placard posted on the bulletin board of the locker room to the effect that all parts of the body were to be kept away from closing elevator doors. The ribbing I received went on for some time, but the notion of firing me never seemed to have entered the management's thinking. Because of my good record and my connections in high places, my job was secure. It was me who was not secure.

My colleagues on the usher squad were characters of whom my mother would certainly never have approved. The job did not attract a lot of very young people. Wages were low and the hours lasted until after the final show, which on a Saturday night could be 1 or 2 in the morning. At that hour on Times Square, lots of strange things can happen. Being one of the group was always important to me, and I tried to fit in even though it often involved doing things that I would not usually do. Occasionally, there was a party at one or another usher's apartment in Manhattan. Usually, it was a walk-up in a tenement. I drank with everyone else as though it was my normal behavior. I experienced my first blackout from alcohol at one of those parties. Sitting on a dingy couch, I remember going in and out of awareness while the party continued. I felt very uneasy but tried not to show it. I was grateful when finally I managed to drop safely in my bed at home to sleep the revelry off.

Some of the guys and girls definitely had rough edges. I was embarrassed by their blatant sexuality and immorality. *This* Lutheran boy virgin was not used to girls going into Times Square bars to pick up men who would ply them with drinks expecting a fun time afterward. Often, the girls climbed out restroom windows and ran down alleys to escape rewarding their new "friends." I remember one girl disappeared from work for almost a week. She was locked in an apartment in the Bronx for the duration. Liquor and sex were a way of life for these kids. They were free-living, with little money but plenty of time to experiment. I hovered on the edge without getting involved. It was a hard road to walk: being friendly without committing to intimacies. I did not want to seem goody-goody or innocent, both of which I was. I hoped they thought I was worldly, and in a way they did. They sensed both that I lived in a different world and that I was not condescending toward the wickedness in their lives. I felt like a voyeur, and I knew how much growing up I had to do.

Chapter 2

NICE BOYS DON'T

There were many pros and cons to attending a special all-boys high school in lower Manhattan. Taking the subway (elevated from Pelham Bay until around 149th Street) to the 14th Street station took at least an hour, sometimes more. I had a few classmates who made the daily journey, which usually made it more bearable. It was always wise for us to stick together from 14th Street to the school on 15th Street near First Avenue, as there were often ruffians on those streets. Stuyvesant boys were singled out as brainy, special kids whose privilege seemed an offense to the street kids. We were easy victims for the toughies. The Third Avenue "El" still rumbled overhead as we ambled to school.

My family had moved a few miles farther east to the Pelham Bay area during my last two years of elementary school. After switching from P.S. 78, I had taken up the fife in elementary school and participated in the fife and drum marching band at P.S. 71. The year of my graduation, I was elevated to sergeant of the fife section, which made me their leader. I would have been thrilled to be the band's leader but I lacked the courage to attempt it. I continued music in high school. Playing the piano was what I really wanted to do. My father was totally against that, the expense and the very notion of having a piano made it out of the question. The cello was settled on, as the school was willing to lend me one free of charge and I could take it home. Perhaps there was a shortage of cello players at school. Whatever the reason, I was encouraged to take up the cello by Dr. Stoffreagen, head of the music department.

Lugging the cello home, I worked on scales and the complicated business of bowing with one hand and fingering the strings with the other. It was much easier to blow the fife, as both hands did the same thing. When it was lesson time, my insecurity was so great that I perspired down the fingerboard. Dr. S. was vastly annoyed with me and finally suggested that I help him run the music department office instead. This was a beginning to my involvement with the administrative aspect of the arts. I did once fake my way through a concert in the symphony orchestra, "playing" a Mozart symphony. When an arpeggio began, I played the first note, skipped to the middle of the phrase, and again to the end, thereby playing three of the notes in a passage of a dozen fast notes. It was a relief not to have to fake my musical talents after that.

After the cello misadventure, I became aware of dance. Aside from the flyers in the lobby of the City Center advertising the New York City Ballet, I had the thrill of seeing a ballet on screen. *The Red Shoes*, starring Moira Shearer and Robert Helpmann, was playing at a Broadway movie house. I tingled with excitement to see that glorious red-haired ballerina dance *en pointe* to her tragic death. All the elements my sensitive, yearning romantic soul needed for stimulation were present in that film. The drama, glamor and dancing were magical to me. A new horizon appeared in my life: the ballet. Needless to say, my father deemed it out of the question that I even consider studying ballet. My options narrowed. I still went whenever possible to the opera, theater and even the ballet. Both New York City Opera and Ballet were housed at the City Center, long before Lincoln Center was built. I became adept at sneaking into performances either during intermissions or by prying a balcony door open from the fire escapes at the back of the City Center.

Queens College: Helen Athos and Bob with their charleston flappers.

Saturday matinees were a perfect time for me to attend Broadway plays and make exciting discoveries in Broadway musicals. With utter abandon, I bonded with Lorelie Lee in *Gentlemen Prefer Blondes*, I swooned with enchantment at the exotics of *Kismet*, especially the production number "Baubles, Bangles and Beads," and a little later I dreamed along in "Some Enchanted Evening" with Ezio Pinza and Mary Martin in *South Pacific*. I *was* Gertrude Lawrence in *The King and I*. And so it went. From matinee to matinee, I dreamed of other places, other worlds as I had discovered on the Silver Screen. Wearing the wonderful mantle of fantasy, I transferred myself from the Bronx to other lands experiencing thrilling, grown-up emotions.

I managed to coerce Flo or some other young adult to accompany me to many of the events if Nancy was not available. My first straight play was *A Tree Grows in Brooklyn*, starring Peggy Ann Garner. It was on tour, playing near the Grand Concourse in the Bronx, very accessible to me. On Broadway, I saw *The Happy Time* with Eva Gabor and Claude Dauphin. I even got my mother to attend an evening performance of *The Royal Family*, with Eva Le Gallienne, at the City Center.

The old Met was the hub of operatic glamor. The only way I could afford to attend was by securing a standing-room ticket. I waited in line for hours for a $2 ticket. I was the youngest person in standing-room, a distinction which gave me pleasure. The interior of the Met was beautiful. Standing there while the overture played, I noted the glamorous people in the dimly lit boxes that formed the diamond horseshoe. Sometimes, I recognized a celebrity such as Jean Simmons or a famous socialite whose life I read about in the *Daily News*. Sherry's Bar was thrilling to peer into, with the rich and famous imbibing during intermission. One day I planned to be able to sit there and enjoy the ambience from the inside. There was no doubt in my mind about that.

If ballet lessons were forbidden, I did have another outlet for my terpsichorean efforts. There was a Swedish folk dance club I was allowed to join. It performed at the various Swedish festivals in and around New York. Once a year, around Midsummer's Night, we danced at a place at the end of Throgs Neck. A maypole was erected on the grassy field. Inside a large building there was a dance floor crowded with "festive" Swedes filled with old-country food and drink who schottisched, polkaed, hamboed and waltzed into the night. Vasa Castle Hall on West 149th Street in the Bronx was a meeting, rehearsal and sometime performance space for our dance club. Once a year, a costume ball (often turning into a brawl) was held with prizes awarded. Helen and I often entered, although I later participated with Nancy and our Swedish-American peers. Thanks to Flo's lessons, I shone on the dance floor, doing all the Swedish dances and popular American ones like the Lindy and the foxtrot.

I never felt comfortable performing the folk dances, but I liked my costume: blue knickers and a red and blue vest. All the other guys wore the traditional yellow knickers, but I found that blue was used in one province of Sweden. Mother complied with my wishes. After consulting the picture I found of my costume, she deftly ran the fabric through her sewing machine and sewed on the shiny buttons. We were both pleased with the result. Mother did it with a pride of accomplishment, unwittingly assisting me in my need to be different or unique. I shone at things that took individual imagination but I had great resistance to organized routine. My folk dancing was a group activity; the steps had to coordinate perfectly with the other dancers. It terrified me. I was certain that I would misstep. A fast Viennese waltz did not faze me; being part of a chorus panicked me, the fear of error within the group. I preferred improvisation on my terms.

Meanwhile, back in the school gymnasium, I managed to climb ropes and work out on the exercise horses. The basketball court was my undoing. I got so flustered trying to run with the ball, fake left or right and then sink it into the basket that I ended doing balletic pirouettes and leaps, creating great mirth among my peers. Locker-room time and showering were kept to a minimum; I was very uncomfortable exposing myself to the boys. My prudishness was paralyzing.

It was mortifying for me to recite in class. During a grammar slip in English class involving the nominative case, I was commanded to learn "After 'than' or 'as,' use the nominative case . . . I, you, he, she, it; we, you, they.'" The very next day, I stood and recited the rule. It is indelible in my mind, coming out whenever someone makes a similar error. Science classes were a mystery to me and I did poorly in them. English, music and art were my favorites.

The question of college was never very far from my consciousness. What in the world was I to become? What course of study would I pursue? I was not going to follow my brother into the construction business and therefore would not get financial support from my perplexed father. Where would I go to school? Getting a scholarship to one of the city colleges was the answer. The choices narrowed to Hunter College in mid-Manhattan or

Queens College in Flushing. Anita Carlson, a friend from the Swedish folk dance club, was going to Queens. After visiting the college with her and knowing that I would have a friend there, the decision was made. The campus was almost like an out-of-town college campus. There were trees and grass, and on the horizon the Manhattan skyline, beckoning to me.

During that period, a thrilling event burst upon the world. Not far from where I lived in the northeast Bronx, a young man, not happy in his own body, went to Copenhagen for a sex change. When Christine Jorgensen returned home, it made the cover of the *Daily News* and most of the other papers. A sensational notion for me—a man turned into a woman, and how lovely she looked! Flo remembered him from the neighborhood. Shortly afterward, a Scandinavian-American society honored Christine Jorgensen as "Woman of the Year." (Around that time, Ingrid Bergman was honored in like fashion.) The ceremony took place in a huge ballroom at Manhattan Center near the old Pennsylvania Station. I attended with some of my peers, my brother with his friends. I have a picture of the crowd with the slim, blond, evening-gowned Christine in the foreground with dignitaries. It was thrilling, glamorous and a bit confusing. I kept staring at her, wondering how that kind of thing happened. She looked the way I had often felt when playing "Princess in captivity" in the back garden with Helen. Years later, my final view of the perplexing creature was at Johnny Carson's birthday party at Toots Shor's. The once perfectly gorgeous Christine had thickened. She seemed coarse, if not unhappy, puffing on a cigarette, barely noticed by the other celebrants. I

Christine Jorgensen, Woman of the Year with Bob looking on.

sensed disintegration, both physical and spiritual, in this wreck of a woman. Time and the transsexual are not compatible.

My own ambiguity continued. I began dyeing my white shirts pastel shades to the dismay of my brother and father. In the early 1950s men did not wear shirts like that. Then, my choice in Easter outfits continued to startle and amaze. I still love color in my clothing. There was defiance in those sartorial statements. Today, there is joy in playing the peacock.

Traveling to school was nothing new to me after years of attending Stuyvesant High School. Taking a couple of long bus rides over the Whitestone Bridge to Flushing, Queens, seemed a prettier trip. I always appreciated nature, and the views of the water were pleasant backdrops for the daily adventure to college. There were quite a few others from the Bronx attending Queens College, girls from Parkchester or the Tremont area. Many of them were from Jewish families, so I got exposed to a lot of Yiddish expressions and humor. A warm, nonthreatening knot of friendships developed on the buses.

Ever thrifty, I lived on a tiny allowance from my family. To augment my finances, I took two jobs on campus. One was helping Dr. Margaret Spiesman teach social dancing to the Adult Education enrollees once or twice a week. Social dancing became a constant pastime. It began with the class offered as part of the curriculum. Having passed it with flying colors, I stopped in during free time to dance even more. I perfected the tango, rumba, foxtrot and the new mambo through constant application. As a natural outgrowth of my absorption, I was given the job of night-class assistant to the dance instructor. I spent time dancing rather than studying or going to class.

Another classmate who loved to dance had insecurities similar to mine. She became my partner. We worked out routines, often winning dance competitions. Helen Athos was lovely, but the fraternity crowd thought her frigid, which was fine with me. I just wanted to "make believe" sexy doing the mambo. We tangoed and did quite an abandoned Charleston, for which we were best known. Her black, Greek, short-cropped poodle look went well with her large dark eyes and pouting lips. Helen was a "flapper." We each donned raccoon coats to complete the effect.

When not dancing, attending class or perfecting my bridge in the school cafeteria, I worked part-time in the cafeteria. Money was never abundant but I managed to stay afloat. Mother appeared every so often, as she did during high school, with a roasted chicken or a stew to add to my Bronx larder.

Hunger for food was not an issue; what I was starving for was to know about the fearful mysteries of life. My sexuality was completely dormant. I purposely kept myself occupied to avoid any action on it. Girls as well as boys fascinated me, but I was reluctant to show any strong sign of interest. Both sexes made advances to me, but I fended off all comers. My androgynous life was rife with confusion. I was an attractive, easygoing young man with a demure exterior. When I was partying and having a few drinks, everything became mellow; I had the comforting illusion of belonging. Drinking became more and more a part of my social life. My fearful God from earliest youth had lessened His control over me during the college years. There were so many other ideas to take His place. Everything was open to question as part of my liberal college education.

Impatient with letting things work out by themselves, I decided to pretend I was just like the other guys. I would join a fraternity where alcohol flowed at every occasion. I would enjoy their dances and their company. Maybe I could really become like them through association. I chose the most popular fraternity. The brothers were campus leaders in sports, campus politics and social events. They were considered the handsomest, most desirable jocks. On a predominantly Jewish campus, the fraternity was remarkably Christian in makeup, which brought its own kind of distinction to the group.

My problem was to convince them I was really masculine

enough to be worthy of their brotherhood. Since I danced and played bridge with some of the leading females on campus, the girls all promised to whisper the right words of encouragement into the frat brothers' ears. It worked like a charm. I was really only shy, not effeminate, I imagined the girls explaining. The classiest girls seemed to like me and they expressed confidence in my desirability. I did not realize it at the time, but I was "acting as if." I tried to look and behave like the other guys. Laughing at their jokes, I often sought similar jokes to share with them. We would drift off to a local bar after classes where I drank with my pals, hoping they would not find out that I was not one of them. I dated campus girls and went to frat parties with the same line of chatter as the other guys. I acted as if what I did and said was genuine. It seemed to work for a while. My drinking bouts provided escape but I still had not accomplished true fulfillment in knowing about life and how I was to live it.

To paraphrase George Bernard Shaw: if you can't do anything else, try teaching. Queens College had a large education department, with vague enough requirements for me to enroll in those courses with a minor in speech. Slowly, I realized that not only did I not find the education courses challenging, I did not want to be a teacher. It was nonessential to my sense of life and awareness of the arts. The theater department was closely allied with the speech department, and it caught my attention as did nothing else at Queens College. Stuttering and splayed palates gave way to Tennessee Williams and stage movement. Ray Gasper, a young professor arrived, holding us spellbound with his theater concepts. I was ripe for commitment.

I managed to get the occasional "extra" position at both the old Met and the City Opera. Time would not permit me to do more than one or two operas a season, but I was thrilled to get into costume and walk onto the stage. At the City Opera, I was a torero in Escamillo's entourage in *Carmen*. Every time I entered downstage right, a young woman with flaming red hair offered me her oranges. Her name was Beverly Sills.

I brought Ted, one of my friends from the Music Department, to be with me in the Met's *Tosca*. I was threatened by the homosexual overtones in the dressing room. That is the major reason why I turned down a walk-on in *Aida*. I was fearful of being stripped to a loincloth and spear. An acolyte with a long robe was safer, I thought. My friend and I both left after the first-act cathedral scene. Somehow, we had it in our heads that it was a one-act opera.

We became known as the *Tosca* lovers by the stage manager and his gay friends. They assumed a relationship that never was, or one that was at least unknown and unrealized by either of us. It was a relationship fraught with possibilities, however. I found him very attractive and companionable. Again, I never explored the possibility of talking frankly with a peer about such personal matters. Instead, we once double-dated, ending up at his Village apartment. We were stretched out on two couches, necking, each couple keeping an eye on the other couple. It seemed that he and I were making advances to the girls, but it was really to each other.

Drama replaced "rah-rah" in my mid-college years. My clothes were theatrical statements underscoring the immense seriousness of my newly found pursuit in theater. Breaking with tradition, I wrote a letter of resignation to my fraternity. I was told that one cannot resign from a fraternity. Utter nonsense, darling! Frivolity was dispensed with. I gave up the dance classes and bridge with the sorority girls.

Life was full of "meaningful" enterprises. I got involved in technical aspects of play producing. I wrote a paper on the works of Eugene O'Neill that my professor claimed was worthy of a Master's thesis. Suckling at the teats of Tennessee Williams and Eugene O'Neill, I hung out with actors and theater technicians when not going to Manhattan to ballet, opera or theater performances. Living and breathing that intense air created an increase in alcohol consumption and depression. I believed an artist drank life to the fullest. Drinking glasses of something to excess made up for not doing the big "it." Worries about my future, my talents, my barren personal life helped to deepen the depression already encouraged by alcohol.

By graduation time, I was preparing to run away to Europe to live in a garret in Paris and suffer for art. Before graduation, I sold off everything I owned to amass enough money for a few months in Europe as a student. Paralyzed with fear and longing, I asked to meet with my young professor for a drink. I thought I was having a nervous breakdown and I hoped for answers. There was little he could do to assuage my condition other than to assure me that I had an aptitude for the theater. I displayed an intelligence and willingness that were assets. He wished me luck and suggested I keep in touch.

My last year or so at Queens College was spent in a rented room with a family who lived near campus. The family was very hospitable. They had another boarder, also a student. He was slightly older, a veteran of the Korean War. We had an agreeable, polite relationship. He bought my tape recorder, which helped finance my European adventure. Summertime jobs helped me save something toward the adventure, too. They also provided me with experiences to further confound my ability to cope with life. I took a job washing dishes in a colonial-style hotel in Wellfleet on Cape Cod. One of the popular sorority girls worked as a waitress there; she told me how lovely that part of the world was. I arrived and settled into what might have been a blissful summer. Dishwashing is a dumb, undemanding job. With it came room and board and a small salary. Our off-time preoccupation was preparing a group theme costume: we saved bones from the kitchen, which we bleached and strung around our necks as part of our savage costumes for the annual Artists and Poets Costume Ball held in Provincetown. With some trepidation, I joined the sav-

ages for a night in notorious P-town. There was always a lot of jok-
ing about the queers there. I wondered if I would be assaulted by
them, or if others would think I was one of them.

I tried to bond further with the group. Parents of some of
the girls were about to arrive. We had a party the night before on
the grounds of the Saltonstall property. There was drinking and
smooching. I remember a rowboat ride in the moonlight with one
particularly attractive blond girl who did not work at the hotel. It
was a pleasant evening, quite well-behaved, overall. The next day,
while talking with a handsome local boy considered the stud of
the crowd, I embroidered the story about the party in ways that I
thought would indicate to him that I was quite the rooster in his
absence. We joked and gossiped about various friends. It seemed
a happy, man-to-man conversation, enjoyed on a summer morning on the Cape. But my inventions took on proportions I had not
envisioned. By the time the girls' parents arrived, the story of our
innocent party had been transformed into a wild orgy. When I
attended the Methodist Church that Sunday, the sermon was
about the Prodigal Son. The minister and the congregation meaningfully turned their gazes to me. I was so mortified that I left
Wellfleet immediately. Run out of town for immorality! Ironically, my sin was lying, a pretext to hide my virginity.

It was that summer in the mid-1950s when Ingrid Bergman
got so many Americans upset over her affair with Roberto
Rossellini while filming on the Italian island of Stromboli. Dr.
Lindstrom proved his Swedish mettle by suing for divorce from
his pregnant errant wife. He brought his daughter Pia to Cape
Cod to enjoy summer in seclusion away from the irritating press.
"Jenny" became part of our crowd. All of us made believe to her
that we did not know her real identity, but one look at that profile
brought her famous mother to mind. Many years later, Pia
revealed to me that it might have been me who gave her her first
potent drink of alcohol there in Wellfleet.

The next summer, the one before graduation, was spent on

the UCLA campus in Brentwood, California. I rented a room in
the fraternity house, a chapter of the one to which my brother
had belonged. I had befriended an unusual young lady who lived
in a sorority house up the street. Terry was visiting from New
York and taking a summer class. We were both bitten by the theater bug, and we encouraged each other in dramatic flights of
fancy. One day, we were hanging out in Hollywood, and we
decided to have lunch in a small restaurant. We were seated in
the back. At the next table was an attractive young man who
looked familiar. It was not until later that Terry confirmed my
suspicions that it was James Dean. He was alone and engaged us
in conversation. I thought that most of his attentions were
directed at me, which was fine. It seemed harmless, and besides,
I had Terry to protect me. At the end of the meal, we bid an ami-
cable farewell.

Selling Catholic Bibles was my means of support for the first
part of that summer. Even though I no longer subscribed enthusiastically to the Good Book, I could recommend it wholeheartedly to my door-to-door customers. My clean-cut good looks and
sincerity won me many subscribers. Waiting for my commission
check left me close to penniless. At one point, I remember feeling dizzy from hunger and nearly passing out. There was a church
that offered some repast to participants. I remember going there
and dropping a coin in the collection with a prayer for protection
from hunger and need. I took an orange home with me from that
simple meal and never had a hunger spell again.

My roommate and I spent lots of time in a friend's pool.
Tom often did not wear a bathing suit; he displayed his very
developed manhood in a most casual fashion. I was all awkward
shyness tinged with fascination. Again, we never talked or did
anything in the privacy of our room. I was a master of avoidance.

Promising to telephone Terry in the fall, I departed in an
automobile driven by two girls who were returning to Minnesota.
One had a boyfriend in Yellowstone National Park; we planned to

stop there on our ride east. I planned to continue from Minnesota to New York by train or bus. With my Bible salesman days behind me, I was looking forward to a pleasant trip across the country.

Chapter 3

My Moveable Feast

Yellowstone was incredibly beautiful and, impulsively, I decided to stay on. I asked the boyfriend of my traveling companion whether he could use another gas station attendant. He said I could start immediately. I was shown my bunk and introduced to the gift shop personnel, some hotel employees and my fellow gas station mates. Not daring to reveal that I knew nothing about cars or pumping gas I proceeded to do a series of foolhardy things. The worst of them was truly explosive, clearly a case of being totally mismatched to the task at hand.

All my life, I had related to nature with passionate interest and involvement. Finding myself in Yellowstone National Park was a waking dream. The waterfall in the canyon area of the park where I bunked was awe-inspiring. Brown bears gave me pause, though, and I quickly learned to be alert and respectful. I most wanted to avoid the grizzly bears, and usually did; although once, while hitchhiking across the park, one chased me. A passing motorist stopped in time to avert disaster. Bubbling mud pools and boiling hot geysers added to my fascination with the park. Church services were held in a clearing with enormous pines for walls and the blue sky above for a ceiling. I was no longer Mother's devout Lutheran, but I attended Sunday services reverently. Luther and pantheism intermingled, and I was grateful for the peace afforded me.

My masquerade as a gas station attendant posed some difficulty. I could barely distinguish the front from the back of a car. One twilight, I was pumping gas when I decided to check the tank by lighting a match to get a better look. I know that sounds idiotic, but happily I was prevented from taking a closer look down the tank. "No lighted matches near the gas pumps!" the station manager shouted. Eventually, I figured out where to put the gas without much problem, which is more than I can say about oil changes. We earned extra money by changing tires and oil. When my turn came to do it, I quickly acquiesced. After all, I had watched the others. I pulled the car onto the lift without incident. Then I went under the car, unscrewing what must surely be the oil tank cap. Out poured the most beautiful yellow-green fluid imaginable. As it drained into the tank for used oil, I thought the customer was foolish to want an oil change when the oil look as pristine as that. But it was his money and my tip. At that point, the customer looked under the car to see how I was progressing. "You fool!" he screamed. "You're letting out the drive fluid!" I spent some time replacing the fluid with an eye-dropper. I also paid for it.

One fine but frosty morning it was my turn to open the gas house. The house had just been painted and was still sticky. A customer requested a tire repair. Again, having watched others use the hydraulic tire-changer, I offered to do it on the spot. I was certain to earn a good tip. All was well until it was time to remove the air hose from the nozzle of the repaired tire. It was stuck, and it continued to blow more and more air into the tire, which was growing to alarming proportions. Flo's husband Jack once told me about a man who lost his arm when a tire exploded. I advised the man to back out of the gas house. I, too, started to back away, my eyes fixed on the ballooning tire that showed growing wrinkles of stress. No longer able to accept any more air, the tire exploded, pulling the tire changer out of its cement base. The windows blew out and clouds of dust swirled around, much of it clinging to the damp, freshly painted walls. Bells were ringing for a very dazed me. People from the hotel a mile up the road rushed down. A gaggle of people surrounded me and the bells continued to ring in my head for hours. To this day, I have hearing loss in my left ear. The man whose tire was destroyed repeated over and over again to the station manager that it was not my fault. He explained that I had tried to disengage the air pump from the tire. Kindly, he would not hear of having me pay for a new tire.

Those incidents convinced me that it was time to retire from the gas station business, so I gave notice. During those last days, money was stolen from the station's cash register. I suspected that two new guys were the culprits but said nothing, having no proof. What most offended me was that I was considered a suspect. As the only one from the station who went to the open-air church, I thought my character above suspicion. I might be a misfit as a gas station attendant, but couldn't everyone see that I was above reproach when it came to criminal behavior? The matter was never resolved and I went on my way.

Dressed in smartly colored cowboy duds complete with cowboy hat, I stopped in Buffalo en route to my parents' home in Westchester to visit George and Ellie. My beautiful, if outlandish, costume perplexed and embarrassed them. Solid middle-class values must be respected at all times. One should not dress in bizarre fashion. Adhere to the norm at all times. What would I do after my final semester in college, they inquired. I had hopes of going to graduate school to continue theater studies. Specifically, I was one of ten candidates accepted to the Carnegie Institute in Pittsburgh. It was an honor, but the price tag posed difficulty. Clearly, Father was not about to foot the bill, and my brother was not forthcoming either. He knew it would not be repaid, barring a miracle. I could not deal with that impenetrable problem then, so I returned to Queens College.

Some of the college kids would sneak off to Jones Beach on exceptionally fine, warm days. While they swam and frolicked, I made further discoveries on that lovely stretch of beach.

Stretched out in the dunes, protected from the wind, I felt the delicious sun beating down on my lean body. I was surprised to discover men combing the dunes, looking for tasty morsels of other men. I was shocked at their advances, but I duly noted the activity anyway. It was used to great advantage later.

Tennessee Williams's *The Glass Menagerie* was the major theatrical production that final fall at Queens College. I worked the sound cues for the run of the play, which entailed being at most of the rehearsals as well as the performances. I buried myself in the theater department to the detriment of my other studies. Now that Williams's work had become a staple in my life, I went to a production Off-Broadway of his new play, *Garden District*. A friend who lived in Queens played one of the roles. I went backstage to visit with her after the performance and had my first meeting with the playwright. We would cross paths on several occasions in the coming years. Patricia Ripley was also in the cast; she became my good friend in recovery in New Mexico more than three decades later. The double bill featured *Suddenly Last Summer,* later made into a film with Elizabeth Taylor and Montgomery Clift. Life has a curious way of weaving people and me together over a period of time, as was the case with both of those stars. I am convinced that if I live long enough and continue to be "available" to life, many of the same people will reappear. Circumstances change along with relationships, but recurrence makes for a surprising spice. Helen Hayes appeared in a City Center production of *The Glass Menagerie* at the same time as our Queens College production. My idolized professor denigrated the performance that we attended with him. He insisted it was crassly commercial, with little inner meaning.

With all the brave-heartedness I could muster, I was going to escape the rampant commercialism of America. I was going to run off to Europe to discover the richness of life there and to experience *la vie de bohème*. My nerve was bolstered by alcohol, and I called it courage. I thought of all the sacrifices the "greats" had endured in the history of the arts. They blended in my head, indicating my dramatic cause: survival before the altar of Art! Booking an inside (windowless) tourist cabin on the S.S. *United States*, I sailed off to the great unknown—Europe. My parents, Flo, and actress friend Rosemary Banks, saw me sail out of New York harbor with no concrete prospects for my future.

Trains in France at that time had three classes, not two as today. The Métro had wooden cars instead of today's sleek metal ones; the wheels were metal, not rubber. The ride was noisier, bumpier and far more romantic. It seemed as though half the occupants were in love with each other; there was always a lot of hugging and kissing. Full of trepidation, I studied everything, trying to make sense of the foreign language and surroundings. In 1957, Europe still had scars from World War II. Paris was still clearing wartime debris and had not yet cleaned its blackened buildings, but the Seine still pursued its romantic passage through the magnificent city, and I was enchanted.

I took refuge in the American Residence at La Cité Universitaire in the fourteenth arrondissement. I told the admissions office that I was a student doing research on the theater. Requests for letters from a couple of Queens College professors confirmed that I was there on a study/research program. Admittedly, I was stretching the truth but I secured a safe, inexpensive and comfortable place to sleep and eat. Tony Davis, an American painter, had a studio on the upper floors. He invited me to visit, and I felt undertones of ulterior motives. I did not encourage anything to develop; I kept myself on the fringe of "it."

With student status, a travel card for the Métro and a special card for dining in student restaurants were available, making daily living expenses much lower. Once in a while, wealthy patronesses invited students to their salons for musicales or conversation. I investigated the lovely apartments in Passy and ate many delightful hors d'oeuvres. I invented a project to interview stars of the French stage, thinking that the Queens College newspaper would enjoy printing insights into the celebrities I maneuvered to meet. I spent time with Jean-Pierre Aumont in his dressing room before Giraudoux's *Amphitryon 38*, and got an invitation to see the performance from the best seat in the house. I neither returned to continue the visit nor wrote it up for the newspaper; fear of inadequacy accounted for both blanks. I could not imagine what I would do if the gorgeous Aumont propositioned me. Rather than be graceless and fumble awkwardly, I chose to disappear.

Everyday living presented obstacles—foreign language, foreign place. Logistics of daily survival canceled writing home about my visits with celebrities, and the project was definitively abandoned. I decided even the postage money could be put to better use. Happily for me and my pittance, theater in Paris was inexpensive for students. The Comédie Française intrigued me with its rich history and reputation for theatrical brilliance. Jacques Charon, one of its stars and a *sociétaire* of long standing, invited me to visit his extraordinary dressing room. I have never been in so elegant a backstage, with paintings and antique furniture in the hallways. Every performer had a dressing room done to their taste, for their personal use alone. The one I was in had a crystal chandelier, a zebra rug and an antique chaise longue. The dear, aging "auntie" of drama treated me with great courtesy. As my French was nearly nonexistent, we conversed in English. After getting an eyeful, and learning more about the venerable institution, I excused myself as politely as possible. Had I been a bit more worldly, I am sure I could have prolonged the visit.

The Hungarian uprising had just happened, bringing many young people, refugees from that horrible scene. I met a beautiful, exotic actress who shared some of her experiences with me. She introduced me to others in the theater and, on occasion, invited me to go the theater to meet a director or actor.

Imagine my thrill upon discovering that Alice B. Toklas still held court in Paris! Gertrude Stein had long since died; her legendary lover remained. I thought about going to see her, but I never did. I did not think I had anything to share with her. My lack of self-esteem made me believe that nothing I had to say to her would be of value, so why should I take up her time.

I could not afford expensive, elegant restaurants. However, my student bill of fare was delicious, if simple. It did not seem one could get a bad meal in Paris then. A flavor of old Paris was very much in evidence. I could easily imagine the world of Toulouse-Lautrec, Mistinguette and Piaf. The Montparnasse tower and other modern buildings were unimagined things of the future. Accordion music, *pissoirs* and smells of freshly baked bread had not yet disappeared, to be replaced by blaring rock sounds, pay toilets and fast food. I do not know what impressions or hint of *le temps perdu* a foreign student today could experience in the Americanized Paris.

In the spring of 1957, Queen Elizabeth II and her husband, Prince Philip, so young and attractive, made their historic Paris visit. I watched from beside Nôtre Dame as they arrived by boat. Paris put on a fireworks and waterworks display with barges on the Seine as a welcome. It was the first time in years that the ruling head of England had come to France. The crowds were jubilant. We drank lots of wine.

I then planned to take the train to Rome, see a bit of Italy, then go back north and visit the British Isles as a completion to my first European adventure. Money was short, as always, but I had a travel card that gave me train travel for a specific period. I wanted to get home before summer to prepare for the start of graduate school, even though I still did not know how that was to be achieved.

The trip to Rome was long, but when you are young and everything is a new experience, it does not matter. I took a cheap room in a pensione on the Via Babuino, where I met other young Americans and English. There was talk of the movies made at Cinecittà on the outskirts of Rome. Michael Redgrave was starring in one film and a young American actor, Anthony Perkins, in another. Work as an extra in one of those films paid about $20 a day, a fortune. I could live on that for days. I just had to get into Cinecittà, but a stern custodian guarded the entrance. While he was on the phone, I crawled past his door—only the upper portion was open. I was not apprehended! Upon entering a sound studio, I ran into the great Redgrave himself. He carefully sized me up, then asked me to wait while he was called onto the set. A gruff Italian came by and demanded that I leave. There was no way to explain to him that I had been invited to stay by the star. I was also uncomfortable with the impending "compromise." What would it take to unstick that closet door?

I found the other studio, where Anthony Perkins was filming. Without a notion as to what he looked like, I inquired and someone pointed him out. I waited for a propitious moment and approached. I blurted that I studied theater in the United States and was in Rome in very reduced circumstances and that I would be grateful if he could arrange for me to be an extra. Perkins looked at me and requested that I remove my dark glasses. (Since then, I dislike talking to anyone with dark glasses on.) "Wait here," he told me. He returned with a flunky, who told me I could start the next day. We would be filming in a hotel in the elegant Parioli section of Rome. At dawn, there I was, along with many others trying on clothes. Within minutes, the director's assistant approached me and asked me to do a bit part for which I was perfect. Some actors would kill for the many opportunities that presented themselves to me accidentally.

The work was boring. Filmmaking can be tedious—takes and retakes. In the hands of Italians it is multiplied in confusion and time consumption. Add to that the fact that the director was French, René Clément and the cast comprised Americans, Italians and a potpourri of other nationalities, causing the entire film to be dubbed. Everyone spoke their own language. Richard Conte, Jo van Fleet, Valli and Sylvana Mangano were the leads. Dino de Laurentis, Mangano's husband, was the producer.

My performance, in a word, was terrible. I was so bored that the only things I took seriously were the money and quitting time. The young American girl I had one scene with was terribly annoying. We were a backdrop for Mangano's entrance (I picked up the handbag she dropped and returned it to her). I had to read the girl "the love letter," but as I looked passionately into her eyes, I would instead tell her what foul breath she had or that her face was hideous. Since we were dubbed it didn't matter what I said. Alas, it did in my performance, and I wound up on the cutting-room floor.

Tony Perkins was known to be gay and I felt he might impose himself upon me, since he got me the job, but that was not the case. He lived at the plush Hotel de Ville, next to the Hassler at the top of the Spanish Steps, and I lived below on the Babuino. We were often on the street at the same time, but we each elected to avoid the other by crossing the street. We made each other very nervous. It was better to stay at a distance. It was not until many years later that I had a chance to thank him for his kindness in keeping me from hunger and destitution. It was at a Valentine's Day party given by Mia Farrow. He was there with his wife, Marissa Berenson. Perkins demurely accepted my expression of gratitude with modesty. We both seemed more comfortable with ourselves and each other.

Rome was a small, beautiful town in those days. Fruit vendors sang on the streets and life seemed especially colorful and warm. What joy to stroll the cobblestones in central Rome, with fascinating shops and studios where artisans carved or chipped away at soon to be "antiques," with a backdrop of decorated churches, splashing fountains and the ubiquitous fragment of Roman ruin.

It was time to wave *arrivederci* to the Eternal City if I wanted to catch a glimpse of Cannes en route to Paris. I located a youth hostel just outside the beach resort. For a small amount, chores sometimes requested, one could rest and bathe. I set out to investigate the famous watering hole for the international set. While sunning on the beach, I became fixated on a young man in a small white bathing suit sitting nearby. He told me that he was an American with the Ballet Russe de Monte Carlo. That explained his gorgeously sculpted body. He invited me to meet him later that evening after the company returned from a performance in Monte Carlo. Memories of *The Red Shoes* flooded my imagination, mixed with the thrill of a rendezvous with a ballet dancer on the Riviera. I was told to be in a certain bar after 11:00 p.m. I planned to return to Paris the next day, so I could save the small amount I would pay at the hostel by staying in his apartment. Also, there was a curfew at the hostel that would not accommodate that late an appointment. Daringly, I agreed. The man at the hostel let me out of paying for the night, even though a space had been saved for me and it was late in the day when I told him my change of plans. He was doubtful about my arrangement, but wished me well.

Since it was too early to go to the bar, I went to a cinema. My legs were crossed when some people came in to sit in front of me. My trouser leg got caught in their seat but I did not know how to explain the predicament in French, so I sat there fixed in place until they got up, only adding to my growing apprehension. To make matters worse, my new friend was not at the bar. I waited and waited. A couple of people there knew who I was waiting for, and it became a source of mirth as to whether or not I would be stood up. I did not know where I would go if the arranged meeting did not materialize. Tense and fearful, I was thrilled when he finally did appear. It seemed as though he had half forgotten our rendezvous. He muttered some excuse about being held up in Monte Carlo with ballet business. When we got to his apartment, he questioned me about my experience. It was clear that I was "green." The beautiful dancer hugged me and suggested that I get a good night's rest in preparation for my trip to Paris. We both accepted some sort of excuse about not indulging in sexual investigation. My initiation would have to wait, for which I was both glad and sad. I was overripe for plucking.

Chapter 4

STIFF UPPER LIP AND . . .

London in 1957 still had blitz scars from the war, and the food was not as delicious as in France; it was overcooked and bland, in the English tradition, although that was soon to be modified by the demands of increased tourism and the sweep of American influence. I took a cheap room in a boarding house near Bayswater Road. Most of the other boarders were young people. Down the road was a delightful pub with music and singing.

From time to time, I hitchhiked to Eastbourne on the Channel, where I stayed at a lovely hotel managed by the parents of an English girl I knew from Queens College. Angela had been very popular with the boys and some of the male faculty. Perhaps her coziness induced her return to England, pregnant. When I arrived the first time, I was on edge for signs of a baby or some indication as to what happened to her pregnancy. Never a word was mentioned. We visited her friends in the country. One was Brian Shiner, son of England's singing actor Ronald Shiner, who made popular the song "Now maybe it's because I'm a Londoner." We went to the pub Ronald owned in the Sussex country-side. Brian had a coming-of-age party in London the night before my return to the United States. Angela and I attended. My tuxedo was borrowed from friends of Angela's parents in Eastbourne. As they had no need of it in the near future, I borrowed it for use aboard the French Line's *Ile de France.* Later, I realized that was very clever planning.

While in Eastbourne, I attended old-fashioned country dances. They reminded me of a more formal version of American folk dancing, and they seemed very proper, very nineteenth cen-tury. The whole resort was old-fashioned, mainly because it was populated by the elderly—"See Eastbourne and die." At that time, an Eastbourne physician was on trial for murdering dozens of his clients. His office was called "Bedside Manor." He was very charming, according to accounts; he got his patients to endow him nicely in their wills before he helped them find eternal rest.

Despite it being close by, Brighton was not on my itinerary. It was a noted hangout for gays, a word not yet in use: "pansies," "poofs" and possibly "queers" were the terms of the day. Some-times, while hitching, I would turn down rides to Brighton from guys; it was not on the same route as Eastbourne. More than once I was told I should change my mind and go to Brighton. It might have been a livelier place, but I just was not ready, as intriguing as it might be.

There was a manpower shortage in England after World War II. Temporary stagehands were needed for Wednesday mat-inee performances in the London theaters. That suited my needs and interests very well. I managed a couple of stagehand stints at the Royal Court Theatre on Sloane Square. The play was John Osborne's *The Entertainer.* Its star was Sir Laurence Olivier. I thrilled to study him preparing for his performance. Here was the gorgeous Hamlet, who had won me over when I was a youth. Now he was much older, pudgier, and he perspired a lot, but he was a living legend whose mere proximity I enjoyed. My shyness kept me from conversation. His intense focus on the work at hand discouraged interruption.

I also hitched rides to St. Andrews, Scotland. I heard that a young American couple were running the Old Byre Theatre there. I would surprise them. It seemed a fine opportunity to see Scotland and gain more theatrical experience. One evening on the road it began to get dark and I saw no place to spend the night. I entered a pub to ask about inexpensive lodging in the neighborhood. A youth hostel, perhaps? No, nothing. A young man advised me to do what he did from time to time when he did not feel like going home. Sleep in a haystack was his suggestion. There were haystacks at the farm just down the road. I took his advice. I had no sooner settled into the straw when I saw a lit cigarette in the near distance. Someone was approaching. It seemed very likely that it was the same lad. I was not comfortable revealing my location; it might have led to an awkward situation, so I snuggled closer into my straw hideout. He gave up his search and I pondered the stars until I fell asleep. I was awakened by birdsong. The sound was very like that of Mother's cuckoo clock. It was the first time I ever heard that sound live and I was delighted. When I arrived at the Americans' home in St. Andrews, they were excited at my news of the cuckoo. It seems it is quite an honor to be the first of the season to hear the bird's song. They called the local press who came and interviewed me. A photo and story of my theatrical quest and the cuckoo song appeared the day I was to hitch to London to keep my date with Sir Laurence Olivier. I had no difficulty getting a ride as I was recognized from the newspaper story—a lovely feeling, being a celebrity, even for a short time.

Bell, Book and Candle was being performed at the Old Byre Theatre. A young man in the company befriended me and we spent much time talking about life, growing up and theater and, finally, after some hedging, same-sex relationships. In spite of coaxing to expand my horizons and my attraction to that nice

Scottish lad, I could not permit myself to step out of my shell and let life happen. Regretfully, we walked back to where I was staying. I remember our footsteps ringing hollow on the slate sidewalks. We spoke of the preponderance of ghosts in St. Andrews, emphasized by our footsteps. I would miss my new friend and wonder "what if?"

Farewell to jolly London with Brian Shiner's party, and off I went to sail home on the famed *Ile de France.* The tender took me from the Southampton dock to the luxurious liner. Didn't Lorelei Lee sail on her in *Gentlemen Prefer Blondes,* as well as celebrities from the arts and society? Light bulbs spelled out the ship's name from the upper deck. It was dark, so that the name glowed in the English fog. I was spellbound, and I had a tuxedo packed for the finale to my first trip to Europe. The exquisite decor aboard the *Ile de France,* in impeccable French taste, was elegant, lavish. Tapestries and etched glass panels decorated the public rooms. Fine carpets laid out on the highly polished floors muted footfalls and added splendor. Bouquets of white French lilies bobbed from countless vases. And, of course, the champagne flowed.

My heart skipped a beat when I perused the guest list. On board was Ruth Warrick, the Hollywood actress I enjoyed seeing in many films. Now, I instructed myself, I must not say to her when we meet that she used to be my favorite actress when I was a kid. I must not embarrass her that way. No, no, no! "You used to be my favorite actress when I was a kid," I blurted while we were dancing in First Class. I had sneaked in the night after sailing. She was pencil thin with small breasts, her hair Maureen O'Hara red. I was very nervous. It did not help that she kept darting her tongue in and out like a salamander catching flies. Years later, she told me it was a nervous reaction. Ruth was insecure herself, and she was not sure how to handle the attractive, enthusiastic young man who asked her to dance. Her skimpy black evening gown had spaghetti straps she tugged in an effort to catch the Styrofoam balls onlookers were tossing into her bodice.

Ruth had been given a suite by the purser, as there were only a handful of passengers in First Class. This was a "ghost" voyage: the ship was not scheduled to sail as it had been undergoing repairs, having run aground off Bermuda. With repairs completed in less time than expected, the French Line decided to sail her to New York. Only those who booked at the last moment had the rare opportunity to sail on one of the most glamorous ships ever built, with no crowds. It was like a private party for a handful of pleasure-seekers. The staff were determined to keep us happy and content.

Ruth harbored a stowaway named Clandestine in her suite. The intrepid beauty was discovered by Ruth while at the Marché aux Puces on the outskirts of Paris. On the flea market's barbed-wire fence was propped a blond mannequin with moveable fingers, elbows and knees. Life-size, she was the perfect gift for Ruth's husband, who requested that she bring him back a French maid. An enormous wicker basket transported "mademoiselle" from the Hôtel Georges V in Paris to the boat train. Her limbs splayed out of the top, mounted atop a taxi. It looked like a murder had been committed and the body was being transported. Bob Hope helped Ruth get packed for the steamer home. As there were so few passengers, Clandestine's existence could not be kept secret. Playfully, Ruth gave a cocktail party in her honor in the suite. The ship's doctor bore a vaccination certificate as a gift; the captain and purser winked at the stowaway status and officially welcomed Mlle Clandestine. She was a vision to behold at the door of the suite, welcoming startled visitors. Her golden tresses were carefully coiffed and the scent of Chanel No. 5 filled the air. Ruth lent Mlle Clandestine a flimsy negligée that revealed freshly rouged nipples. She held a small revolver (another gift for hubby) in her right hand and in her left a small nosegay of violets. Champagne and mirth accompanied the

unusual reception. I was in a fool's paradise with constantly flowing bubbly, in the company of an acclaimed performer and a cast
of international characters afloat in a pleasure palace—the life I
had yearned for so long.

One of the Cabin Class passengers was Gordon Merrick, a
writer of gay fiction that usually involved the rich and famous in
torrid, compromising plots. Gordon, from the Main Line outside
Philadelphia, was enormously attractive. When he was not writing, he took an interest in me. I loved listening to his tales of
encounters with notables. The last night out, I consumed a number of drinks. I remember Gordon walking me back to my stateroom. I woke up in a state of disarray. I remember nothing that
transpired. Some of my clothes were on and I had a nibbled dinner roll in my hand. Had I tried to put myself to bed but given up
while munching on a dinner roll? I did not remember if Gordon
had a hand in the disrobing. I visited him shortly afterward at his
Manhattan walk-up near the Hudson River in the low 50s. It was
not at all a chic apartment or address, just a simple pied-à-terre
he used when in New York. Gordon's male friend was there taking a shower when I arrived. I gasped at how beautiful he was,
while trying in vain not to stare at his gorgeous body (which he
made no effort to conceal). I was paralyzed with shyness and insecurity. I had Gordon sign a couple of his books I had bought and
exited hastily.

Maria de Kosenko, a Russian-American designer of wallpa-
pers in the eighteenth-century manner, was aboard the *Ile de
France* as well. Upon our return, we had many hilarious parties
with Ruth and Mlle Clandestine, culminating in the engagement
party we threw for Mlle Clandestine. Maria rented a male mannequin for the event. He was dressed up and given the identity of
an Italian nobleman. We gathered at Maria's East 71st Street
apartment for the happy event, celebrated with much champagne, as always. We humanoids went out to dinner, probably at
the Gay Vienna, which offered zither music with dinner. When

we returned, we thought the two mannequins had moved, changed positions and had a cozy life of their own in our absence. Maria was very old-world in her behavior. She used a pince-nez when perusing a menu, and crayon-colored her hair, which was pulled into a chignon. Full of amusing stories, Maria lived by her wits. Her early life was one of luxury, but her present circumstances were greatly reduced. Later, I myself would bail her out of a few dire straits. On one of our nights out dancing and sipping champagne, Maria and I went to a nightclub on East 14th Street near Luchow's. The Two Guitars featured Russian-Ukrainian music and had a nice-size dance floor. Sitting at the next table was the handsome and magnetic Aly Kahn in the company of a gorgeous brunette. Maria knew him from Europe and we joined them for a while. He was splendid to look at and I knew why Rita Hayworth had married that prince, who was also the spiritual leader of the Moslem world.

Does fanciful living bolstered by gushes of champagne encourage a peculiar view of life? The amount of alcohol I consumed certainly colored my verve for "life" and helped me achieve comfort with the cast of characters around me. I was no longer on the outside looking in. I was awash in the excitement of my colorful life, even if most of it was make-believe. Drinking was still fun at that point, but over the years the fun diminished and it became a nightmare out of control.

Rosemary Banks, an actress I had known since graduation from Queens College, lived in a walk-up in the East 70s. A few other struggling actors and a director also lived in the building. It was an enticing place for me to hang out. The director was doing a play out of town, and he offered me his apartment. I stayed and kept staying even after Royal returned. He fascinated me, and I remained long enough to finally acquiesce to "it." His gentle coaxing led to opening the floodgates of my yearnings. What a revelation! There was clearly no relationship in the making, but the meaningful interlude started me off on a new direction in life.

Ruth Warrick and young hopefuls
(Steve, Helen, Rosemary, me, Ruth (seated).

I wasted no time in trying my newly acquired knowledge out on the attractive actor Steve, upstairs. Yes, it was just what I had been waiting for. Suddenly, my horizons were not only expanded but seemed splashed in gold and vermilion! Intimacy with another man excited me. I liked the strength of my partner mingling with passionate beard-burning kisses. It was summertime and our perspiring bodies reveled in the released energies we were sharing. I related to Steve's muscularity and wanted to be strong, too. At long last, I felt tangibly connected with someone. It might have lasted a bit longer had it not been for Steve's lover who returned from a trip, alas.

I took a job at Walgreen's as a soda jerk. Graduate school loomed ahead and I still had no idea how I would manage the tuition. Things were bound to fall into place. After all, I was beginning to understand my own sexuality after years of questioning. Time would surely provide answers. I worked the night shift at the Walgreen's on Times Square. Post-theater tourists were replaced by the hookers, pimps and other characters that filled Times Square in the wee hours; the underbelly of the area was exposed nightly at my counter and I was fascinated. I did not relate to all the people, but my imagination was inflamed by their stories.

Finally, I had to accept that there was to be no miracle to give me tuition to the Carnegie Institute in Pittsburgh. I had to

A family portrait: George, Flo, Helen, Bob-Eric standing with parents seated.

relinquish my claim to admittance, but I did get a promise of acceptance for the following September. That gave me a year to organize myself. Getting a regular full-time job for the coming year seemed a good way to start. Flo had once worked at U.S. Plywood on West 44th Street, so why not ask them for a job? The personnel manager seemed affable to my request. He suggested that I might be right for the import-export department as an assistant to its secretary. I would have to pass a competency test first. Clearly, the young man liked me and wanted me to work there. He gave me more test time than was allotted and made sure some of my answers were correct (or corrected). He asked me to join him for drinks and dinner later. Would I be amenable to spending the night in the hotel next door afterward? I got the job, had drinks, dinner and my first one-night stand. The best thing to come out of the position was a long-lasting friendship with the boss's top secretary, Ilse ("Illa") Marum. She was a plain, bespectacled woman from Cologne, Germany, a refugee from Hitler. Illa became a very close friend until she died, some thirty years later.

I found a small room with a shared bathroom in the penthouse of a building on 76th Street, just west of Lexington Avenue. It had previously been a maid's room. The view was lovely: the rooftop and dome of St. Jean Baptiste Church, with an eastern exposure behind to view sunrises. I used the large wraparound terrace to entertain.

One day during lunch, I bumped into a girl I had known at Queens College. I had always thought she was very intellectual, with a serious bent that did not click with my fervent fraternity carryings-on. Then we had lost touch. Now, Lucia Pisacane dressed with verve and a simple sophistication that impressed me. She had a comforting, easy directness. We went to foreign movies and talked of art, theater and Europe. My excursions into sex had been minimal and, for once, I did not feel threatened by a woman. Little by little, I was working out my confusion. I began to believe that here was a female who did not panic me or threaten me. We seemed to share a gentle awareness of our vulnerability. With time and gentle effort, it might just be that Lucia and I could make a meaningful relationship. Surely, if the two of us tried with support and love, we could overcome my hang-ups and hers, too. After some months of seeing each other, we decided to get married. She was going to keep her job while I went to summer stock. Then we would move to Pittsburgh, where I would finally get to go to graduate school. She was going to find employment in Pittsburgh.

Despite my good intentions, there were constant temptations to lure me astray. At that time, a kindly, elderly doctor amused himself by tending to the needs of actors, both famous and struggling. At lunchtime, between morning and afternoon appointments, Dr. Fred Stern held court at the cafeteria of the Central Park Zoo. Young boys would gather around him and he would introduce the newcomers around. He dispensed his services free of charge to those who could not pay. I suspect his pleasure was in examining young men in his Fifth Avenue office in exchange for their shots or medicine. He introduced me to many interesting young men. One slightly older man befriended me. Noel Davis was the personal secretary and dresser for Edward Mulhare, the Professor Higgins in *My Fair Lady* after Rex Harrison left the cast. Noel invited me backstage to see the show, and he took me out afterward. Then we went back to Edward's fashionable East Side apartment, where he had his own living space.

My theatrical network expanded greatly. Noel introduced me to Mulhare and many of the cast members of *My Fair Lady*. One day, he took me to have tea at the apartment of the opera star Jennie Tourel. She was a delightful woman. Everything about her was round: figure, fingers and lots of rings. She regaled us with operatic vignettes that I devoured avidly: her opening-night performance at the Met as Manon, for example, when she

emerged from the coach in the first act and was blinded by the
lights. As a star, she did not have dress-rehearsal time, which was
thought unnecessary, to acquaint herself with the setting. She
faked it and achieved great success. Naughty in her recounting,
Jennie would sing the Purcell aria "Dido's Lament," "When I am
laid, am laid. . . ," with great significance. I enjoyed her charming,
lively company.

Through Freddie or other friends I met more actors, dancers, and "wannabes." André Prokovsky, the ballet dancer son of
the woman who had befriended me at the American Residence in
Paris, came to town with Roland Petit's Les Ballets de Paris, starring Petit's wife, Zizi Jeanmaire. I went to the ballet almost every
night and, through André, became friendly with the company of
the Ballets de Paris. I began to go out with other members of the
company. André was on the dull, straight side; the others had
more flame and pizazz. We went to the many parties given for
them, and even I managed to scrape enough money together to
invite them for sherry and cheese on my penthouse terrace, simple as it was.

I also remember the gorgeous star of the London Festival
Ballet, John Gilpin. He was with his benefactor, the head of the
ballet company, Anton Dolin, familiarly known as "Pat." We met
in the dressing room of Tony Randall, then starring with Alexandra Danilova on Broadway in *Oh, Captain!* It may have been
Noel who brought me there. In any case, I was intrigued with
dazzling Gilpin and world-renowned Dolin. I must have made an
impression on them, too, because they came to my terrace for a
visit.

Sylvia Tysik, a Canadian ballet dancer lived in New York at
that time. She commuted between Toronto and New York as she
had her own television program in Toronto but was pursuing a
career in New York. We met backstage at Les Ballets de Paris and
became friendly. The petite redhead went on to appear in *Stop*

Springtime wedding: Lucia and I plunge.

the World, I Want to Get Off! and the London production of *West Side Story*, playing the part of Anybodys.

Summer approached, and with it my stint at the Lakes Region Playhouse in Laconia, New Hampshire, near Lake Winnepasaukee. Lucia came up to help me get settled in the little cottage I rented. Shortly before leaving New York, we had had a simple Justice of the Peace ceremony in Yonkers, with Flo as matron of honor and Henry, a floormate from my penthouse, as best man. My brother George and his wife attended as did Father and Mother. I do not recall whether Helen was there. I do know that none of Lucia's family attended, as they heartily disapproved. They had received an anonymous poison-pen letter warning them of the disastrous mistake the marriage would be. It bothered me and I had many uncomfortable suspicions as to the sender. After the ceremony, we went to my small apartment on East 75th Street for food, provided by Mother, and lots of champagne. Lots of champagne was my answer, remedy and solution to everything. Then Lucia and I went to see the Russian ballet film *Romeo and Juliet.* That was our "honeymoon," and perhaps our first marital mistake. We should have taken a real honeymoon, alone. Maybe we would have really connected. Our marriage was vaguely defined, with a great need for closer communication.

There were a half dozen productions that summer at the Playhouse, each with a different star and cast. Eight or ten of us worked on sets and costumes, jumping into acting roles when needed. I was highly self-conscious while acting, but managed to attract the attention of a couple of directors and was cast in roles that made me very uneasy. I remember telling them I could not act. Invariably, their ego encouraged them to allay my fears with promises that they would help me turn out a wonderful performance. Usually, the wonderful performance they wanted was between the sheets.

David Halliday, a handsome and desirable young man from the Midwest, was in charge of scenery building. He had a girlfriend there with him, which led me to believe he was straight. His obsession was singing Tony's songs from *West Side Story,* which had just opened to rave reviews on Broadway. To everyone's surprise and delight, when he auditioned that fall for the role of Tony in the London production, he was chosen.

Many exciting things happened to me that summer. I met Tallulah Bankhead, who appeared in *House on the Rocks.* Every time she heard me speak backstage, she thought it was a great friend of hers that had come to see her. "Son-of-a-bitch" was her nickname for me because that is what she uttered when she realized it was not her friend. It was said with some affection: "Oh, Eric, you son-of-a-bitch!" She astounded everyone at the theater with her performance and her compulsions. She demanded that a lovely, young Iranian girl bring her glasses of bourbon when she exited the stage. The girl was a bit embarrassed, as it was obvious that Tallulah had taken a gratuitous attraction to her. Craven A cigarettes, her favorite, at which she puffed constantly, had to be in the cigarette cases on stage at all times. Clothes and Tallulah were not always compatible. She loved to sit stark naked in her dressing room with the door wide open. I spied her many times, always looking like a raisin. Tallulah kept her makeup on ice even though only minutes after application the hot lights would undo all the tightness she had achieved. Ritual tainted with denial perhaps explained it. By curtain call, Tallulah was flying high. Her last-scene costume was a long crino-

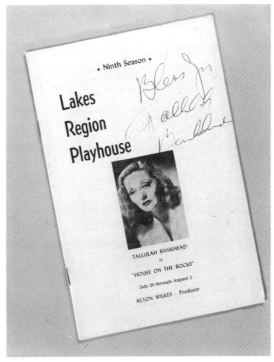

Tallulah at summer stock

line gown, which she would gather up in front to swoop down to the footlights. In her exuberance, she would lift it so high that anyone in the front of the house could enjoy a revealing gander at Miss Bankhead's thighs.

Veronica Lake was one of my favorite stars that summer, appearing in *Cat on a Hot Tin Roof.* She quickly lined me up as her beer supplier. Her most recent husband was determined to keep Ronnie sober. When no one suspected it, I slipped her a forbidden beer. One day, she invited me to visit them in their lakefront apartment. My co-workers were critical of my palling around with the stars. One of them had agreed to drive me to the lake but purposely disappeared when it was time to go. I was all dressed up but had to walk there, getting perspired and flustered.

Ronnie's husband offered a drink, and I joined them in brief conversation. Perhaps I had been invited there so she would have an excuse to drink. I was instructed by her husband that I was not to supply Ronnie with alcohol. She had tried to give up drinking by going into seclusion in the Sierra Nevadas, to no avail. Veronica Lake did not have the long, peek-a-boo blond hair we saw in her Hollywood films with Alan Ladd. She wore a short, feathery cut. Her face was puffy, filled out with time and alcohol. It was only in profile by a campfire at a picnic she threw for the crew that one had a notion of what Veronica Lake had once looked like. She was the only star who bothered to thank the crew with a party on an island in the lake. It was generous of her. I sensed she had a good heart but was vulnerable both to a cruel world and her own addictions. Not long afterward, I heard some queen bragging about being at a party in New York where Veronica Lake was very drunk. She had taken a job in the restaurant at the Martha Washington Hotel near Gramercy Park. Then there were stories of the Mafia beating her up for bad debts. Tales of her unbridled licentiousness during her movie-making days completed the picture of an unhappy, needy woman driven by compulsions.

Damn Yankees was the musical event of our season, and I was deliriously happy to work on that show. The cast was especially attentive to me. The fun of being around a musical every day delighted me. Some of the cast members went on to be long-lasting friends. The crew greatly resented my instant bonding with the actors, singers and dancers, but I did not care.

Groucho Marx arrived with his young wife to star in *Time for Elizabeth*. Because of my determined networking, I was the only resident member invited to a luncheon that Groucho hosted at a nearby restaurant. A fan approached him and offered to shake his hand. Groucho placed a clean, white napkin over his hand before shaking the stranger's hand. He introduced his stage wife to the fan as his wife, rather than the much younger real Mrs. Marx. The master comedian was a ruthless top banana in the production. A character actress decided to do a new piece of business with her costume during a rehearsal. Our uproarious laughter caused Marx to forbid her to do it again. She was annoyed that we had betrayed her intentions through our laughter.

One night backstage, Ruth Manning, who was in Groucho's cast, looked me over and asked me if I had a name other than Bob, my first name, which I still used. When she discovered my middle name was Eric, I was instructed *never* to use Bob again, Eric was far more fitting. At my invitation, she came to my cabin for a drink early one evening when the theater was dark. She regaled me with Hollywood stories involving Errol Flynn and others. I was entranced. We went to her place, too, and I made myself naively oblivious to her enticements. I went home an innocent babe, grateful for the sophisticated attentions I had received.

Once, restless around 2:00 a.m., I dressed and walked down the road about a mile to where many of the cast members slept. I knew which bed Wyatt Cooper occupied. Steeling myself with imagined courage, I sneaked into the room. Slipping out of my apparel, I snuggled next to the male god. Gratified by the attentions I received, I slipped out past the sleeping cast members before dawn. It was a very forward, aggressive act to gain affectionate attention. We never spoke of the event. I loved possessing the young, romantic leading man, even for a short time. About a year later, I was surprised to see his glamorous face on the front page of the *Daily News* as the new husband of Gloria Vanderbilt. Lucky "poor little rich girl" was she to have that hunk every day and night. I had many occasions to visit friends over the years at the United Nations Plaza where the Coopers resided. I would greet Wyatt and his young son coming in or going out. Occasionally, I saw Gloria with him, too. She also maintained a studio next door to where I would live for six years in the early 1960s. New York seemed like a small place where one saw the same 100 or so people all the time.

Summer stock came to a close with Ann Sheridan in the final play of the season. I left a bit early to go with Noel to Kennebunkport, Maine, for a little holiday. I remember a quaint, white guesthouse, sunning on ocean-sprayed rocks, eating raw oysters and sipping champagne while champagne was drunk from my navel. Noel had a couple of acquaintances there who joined us for a ride down to the new Shakespeare theater in Stratford, Connecticut. Fritz Weaver and Inga Swenson were playing in *Hamlet*. I was fondled the entire trip down in full view of the others in the car and any interested driver-by. I thought it daring and fun.

Noel was to leave a few hours before Lucia's arrival; their trains would pass each other. He did not depart without leaving his mark, perhaps more for Lucia than for me. I discovered that I had picked up "crabs" and Noel insisted on shaving off all my pubic hair. It was my first brush with the creatures. We purchased a strong solution at the pharmacy and applied it. Noel maintained that shaving was necessary, too. I think it amused him to ponder how I would explain it to my wife. It was the first clue of a mean streak that would later take a vicious turn.

My reunion with Lucia was polite but awkward. A shaved crotch, a case of crabs and a reluctance to intimacy was not the best mix for young marrieds. We kept all our issues on the back burner while trying to put on a pleasant front for ourselves and the world. It would take time, but it would work out, we assured each other. With that hopeful promise, we set off for Pittsburgh, where I could finally approach graduate school and the challenge of my future. Lucia found a job and cheerfully helped to keep the bills paid and food on the table. There were mounting liquor costs, too.

For years, my wife had resented living with her family in Forest Hills over a store. She felt her life would blossom, away from that environment. What did I do? Against her bitter protests, I took an apartment over a store. It had good space and light and was near school. Surely, she would get over her adversity to that situation. Add disappointment over our sexual inexperience and incompatibility, which we thought would change miraculously, and the scenario was not the happiest. My self-absorption with school and my needs overshadowed Lucia's needs. We began making unpleasant scenes in front of friends. Someone called me on the phone one evening when we had a few people in. I was lying on the floor talking in a cozy, confidential tone to the gentleman caller. Lucia left the guests to see what was up. Having dumped her glass of red wine on my head in despair, she went back to the guests. Outraged by the impertinence, I reentered the party and, in front of all the guests, emptied *my* glass over *her* head. The guests were shocked and beat a hasty retreat. I am not sure if I went to the party that the phone call was about. It was clear that our rift had become deep and troublesome.

Christmas break was coming. I decided to go to New York and stay with Noel for part of the time. I would visit my family in Montrose in Westchester, but allow ample time for New York carousing. With money tight, Lucia would stay in Pittsburgh, since she was holding down a full-time job. There was acrimony about my going and my inability to resolve my problems with the marriage. A break might be beneficial for both of us. Lucia was beginning to make friends both at Carnegie and in the community. She was befriended by a couple who were affiliated with the Pittsburgh Symphony, which gave her a source of interest.

My Fair Lady was a constant in my life, then. I must have seen it ten times from the front of the house and as many times backstage with Noel. My holiday drinking sky-rocketed. It was thrilling to sit in the overstuffed chair in Professor Higgins's dressing room, a scotch in my right hand. In came Liza Doolittle (Sally Anne Howes) with an open bottle of champagne. When I was offered a glass, someone said, "Oh, Eric doesn't need champagne, he has a glass of scotch." I hastily replied, "That is in my right hand, my left hand is free!" I gleefully took the glass of bubbly and drank both. That was fun. That was exciting. That was validation. Not only expensive scotch and costly champagne, but both offered to me by Broadway stars. Surely, I had arrived at a pinnacle of personal success. Pittsburgh now seemed distant and drab compared to the breathless excitement of New York. My experience with the mighty and glamorous was heightened to dizzying proportions.

The young composer and conductor of the New York Philharmonic had just returned from a triumphant tour of Russia. There was a parade in his honor and every department store on Fifth Avenue displayed huge photos of "Lenny." When Jennie Tourel was at her peak as an opera singer, she had helped Bernstein in many ways. As he grew in stature, he protected and aided her in true friendship and admiration. Tourel gave a supper party in his honor to celebrate the successful tour and return to New York. It was at the time of a newspaper strike in the city. *West Side Story* had just opened in London and Bernstein was eager to read a review about his musical creation there. I was backstage in Mulhare's dressing room enjoying a scotch with Noel and Edward's mistress, Jean Suskind, who was the wife of a conductor in Canada. The phone rang and Edward greeted Lenny. Yes, he had the London *Times* but no, he was unable to go to Jennie's party. However, he would entrust the paper to Jean and Noel, who would be leaving shortly to attend the supper. I was about to meet Leonard Bernstein!

Each of us was clearly excited about the prospect of the night ahead, even though they had met Bernstein before. I contemplated what I might do to make an impression on him. He was overwhelmingly attractive and perhaps he might find me of "special" interest. Surely everyone there would be hanging on his every word. How would I manage to compete? On entering Tourel's apartment and giving the butler our coats, we saw the esteemed Lenny on the couch, everyone either clustered around him or sitting at his feet, as was Tourel. Jean whispered to me that we should go to the bar, where a radio was gently playing dance music. In full view of the maestro, we took our drinks and placed them on the bar. We danced cheek to cheek, ignoring the crowd in the other room, but aware that the center of attention had caught sight of us, seemingly indifferent to what was happening in his circle. "I think he might like a threesome," she murmured in my ear.

A short while later, Noel, Jean and I were in an area not far from the throng. Lenny approached and asked Noel for the London *Times* Edward had sent along for him. I purposely turned my back on the guest of honor. Bernstein must have been surprised, perhaps piqued at my indifference because he demanded to know, "Who's the guy?" Alcohol-bolstered courage pushed me on. Calling upon my theatrical training, I tried to seem sophisticated and alluring. Spinning around and looking him squarely in the eye, I extended my hand, which had a bowl of nuts in it. "Nuts?" I offered. Within minutes, Noel sidled up to me and confidentially told me that he thought Lenny wanted a foursome. It was not until after a supper of beef stroganoff that I knew for sure. A young Israeli singer was encouraged to perform a cappella. Lenny had just come from the bathroom, doused heavily in perfume. He sat next to me and proceeded to squeeze my leg. He did not want a threesome or a foursome, he wanted a twosome. Alas, he could not ditch the Russian musicians who were there in his honor; I was not sure what to do with Noel. The evening wore on, and finally Jennie reminded always-ready-for-a-party Lenny that he had an afternoon concert at Carnegie Hall the next day and that he should try to get some sleep.

Tourel lived around the corner on West 58th Street north of Carnegie Hall. Bernstein and his wife (who was not at the party) lived at the Osborne, diagonally across Seventh Avenue from Carnegie Hall. The Russians (damn them), together with Jean and Noel, joined me in walking dear, desirable Lenny around the corner to his home. He kept a separate studio in the building and was not ready to call it a night yet, suggesting we come up for a nightcap. It was clear that we would never get rid of the others, so Lenny invited me to have Noel come with me to the concert the next day and sit in his box.

Grievously unhappy events unfolded in the predawn hours upon return to the Eastgate that morning. Jean did not come back with us as Edward had gone away somewhere. Noel began needling me about my interest in Lenny. He provoked such distress that I finally became nauseous. At that point, Noel desisted from his tormenting comments and became affectionate. It was such a strange turn of events that I repelled him and fled to Edward's empty bedroom, locking the door behind me. After vain attempts to get me to return to his bedroom, we slept a few hours. I was torn with emotions having to do with marriage, an untrustworthy "loving" friend and the promise of a liaison with the most dynamic man I had ever met, Leonard Bernstein. That morning I telephoned a longtime friend, Walter Ash, who invited me to come stay in his apartment after the Bernstein concert until my return to Pittsburgh.

Strained and quiet, Noel and I went off to Carnegie Hall for the Bernstein concert. With pride, I settled into the maestro's box, looking forward to seeing him in the green room afterward. I had a recut camel's-hair overcoat that I wore jauntily over my shoulders in the most casual attitude I could muster. Noel, Lenny and I had a brief conversation and I was full of anticipation. Then, we said farewell. I, sadly, walked a few steps feeling heavy with rejection. Then Lenny called me back. He asked whether he could reach me later at Edward's apartment. I told him that I had left the Eastgate and gave him the Murray Hill number of my new host. Triumph after all! It was with a new attitude that I returned to Pittsburgh. For the first time in my fearful life, I had tangible encouragement from the demigods themselves that I was desirable, attractive, interesting, worthwhile and, maybe, even one of them—the glitterati of the world.

Wanting to be released from the marriage and trying at last

to be fair with Lucia, I suggested to her that we get a Mexican divorce. She was more than startled but knew that I was firm in this conviction. Her final indulgence to me was going to Mexico and getting a legal divorce. It was a nine-month fiasco, but now each of us could go about making a new direction, a different life.

Married at twenty-one, divorced at twenty-two. To make ends meet at the time of the divorce, I volunteered (for pay) to be a guinea pig in an experiment at the University of Pittsburgh. I had moved farther down Forbes Avenue to an apartment adjacent to a local gay bar. I had the back apartment on the ground floor of a building inhabited by "colorful" individuals. The front apartment was occupied by a doctoral student at the University; Audrey Holland put me up for the experiment, to assist me financially. The experiment consisted of isolation for twelve hours at a time, three sessions, and was one of the most fascinating experiences of my life. Most of those who started out in the experiment left after the first session. I, on the other hand, loved it. I discovered that being isolated in a room devoid of light, sound or movement was a challenge, a mind-blowing adventure. I was taken into a small room and asked to sit on a cot. I was administered orange juice in which, I suspect, was some drug. I was told that I was expected to lie still in the dark for twelve hours, only to get up to go to the toilet or to eat what was on a tray under the cot. I would know when the food was slid in on a track by the trembling of the cot. I did not have to drink the milk or eat the sandwich or cookies if I chose not to. After finding the bathroom with the lights on once or twice, I was left on my own with the lights out.

I prepared a few different projects to hold my attention during the sessions. One was the creation of a mental map of Western Civilization from as early a date as I could recall. It was amazing to dig around in my mind, filling in pertinent details (rulers, wars, writers), free of distraction by the senses. My mind swung open, revealing information I had either forgotten or never knew was there waiting to be tapped. To make sure that what I conjured up was indeed based in fact, I went to the school library after each session to check up on myself. My mind, in isolation, was capable of dredging up enormous amounts of data. Second, I amused myself by directing a cinema version of *Cyrano de Bergerac* using talents both alive and dead. My cast included Anna Magnani as the baker's wife and Marilyn Monroe as the leading lady, Roxanne. Then I moved them about the set, creating the most theatrically wondrous scenes. A third project was analyzing personal relationships. Family and friends were scrutinized and evaluated. That project was the shortest and least worthwhile. It is possible that my ingrained sense of denial would not permit clear examination.

Once in a while, just to create an effect, I pressed the red button at my side. Each session was in a different room and had a different kind of machine overhead activated by the red button. One day, for example, the button created a blinking of red and white flashes moving along a wire. Another day, it was a stationary blinking of just red. The blinking was dull, certainly no substitute for television or any other kind of technological distraction. I was told that it was an outer-space experiment to see if machines would amuse spacemen. No way! I do not doubt that my responses surprised the supervisors of the experiment. I was truly enthusiastic about the isolation and fascinated to discover clues about my "brain trust," not that I would ever use it in everyday life. The project bought me much needed champagne and salami for the refrigerator à la Zsa-Zsa Gabor, who believed in stocking only those two commodities in hers. I did not realize it then but the isolation was not really a change from my interior landscape. All my life I had retreated into my own fantasy world. The ominous undertones of alcoholic consumption encouraged my taking to this scenario so readily.

The last part of graduate school was spent delving into the Japanese Noh drama, even though the head of the department and my adviser thought it a noncommercial waste of time. I was

fascinated by Zen Buddhism and the intricacies of the tea ceremony, both related to an understanding of Noh. I put myself on a
prescribed study time between midnight and 7:00 a.m., often culminating in a dawn walk along the railroad tracks, lined with
spring forsythia, cherry blossoms and pussy willows. Nirvana and
euphoria alternately transported me, in sharp contrast to the crass
earthiness of the gay bar next door. That contrast became a
repeating pattern for the rest of my life.

Audrey, my speech pathologist neighbor, was often whisked
by me "out to get a breath of fresh air." With raincoat over her
nightgown, I brought her to the smoky bar next door for night-
caps. Other flamboyant characters in the house on Forbes Street
included the girl on the floor above Audrey in the front. She
painted her studio apartment black and had a red light in her window. Jackie was a free spirit who rarely wore more than a frilled
shorty nightgown. Her colorful career simmered down when she
married an undergraduate from the Drama Department and had
a mulatto child. On the top floor lived Dawn, a drama student
who had a tempestuous love life. Once, we saw her ousting a gentleman caller, hitting him on the head with an iron frying pan and
pushing him down the stairs amid screams of abuse. She always
used a palette to mix her lipstick, applying it with a fine paint
brush.

I developed strong likes and dislikes for some of my professors as well as my peers. I was attracted to the dramatic drinking
queens of the school who closed the off-color gay bar downtown
at dawn and barely had time to change for class. Some days I was
on my midnight-to-dawn study regime; others, I was crawling
about until dawn in search of fresh pleasure. Life was extravagantly two-dimensional: either crass and decadent or ethereal
and profound. Alcohol brought me to both places very well, but I
did not clearly see the road to my directing career or any career
for that matter. Answers were not forthcoming. My fears,
although I was reluctant to admit them, convinced me that I sim-

ply did not have the courage or stamina to be a theater director, despite my talent. I would take time to let things sift. Needing money, and knowing how to network and earn good tips as a waiter, I decided to go to gay Provincetown for the summer. I thought it would be a good start for "je ne sais quoi," and in many ways it was.

Chapter 5

OFF AND RUNNING

Ocean rollers washing sea cliffs, beaches under a torrid sun and a wide selection of gay men seemed like a good way to spend a summer. In Provincetown, I was certain I could earn money as a waiter and enjoy "the scenery," too. I believed my entrée into the world of gay men would easily be achieved by waiting tables. I met an artist who later became my mentor, protector and lover. Douglass Semonin was emphatic about my not needing to be a waiter to be noticed, needed and accepted by the network of men around me. My insecurities would not permit me to be convinced, but I remembered his admonition.

I loved going to work in my sailor-striped shirt, cheerfully waiting on customers, sharing information about the area as well as my enthusiasm about life there. During my free time, I wandered around the tidal basin, singing to myself "Summertime, and the livin' is easy" or "It's a lazy afternoon." I went over the dunes to Herring Cove or to the sea cliffs at Long Nook, Truro, where I sunned, swam and flirted. I did not go unnoticed, which helped to reinforce my self-esteem. I was attractive and desirable after all. Moreover, I had a brain. I convinced myself that it was my brain that my chosen guys responded to, not just a pretty face.

Saving money was easy, as I lived in an inexpensive rooming house that was neither chic nor on the tourist map. My food came mostly from the Moors, the restaurant where I worked, consumed between tasks. On my nights off, Douglass or someone

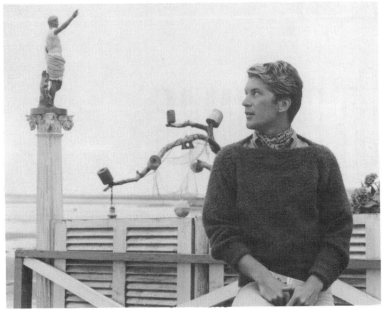

Rising tide from Jones's Locker, Provincetown.

else would invite me out. Boston blueblood Nat Saltonstall became one of my platonic admirers. I was the young, new face in his group.

Jones' Locker was the smart gay place to stay. Larry Jones, a retired Navy captain, created a maze of apartments on the west end of town. They clustered around his deck, which led to the beach. A bar was conveniently located on the deck, full of vacationing gays with money. Larry took a shine to me, helping me add to my European travel fund by paying me for various odd jobs. We collected washed-up planking from the beach and then nailed it down as a hardwood floor in another addition to the Locker. It was hard work getting warped planking to dovetail into a presentable floor. Perseverance and a sledgehammer helped a lot. Larry was very creative, but he did not pay much attention to the finer details of building those odd apartments. It was easy for him to furnish them whimsically with a conglomeration of odds and ends, junk and treasure. Closer inspection was inadvisable. The electrical wiring and plumbing were jerry-built and improperly affixed to the outside back of the building where they were not visible. What went on inside the wallboards or under cupboards was makeshift at best. He was also indifferent to deep cleaning. Everything looked charming on the surface, but I did not move anything or look too closely.

Driving Larry's gold Mercedes 300 was a great honor. Once, drunk, I almost wrecked it taking the Orleans Circle too quickly. Larry was approaching fifty, more than double my age. It was clear that he wanted to become familiar with me. On the upper deck of one of his apartments one late afternoon after work, oiled with gin, he gave me a deeply pained look. "Is it because I am almost fifty that you hesitate?" The agony in his face melted my resistance. We began an intimacy that was not meant to be a monogamous affair, rather a friendly consensual rapport that served the moment very well.

He had had a most amazing long-term relationship with the ultra-flamboyant Jamie Spilman, who appeared in Provincetown from time to time. Jamie was a vivid character and I grew very fond of his way with people. He smoked, drank and caroused with both women and men. He had had a long-term relationship with Tallulah Bankhead's sister, Eugenia. Previously, Jamie was involved with one of the Hearst heiresses. One expected the unexpected from Jamie, and he never disappointed. His whims included traveling with a trained monkey that he would dress up in tiara and ballgown for parties. His own attire was startling as well. Jamie had a well-proportioned physique, despite enormous alcohol intake on a daily basis. Loving the androgynous, he dressed up his butch outfits with bracelets and fur around the neck. Always with a cigarette holder, he could flirt outrageously with a straight redneck, often seducing him. Utterly fascinated, I thought Jamie led the most dramatic and colorful life, so naturally he became a role model.

My second taste of Europe was postponed, as I lacked money. I spent the autumn of 1959 working as a window dresser for Macy's in Parkchester, where Flo lived with her alcoholic husband Jack. By now, they had a child, my niece Lori Ann. I think I got the job there in the Bronx just to be close to my sister.

I shared a walk-up apartment with a swishy guy on East 52nd Street, just down from the famed El Morocco. He introduced me to some of the current East Side fluff, increasing my network considerably. Someone in the group asked me if I would like to meet Joan Crawford's daughter, Tina. Would I? I jumped at the chance.

Tina Crawford lived in a simple ground-floor apartment nearby. I remember our conversation and laughter clearly. She sat cross-legged on the floor in front of a blowup poster of Joan. Although Tina was adopted, she had incorporated a way of smiling similar to that of her infamous stepmother; you would swear you saw a family resemblance. Her stepbrother Chris worked in the display department at Bloomingdale's. What a difference there was between the two adopted children of Joan Crawford. He was painfully shy, with a poor complexion and a submerged personality. Tina was bubbly and pretty. It would be a few years before Joan Crawford herself entered my ever-expanding world, to complete the family picture.

A lovely English girl with long blond hair worked in display with me at Macy's. She was so gentle and pleasing that I was drawn into an easy friendship with her. There were no illusions about our having a physical relationship, but we enjoyed each other's company and we became like brother and sister. Wanderlust overtook us and we decided to buy an open round-trip bus ticket to Mexico City. Both of us had a little cash from our Macy's indenture and Deidre had been posing as a nude model for the Art Students League. I had been in touch with an actress friend from Carnegie who now lived in New York City. Her parents managed a residence hotel in Dallas, and they were informed that Eric and his sister would be by for a visit en route to Mexico City.

Laura took an immediate shine to me, and she and her husband adopted Deidre into their hotel apartment. Laura gave me her son's MG sports car to use while in Dallas. He had just gone into the army and would not be needing it. I garaged it at the hotel and found a room nearby, my choice so that I could have more freedom. Deidre and I decided to build up funds by staying in Dallas for a while. She worked in a coffee house; I picked her up after work and brought her back to the hotel. I got a waiter position at a posh restaurant, where I learned the intricacies of French service, how to prepare a Caesar salad dressing and which were the latest fine wines. I shared the top floor in a nice house with a handsome, sexy young cabaret pianist. I was infatuated and employed, as well as delighted by the nice prospects that Dallas offered me.

Often drunk, Laura got more and more obsessive about me. Her husband ignored her; he was in the bag himself most of the time. They both wondered about our brother-sister relationship, but Laura chose to accept it so that she could continue her flirtatious advances. Friends advised her that I was probably gay. Deidre was cross-examined, but she denied it, as I, too, did when asked about it.

After a month of swimming pool, sports car, fancy restaurant and waning romance with the pianist, I decided it was time to continue on to Mexico. Laura made scenes at our leaving, but finally let us go, with the threat that she and Johnnie would be down at some point to visit friends in Mexico City. And arrive they did.

The bus trip seemed endless, with poor sanitary facilities and dubious food. We found cheap accommodations somehow, and met Mexicans who showed us around. One guy fell for Deidre and drove us to Acapulco via Taxco and Cuernavaca. I sat

on the floor of the car on the way through Cuernavaca to avoid
being seen by Barbara Hutton. I had been told just before departing New York by Doris, a fortune-teller, that a world-famous
woman with an enormous fortune would become attracted to me.
From what I had read in the press, I did not want to be involved
with that notorious woman. I dreaded the notion.

Taxco was in disorder because Cantinflas was making a film
there. I could not pass up the opportunity to be on the periphery.
He was said to be one of the all-time great comedians. My fascination for superstars prompted me to hang around the shooting
to catch glimpses of the great performer.

Mexico was affordable then, and Deidre and I enjoyed
many sights and pleasures of Old Mexico, including a stay in a
simple house on the outskirts of Acapulco. When I told our young
Mexican friends that we were going to meet a couple flying in
from Texas for the weekend, they agreed to come to the airport
and sing for Laura and offer her a shawl I bought at the market.
She was stunned at the reception, at first refusing to take the
shawl. Drunk, Laura was convinced they were trying to sell it to
her. She was a thoroughly kindhearted woman, afraid of growing
old and undesirable. She craved attention and romance. Her
Texas lifestyle revolved around drinking, which was not only a
social lubricant; liquor afforded her flights of fancy and bolstered
her courage in persuing her current romantic obsession—me.
We had several awkward, strained days while Laura and John
were in Mexico City. However, we managed to see a couple of
grand homes, and we enjoyed their hospitality in high-class restaurants.

Mexico was a terrific adventure but it was time to wend our
way back to New York. I returned to my family at Montrose in
Westchester. Plans were to prepare an early start for summer season in Provincetown. I wanted to plump out my travel money for
a fall trip to revisit Europe; it had so bewitched my imagination
and my heart.

I got my old job back as waiter at the Moors, and I managed to get a floor-through right on the water in a house needing repairs. It was on the west end of town near Larry Jones' Locker, which made helping him out easier, too. Alice and Hazel, the new owners of the property, became Mom and Mom-in-law. I paid something like $15 a week for the floor-through that Deidre and I occupied. We made small repairs as part of the deal, a bargain for all concerned. Alice, large, mannish and of Italian descent, was my banker. Every day, I dropped a wad of bills in her lap for my account. Being a waiter, helping Larry part time and posing for artist Robert Hunter kept money coming in. My expenses were small, as I was always being taken to lunch or dinner, or enjoying tidbits at the Moors.

I am amazed at the amount of energy I expended on three jobs and keeping several admirers pleased on a continual basis. Anonymous, indescrimate sex was distasteful to me. Part of that had to have been caused by the inconvenience of yet another energy-sapping activity. I was nearing overload. It was not a question of morals, as I would have had myself believe. It was a practical impossibility. I was acting out a badly needed sense of validation. I just could not develop my talents in the theater. I craved attention and adulation from customers and distinguished friends like Nat Saltonstall, Larry Jones, Robert Hunter and others, mixed with the continuous flow of alcohol. It defined my life with a classy stamp of approval. I thirsted for love and the grand illusion of fun and glamor. Alcohol encouraged me to feel brave, beautiful, alluring and witty.

The 1960 season in Provincetown was the last one of high caliber I enjoyed there. Larry Jones's annual costume party soon went out of fashion. The splendid cast of characters including "Baby June" MacFarland and her Boston Brahmin lover Harry Snelling, Jamie Spilman, Larry himself, Marjorie Oliver and many others were soon decimated by death, illness and old age. A few made escapes to the Caribbean to further indulge their alcoholism. The times gave way to the hippies, an outgrowth of the charming, delightful but short-lived flower children. Style and verve went out the window in Province-town as elsewhere.

Nina Micheleit is a personal treasure I have managed to keep in my life when all the others disappeared for the reasons above. Nina ran the Shore

Nina in Shore Gallery, Provincetown.

Galleries for Bob Campbell, her sister Grace's husband. The Shore Galleries in Boston had a branch in Provincetown, at that time on the deck next to Larry Jones' Locker. One day, Larry was on the deck of the gallery talking with a woman whose hair was pulled back into a bun. She was smoking a cigarette and she seemed cordial and earnest with Larry. I had been in the water swimming and noticed him beckoning me to join them. Nina claimed that I looked like a Greek god emerging from the water onto her deck. My taut, bronzed body glistened with salt water and my sun-bleached locks clung around my smiling face. I remember feeling on top of the world, and I must have shown it. Since art was always high in my esteem, I was glad to meet the earnest, cheerful woman without pretense or affectation. We began to see lots of each other in our spare time, especially since I lived and worked in the same part of town as she did. We were neighbors and colleagues and seemed to be of one mind on many things. Many evenings we shared scotch on my upper deck, lis-tening to the clanging of buoys and watching the tide and the blinking of the lighthouse. In this starry seascape, metaphysical questions dared our investigation, fueled by innumerable libations. We discussed the nature of man, his fallibility and the state of the world, problems we assumed were our province to explore and conquer. Today, when we meet in Onset (Buzzard's Bay) or in St. Petersburg, Florida, some of those monumental problems still present themselves, daring miraculous solutions. We know better.

That summer, it became clear that Douglass could no longer be considered a lover. As much as I desired him as a close friend, anything more was not feasible. It was so difficult to explain to him. We had some strained words, which hung heavily between us. Douglass decided to take a walk out along the flats provided by low tide. I had to get to the Moors for work, but I was worried about his mood. I left him a note telling him to go see Nina at the gallery. Nina told me that she would talk with Douglass, who had great regard for her. She helped me get him over the parting with her gentle, caring manner. We were both grateful, and we managed eventually to continue as warm, devoted friends. When I departed for Europe, Douglass brought me a silver and gold Tiffany cigarette case, engraved "Prince Eric Gustav." A few years later, he painted a full-length nude portrait of me. Years later, I noticed there were six toes painted on each foot. Douglass claimed that royalty like the Bourbons often had six toes or fingers.

The French Line had so impressed me during my return on the *Ile de France* that it was a clear choice for my second trip to Europe that I must further sample French hospitality. What could be grander than the impressive *Liberté*? It had been converted into a troop ship during the war by the Germans, yet the French managed to fix it up with elegance and panache. My parents, Douglass, Deidre and a couple of other well-wishers sipped champagne with me in the large, elegant lounge. I fingered my new Tiffany cigarette case with studied nonchalance and gaily waved goodbye to all of them all, streamers flying dockward, band playing.

As we pulled out, I noticed an elegant youngish matron on the upper deck next to me. She introduced herself, announcing that she was from Cleveland, going to study cooking at the École Cordon Bleu in Paris. She was a First Class passenger, but I knew I would see lots of her and the other First Class passengers, since I planned to crash the barriers from Tourist Class at every opportunity. It was easy to do, as I quickly made friends in First Class and they invited me to join them after dinner for dancing and parties. The crew did not mind that I was welcomed by their elite passengers, and I added pizazz to the evenings.

There was Hermione Gingold's name on the list of passengers. The small group of First Classers that adopted me were pleased by my company, but they were reluctant to include "that actress." That surprised me, but I persisted, as I found her very funny. She had injured one leg, referring to it as her "mauve" leg. Hermione spoke with an English drawl, the result of a pronounced underbite. The sound was exaggerated, adding to her comic effect.

An elegant Iranian woman sporting emeralds was in the group as well as a couple of women from the Midwest and Mrs. Cleveland/cooking-school. The men were outnumbered and forgettable. No wonder a young, vibrant guy who liked to dance and party was encouraged to partake.

Sticking close to her stateroom was the American wife of the French actor Claude Dauphin. Norma was young and beautiful but emotionally fragile. Little did I guess that a few years hence she was to dominate my life in what at first seemed a fortuitous, frivolous way, but that turned into a willfully destructive relationship. For this trip, our agendas did not coincide.

Mid-Atlantic revelry spurred on by the unrelenting Eric continued for the week. As I was going to Paris to celebrate my twenty-fifth birthday, I had booked to Le Havre. Hermione's insistence swayed me to change plans and escort her on the boat train to London. I could still get to Paris for my twenty-fifth, but I might be a little rushed. I agreed to disembark in Southampton with her. It was not everyday that I got to escort a famous actress into Victoria Station with a battery of press on hand to record the event. As she was making a comeback to English cinema after many years, she was apprehensive. The film costarred Marlon Brando, and Hermione was very nervous. She asked me to go over her lines with her in the train. Script in hand, I cued her but I was distracted by her disconcerting habit of taking out and putting in her false teeth. I remember ordering a brandy for my nerves, which were rattled by her fidgeting, which increased mile by mile as we neared London.

"Do you think I should wear leopard tomorrow for my arrival?" she asked me. Answering without pause for reflection, I dismissed that idea as old-fashioned. I did not realize that she had a complete ensemble of leopard and had no intention of settling for anything else. In the early a.m., Hermione prepared to disembark, proudly covered from head to foot in spotted leopard. She asked me to escort her to a fancy event in her honor that evening. I had a tuxedo with me, hastily packed the night before leaving. It was a crumpled wreck that would have to be pressed before I picked her up at the Plaza Athenaeum in Mayfair. The train pulled into the station. I carefully allowed the English actress to descend (as though she would have it any other way) into a battery of flashbulb explosions. I loved posing demurely behind her. She rattled on with agent, press and others, completely ignoring me. Finally, she turned to me and demanded, as though we had just met, "What is your name?" How humiliating from "that actress" I had imposed on my new friends on the *Liberté*.

I found my way to the theater that was showing *West Side Story* and located Sylvia Tysik, my ballerina friend from New York. First she offered me a corner in her tiny flat in Chelsea, but that changed when David Halliday, playing Tony, was contacted.

My summer stock friend immediately suggested I use his apartment, at least for a night or two. For me, it was a delicious notion. It became even more delicious when we spent a very cozy night together, which came as quite a surprise to me. I was always so convinced of David's straightness. Becoming a star in London's West End must achieve marvels of personal transformation.

Totally delighted to be in David's and Sylvia's company, I looked at my crumpled tuxedo and decided to call Hermione at the last moment to announce that I could not possibly escort her that evening. My clothes were in a deplorable condition and there was no help for it in the time remaining. I thought, I'll show her! It was not the thing to do. It would have served me better to meet the luminaries at the event rather than cut my nose off to spite that pretty face. After all, it is just possible that Hermione's nervousness threw my name out of her head. It has happened to me. In any case, I spent the night watching my friends perform in Lenny's *West Side Story*, then with David in his flat. It lasted only that night, however, as he had a "commitment" the next evening and I was off to Paris for my birthday.

While in London, I thought I would spend an afternoon at the National Gallery. Somewhere between Gainsborough and Goya, two older men engaged me in conversation. One was a theater director who was also on his way to Paris. The other, a red-haired man, was an actor. He invited me to join him at a performance of *Oliver!* that evening. Since David was otherwise engaged, it seemed a delightful option. We agreed to have dinner at chic Sheekies in the alley near the theater beforehand. It was there that I first encountered the button-covered buskers who entertain the crowd waiting to enter the theater. Like something out of *My Fair Lady*, it is a curiosity that seems to have died out. Buskers, or "pearlies," were cockneys who covered their entire clothes with sewn-on buttons. Their unusual outfits and songs were part of the West End theater scene for generations, a bit of inimitable color I miss.

My actor friend also took me to meet Alan Bates in his dressing room at another theater nearby. Bates was so pleasant and unassuming. As I had "made a movie in Rome" the last time I was there, I mentioned returning to Rome via Paris and looking for more work in the cinema. Bates thought I was a lucky dog and wished he were me! My actor friend ordered drinks for us in advance, for the intermissions, as is the custom in England. We chatted enthusiastically about so many things. I adored *Oliver!* and I adored meeting Alan Bates in the star's dressing room. I adored my elegant fish dinner and thought I adored my new friend, if with some reservations. It was more appealing to continue our conversation at his flat rather than at David's empty flat, so off we went.

The next morning, the director, who was also staying the night at the actor's apartment, suggested we meet in Paris. He was flying and I was boat-training it. As it was my birthday, he would show me Paris—his Paris. After drinks at his favorite club, we would attend a performance by his friend Gilbert Bécaud, who had a one-man show at the Alhambra. Then we would have dinner. He knew a good pension near the Étoile where we could stay. There was even talk of a country chateau invitation. The actor friend was planning to come in a few days. He agreed to meet me at the pension where we would share a room. It all seemed so agreeable, so glamorous. It would be a sensational first quarter of a century celebration. It was right to want to spend it in Paris. How nicely things were developing.

The director picked me up at the boat train as planned. We checked into the pension, where it was explained to the concierge that I would be staying on and expecting a friend in a few days. Although I did not think the place was very cheerful or pretty, it was comfortable and part of my birthday present from the director. We went to a ritzy club for pretheater drinks. I wanted to order a pastis (Pernod, or its equivalent) as it reminded me of Paris my first time around. He was scandalized, and I had to settle for scotch and soda. I bristled at his overbearing manner. I told him I would really enjoy going to a simple bar along the Seine for a pastis later. He agreed, albeit with a touch of snobby disappointment. We went to the Alhambra to hear Bécaud. Our seats were choice, but I was annoyed. I really did not want to spend my birthday that way and I had not been consulted. The director was, well, directing what I would do at every turn. After all, it was my birthday, not his. I insisted on leaving, which really upset him. On our way to the Seine and the bar of my choice, he pointed out that Gilbert Bécaud might have noted our departure, and that that was impolite to his friend. I had my Pernod and a snack in strained silence before returning to the pension. He stopped the car on the Pont Neuf so I could contemplate the Seine. He indulged me in what must have seemed to him to be childish whims, but he would get his reward together with my comeuppance. Sweet-talked into a night of perfunctory "pleasure," I was informed in the morning that he would go to the chateau without me. I should simply wait for the actor to arrive. Off he went, probably delighted to get rid of the willful, foolish American who just did not get into the swing of things.

Annoyed, angry and disappointed with the director, I was glad to be rid of him and his controlling way. The actor arrived; I was elated to see him again. He thoughtfully brought me a recording of *Oliver!* to remind me of our theater evening in London. He thought the director a cad, and proceeded to show me surprising things in Paris. We attended a performance at Le Boeuf sur le Toit, where we enjoyed a sophisticated, titillating floor show while dining and drinking champagne. One of the star "girls" joined us for bubbly afterward; it was difficult to imagine that "she" was really a "he." At the time, transvestites had license to go around Paris dressed in designer clothes with maquillage that made real women green with envy. Never have I seen such beautiful drag as that night in Paris. Le Fiacre was a popular expensive nightspot for gays and the smart set out rubbernecking at them. Winston Churchill's grandson (who looked just like his grandfather) and Alain Delon were there, adding piquancy to the evening.

Douglass had given me more than a Tiffany cigarette case upon departure: a lover from his dim past was now a noted director in Rome, Franco Brusati. He wrote to him announcing my arrival, and gave me his address and telephone number. Douglass felt that he would be a good ally, as he knew everyone. Upon arrival in Rome, I situated myself in a pensione near the top of the Via Veneto and gave him a ring. An American male voice answered and Brusati came to the phone. Yes, of course, would I be able to meet him at the Excelsior for tea or a drink tomorrow afternoon? The high-class hotel was diagonally across the street from my pensione. Nervously, I awaited the important man. He arrived with a young American man who seemed to be his lover. Compliments fairly flew from the film director. An extra in a movie? Nonsense! He insisted that, with the right tutelage, I was leading man material. On and on he went about my bone structure, photogenic qualities, fine figure and beautiful face. I was flattered, embarrassed and afraid. What did he expect of me? What should I do? I opted, as I so often had, for escape. I politely thanked him and suggested I call him soon, making up an engagement elsewhere. Put it on ice, for now, I advised myself. I returned to my pensione, bumping into a young man from England. He looked at me and announced that he had seen me at *Oliver!* in London. Furthermore, he went on to relate the conversation I had had with my actor friend almost verbatim. I guess he eavesdropped, but I cannot imagine that he would have forseen running into me again!

A surprise awaited me over lunch that week. Alone in a pleasant *tavola calda* near the Spanish Steps, I looked up from my pasta toward the street. On the other side of the window were two familiar faces from New York: my friend Susan Berns, daughter of the owner of "21," and Danielle Weill, her Park Avenue model friend. We had a happy lunch catching up and sharing Roman holiday experiences. They had been there long enough to purchase an expensive car, a Lancia Flaminia. Neither of the girls knew how to drive, however. They were going to learn in Rome with neither of them speaking Italian! It seemed very bizarre to me, but . . . then I got a great idea. I solved their problem by offering to drive for them if they covered car expenses, which they were going to do anyhow. I wanted to see more of Italy and was enchanted by the idea of going to Greece. I would pay for my expenses and drive the car. They were delighted to have a guy with them, especially one they knew and felt safe with. Reserving my room at the pensione for my return, I took off with Susan and Danielle.

Hilarity began with an early-morning start for Sorrento and the island of Ischia. I had a letter of introduction from Don Haggerty (brother of Press Secretary James Haggerty) to an American expatriate who lived there. Don had befriended me when I worked at the Moors. He was amused by me and wrote the guy that I was Lady Brett's son from *The Sun Also Rises*. We packed the girls' fur coats on the top in the trunk and began our exodus from the Eternal City. A white garbage truck seemed to be following us at every turn. It took a while for us to realize that it was not the garbage truck that I saw in the rearview mirror, but our trunk, wide open, dragging the fur coats behind! A bottle of French champagne sat in the rear window for much of the trip; if I had had my way, it would have been consumed at the first opportunity. Susan asked how come everyone knew they were Jewish? I asked what she meant. "Well, every time we ask for directions, they say 'Giù in fondo.'" I explained, barely able to stifle laughter, that they were saying, "There at the bottom (or end)."

With trepidation and careful maneuvering over two planks, I managed to get the car onto the ferry from Naples to Ischia. The man to whom I had the letter of introduction no longer lived there. We found a smart watering hole that evening, however. While I was at the bar, leaving the girls to do their own thing, an assistant to a young German prince brought me a message. The prince would like me to join him. I had sized up the prince as someone I ought to steer clear of. Arrogantly, I turned my cigarette case into the messenger's line of vision, exposing the inscription on the outside: Prince Eric Gustav. "Kindly tell your prince that this prince declines his offer!" Having had enough of the place, I decided to leave, as I had the car keys. The girls wanted to stay, hoping for high adventure. When they saw me make a break for the door, they screamed and had others rush after me to prevent my taking the car. After a bit of mayhem, we all found our way back to our sleeping accommodations.

After a visit to the natural hot springs in the sea, we left Ischia for our trip to the other side of Italy. The dusty port of Bari was where we were to take the boat to Athens' port of Piraeus. In 1960, goats roamed the unpaved streets of Bari and faded Communist banners flapped overhead. It was regarded as the anus of Italy. The trip was long and the boat bowels were hot; my cabin was tiny and airless. To get some air, I opened my door a little but kept it from being opened more by propping luggage inside the door which pressed against a dresser. There was a Quasimodo-like Greek steward who made it clear from the outset that he had taken a shine to me. I had heard about Greek men, and I was terrified that this monster would overpower me, fulfilling his salacious intentions. I arrived intact.

The girls checked into the King George Hotel on Syntagma Square. I stayed down the street at a much more modest hotel. Near it, there was a bar where we met to plan our evenings' activities. One night, the owner of the bar made me a shocking offer. He asked if I would consider being a prostitute at an establishment he owned elsewhere in Athens! The man thought I would provide a foreign attraction, an asset to his enterprise. I immedi-

*Susan Berns
models with Eric
in Corinth ruins.*

ately declined, but the notion plagued me, along with the scenarios my imagination conjured up.

Someone offered to take me to a local gay bar Tria 'Delphi (Three Brothers)—lots of ouzo and Greek dancing. Somewhere, I met a pretty, young Greek sailor. I took him to my hotel room but nothing happened, we were both too shy. I remember taking him back to his base. A searchlight followed the car in and out. He did not speak English, I do not speak Greek, which did not help. So the project was left abandoned and unexplored.

I visited the beach resort outside Athens, Vouliagmeni. I do not know what the girls did during those visits, but I went alone. Once, I met a young Greek boy who insisted we leave that beach for another, more isolated one. Like my sailor, he could not speak English but unlike him, he was eloquent in his desires. We sunned nude and it was clear that he wanted sex. I would not do it, partly because I felt he wanted to be paid and partly out of my usual prudishness. Stifled desires, fear, denial all mixed together befuddled me further. At Vouliagmeni, there was a nightclub that featured one of the dancers I had known from the Ballets de Paris in New York. He had worked up an exotic act in which he was borne on bamboo sticks on the backs of guys. He had always been effeminate, but this was the epitome of queenly fantasy. He plucked his eyebrows and posed coyly like an exotic princess from an outlandish jungle paradise. He had flowers delivered to himself on stage from make-believe admirers.

I drove Susan and Danielle to the monks' fascinating monasteries on "the Needles" north of Athens. We managed a complete swing around the Peloponnese, awed by Delphi and the amphitheater at Epidaurus. I wanted to go north to Mount Athos, which I would have had to do on my own, as women are not allowed. I even got a special pass, but I never had the courage to enter that far-off monastery by myself. The imagined scenarios gripped me in terror.

Two movies were being made in Athens that interested me slightly. The English speaking production would pay better and starred the bleach-blond, buxom Jayne Mansfield. One evening, she sat across from me with her husband Micky, having drinks in a local bar. I was tempted to guide a conversation into the prospects of my doing an extra role in her film but decided against that. The other film was a Greek production, *The Lion of Sparta.* The girls and I decided that neither movies nor prostitution were top choices on our itinerary. Tourism came first and it was nearing time to see the last of things Greek before returning to Rome, where my friends would make provisions for the car to be shipped home.

I returned to my Roman life and speculation about my future. I did not have to wait long for new provocation to action. In the American colony in Rome, photographer Roloff Beny and art patroness Peggy Guggenheim were prominent. Roloff invited me to enjoy the fantastic views of Rome from his penthouse on the Lungotevere. The illuminated Roman ruins across the Tiber made a breathtaking backdrop. Once, Peggy Guggenheim came into the flat, quite breathless, with her little dog. Peggy actually owned the flat but let Roloff use it. She claimed that she had narrowly missed being raped. She threw her sable coat onto a settee and clutched her dog, Sable. Her story was as outlandish as she was. Her nose was bloodshot from years of drinking; she was not a particularly handsome woman. I found her unattractive and could only wonder what kind of demented person would want to rape her! (At that time, I harbored the notion that rape involves attraction rather than power.) The distasteful woman together with Roloff's oily sordidness, playing against the languid Roman background, made me uncomfortable. Things came to a head the evening I went to see *La Dolce Vita* (in English) at the American cinema. I was shocked by the film and by how closely certain details resembled my life in Rome. I knew that if I let Franco Brusati guide me in my career, my life would become like *La Dolce Vita*, and I could not bear that. My denial would not permit me to admit that I was on the run from myself, keeping my fantasies intact.

In the morning, I hastily packed my bags, forgetting my silk pajamas under the pillowcase. I booked passage from Genoa for New York on the S.S. *Constitution*. I left a wad of lire with the startled maid. The signora was out, but I figured my bill and departed, leaving the money in the maid's hands. I later found out that the owner of the pensione claimed I had skipped out without paying. Perhaps the maid pocketed the money. Anyhow, the Englishman living there wrote me, telling me that the signora had filed papers against me so that if I tried to enter Italy in the near future, my name would be on the wanted list!

The *Constitution* was not as nice as the *United States* and not as beguiling as either of the French Line ships I had so enjoyed. I was reprimanded for trying to sneak into First Class; the food was not very appealing; I was disgusted and disappointed. When we got to Cannes, I decided to turn in the balance of my ticket for plane fare back to the States. I remember the flight on Iberia Airways took forever. Back to Montrose I went, with more Europe under my belt.

Securing a nondescript office job on Fifth Avenue in midtown, I rented a studio apartment in the East 80s. One day, on the subway between 86th Street and 42nd Street, I could not help but notice a very handsome, tall young man glancing at me. Later that evening, I sat in the balcony of Loew's 86th Street watching a horror film. Amazing! The same guy was sitting across the aisle from me, clearly giving me the once-over. After a brief time, he slipped into the seat next to mine and asked, "Is there enough blood in this for you?" We left together after the film and talked over coffee and an ice cream soda. David Wallace lived on the top floor of a town house between Park and Madison Avenues on 81st Street. So, we were in the same neighborhood. I do not remember if I asked him up to my place that evening or not. I do know that we found each other mutually attractive and began dining together constantly.

Soon, I gave up my tiny apartment and moved in with David. He had a pharmacist friend sharing the studio with him, who, before too long, decided to move to give us more privacy. Our romance burst into a full-time thrill, an obsession. We sparked in each other a tapestry of mutual enjoyment. Opera, books, museums, cooking and entertaining friends who became *our* friends, rather than his or mine, bonded us. It was a partnership that many thought ideal, admirable and attractive. We looked great together and encouraged each other with fondness and regard. Invitations were always forthcoming, as we made such dependably decorative guests at any dinner, party or social event. Life was a perfect summer's day.

A One-Man Show . . .

One subject, many artists, different times.

Eric nude, portrait by Douglass Semonin, 1969

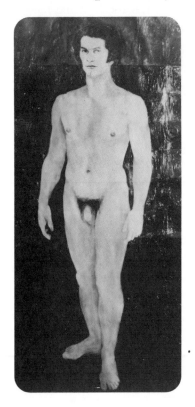

. . . to be continued

Chapter 6

GRAND TOUR

Tall, handsome, aristocratic David was dissatisfied with his Wall Street job. Also, I was none too thrilled to be working a run-of-the-mill office job. We decided it was time for a change. We were both in our mid-twenties, the best part of life in front of us. Youth, talent, good looks and the prospect of available money made us invincible. Spurred on by bequests, we decided it was the perfect time in our lives for a grand tour of Europe. David's uncle, Bess Wallace Truman's brother, died, leaving him a tidy sum. My ear-twisting grandmother died, too, leaving me a small amount of money. With a grandiosity only young queens with social aspirations can achieve, we set out to spend a year in Europe, with the idea of acquiring antiques and collectibles there for a business in New York. We would be instant antiquarians, importers of bibelots for the chic shop we would open upon our return to New York.

Our top-floor flat was leased, the contents sold through *New York Times* ads, adding to the purse for our great adventure. Two girls came to look at the apartment. One was a graduate of Sarah Lawrence, the daughter of the head of Honeywell. She liked the apartment and asked whether we would be kind enough to look up a friend living in Rome while we were there. "Poor Karen is an artist and she doesn't know anyone." David and I agreed to entertain the poor artist and help her as best we could.

Both girls came to our embarcation on the French Line's

Flandre. The *Flandre* was a smaller liner than the others I had enjoyed, but it had every comfort, luxury and more French charm than the larger vessels of the French Line. We received a festive surprise when other friends showed up for the sailing as well. A zany French-Egyptian woman and her American husband, "Bee-ll" (Bill), who came in response to our ad to buy furniture for an apartment nearby they were fixing up for speculation, had mentioned going to Paris by plane, but their plans changed.

*Grand tour begins:
A friend bids
the boys farewell.*

Standing next to me on the upper deck in her white mink was the extraordinary Leila Oteifa Hart. Scintillating and extravagant describe Leila, self-proclaimed daughter of an Egyptian pasha. The four of us were inseparable for the entire trip, together with Piapia and Zuzu, two Tenerife poodles that Leila took everywhere. We were delighted to find each other again so soon. With family and friends on the dock waving farewell amid streamers and blaring music, Leila and I hugged effusively. Those on the dock were amazed at how quickly I attached myself to the lovely passenger. From a farewell photo, taken from the ship by the official photographer, another person standing near my family and friends was caught on camera, limp wrist stroking cheek in astonishment to see me carousing on the First Class deck. It was my roommate-for-a-second when I had lived briefly on East 52nd Street.

Both ads in the *Times* produced amazing results. Not only did we manage to dump the apartment and all its contents, but new friends resulted from each transaction. The repercussions continued for some years. Before leaving for Europe, we had other matters to tend to. Most importantly, David's beloved Siamese, Kitty, was placed in a safe, good home. His mother in Denver was the lucky recipient of that feline, a bit temperamental, vocal and demanding, but beautiful and affectionate, too. Living in posh style, we determined that the only way to Denver was to take the sleeping car from old Pennsylvania Station and head west just like film stars on the Twentieth Century Limited. We were invited by David's aunt and uncle, the Trumans, to stop in Independence, Missouri, for a visit en route.

I had had my memorable meeting with President Harry S Truman and his wife Bess some months before, in New York. It was 1961. They were staying in President John F. Kennedy's triplex atop the Carlyle Hotel. Margaret, their daughter, had a duplex on Park Avenue just around the corner, which made it a convenient location for all. Margaret and her husband, Clifton Daniel, had two little boys. As the Kennedys were in the White House, they lent the Trumans their New York City apartment. Jackie Kennedy had decorated the hotel apartment with furniture on loan from French and Company across the street, next to Parke-Bernet. Upon entering the beautifully appointed apartment, there was a small library on the left. I could not help noticing the red phone sitting there near Jack's famous rocking chair. Imagine picking up that phone and activating "the hot line" to Khrushchev and the Kremlin. It seemed unreal that I could be there in the Kennedys' domain with a previous President entertaining me!

It was with great trepidation that I went to meet the Trumans. Harry made me feel at home immediately with his kind,

open and friendly manner. Bess, however, made me uncomfortable, so nervous that I began to chain smoke, even though I usually did not smoke much at all. Despite my sensing that Bess did
not appreciate cigarette smoking, it was my only crutch. If only
they would offer me a drink. After an eternity, Bess asked
whether we boys "would like something to drink." I knew for certain that she meant water. "I'd be glad to get you a glass of water,"
she continued. "Heck, those boys don't want water. They would
like something stronger," Harry assured her. Bess explained that
they had only arrived that day and had not set in supplies yet. "A
lot my girl knows," said good old Harry. "Come with me." I followed Truman into Kennedy's study, past the red phone and the
rocker. From a shelf behind some books, Harry produced a
square bottle. We proceeded to the kitchen where he poured a
drink for David, me and himself. "Don't you think this is more
like it?" he asked. Our bonding began, and would continue in
Independence.

Most people do not pay attention to the many things in life
that could be thrilling or interesting to note, I thought, while on
the Santo Domingo Indian Reservation in New Mexico during an
enormous Indian festival. Not far away, a California-bound train
sped past. Anyone looking out the windows would have been
impressed by the costumed dancers and singers and their ceremonies. But how many raised their eyes to see? The same applied
to our trainload of passengers as we pulled into Independence
that afternoon. A dark blue Lincoln Continental was the only car
waiting. On the driver's side stood Harry S Truman and on the
other side was Bess Wallace Truman, waiting for David, Kitty and
me.

Harry's conversation was always interesting. How I marveled at his determined affection and admiration for his two
favorite girls, his no-nonsense Baptist wife and their daughter
Margaret, who apparently could never do anything wrong. He
and I sat in his small reading room, talking about books, pastimes

In Independence as housguests of
President Harry and Bess Truman

or history. The greatest sadness in his life was having to make the decision to drop the atomic bomb. He felt he had done the right thing in bringing the war to a quicker end, saving American servicemen's lives, yet the memory haunted him. We both had the habit of reading several different books at the same time. His "walking with purpose" was like my jogging for exercise. We both enjoyed the harmless activity of sneaking an extra drink or two over conversation behind Bess's back; she allowed only one drink a day. Well, we boys had our secrets. Visiting the Presidential Library in Independence with the President himself as our guide was a thrill. If there were Secret Servicemen tailing us and making a continual surveillance, I never noticed it.

The night before we were to continue to Denver, Harry asked me to sit up with his girl and watch television with her. David had an excuse to go to bed early. Margaret was appearing on a talk show. Bess and I sat side by side and listened to her daughter relate the ways she outsmarted her Secret Service men and parents when out on a date. She made a few comments that I would very much have liked to be able to see her mother's reaction to, but it would have been rude to turn and scrutinize her. As I was the only person in the room, I tried to turn my eyes to the right without swiveling my head, to remember for posterity how those comments registered on Mother Bess's countenance. Bess sat with her legs crossed at the ankles and kept an inscrutable smile on her face. We had had a quiet power struggle that day at lunch in a local restaurant on the outskirts of town. An acquaintance of hers came over to the table. I was yearning for another daiquiri but knew none would be forthcoming. Hell, I thought to myself, I'll just order one from the waitress while Bess is talking. I did, she noticed, the atmosphere grew icy.

Before we left for the train, Harry pulled out two belts that had special buckles. They were gifts from the President of Mexico. Harry thought David and I would enjoy having them. My belt buckle had a "T" engraved in the gold, which was studded with rubies and set on a silver base for strength. David's was less flashy, but, then, so was he. That flamboyant Western-style belt buckle has never been stolen, probably because no one realizes that it is not imitation. I love it for its history and for what it represents: my days with one of America's truly great presidents.

We were given a walleyed pike from the famous Truman freezer to take to Christine in Denver. They drove us to the station and we said farewell. I did see Margaret socially, and when she came to a disastrous party that David and I gave in New York, but I would not see Harry again. Years later, when I met "The

Man Called Intrepid," Harold Nicholson, together with the author of the book by that name (same surname, spelled differently) over lunch in Bermuda, I realized how many fascinating things I could have asked Truman about but did not know to ask. Now, when I expect to meet someone that important, I do as much homework as possible, to make the best advantage of the privilege.

I never asked either of them if they knew each other, but I have arranged for both Harry S Truman and Mae West to be together in "my" forever. I have placed each of their autographed photos in a double-hinged frame. There, they enjoy posterity together, as I am certain they would have mutually benefited from each other's company in real life. The only thing one can change is the past. Bess would not approve.

Back to the story, which picks up momentum from the first spontaneous dance on the upper deck of the *Flandre* with Leila, David and Bill watching bemusedly. The ship's captain knew of David's connection with Harry S Truman. When the *Normandie* capsized in New York harbor, President Truman was cooperative in the crisis. The captain made it clear from the first day out that he would honor Truman by giving David a complimentary dispensation on our wine consumption aboard ship. He invited us to a special cocktail party the next night. I told the purser that I did not wish to offend the captain but I had planned a small get-together to celebrate David's birthday. Gallantly, my guest list was requested and the captain made my list into his list of invited guests. One of the bigwigs of the French Line was aboard, Monsieur Andouzferrie. He was enchanted with the irrepressible Leila. I remember Leila standing on the deck requesting the distinguished elderly head of the French Line to "park his leetle sheep in Southampton so we can all go gambling."

A dapper older gentleman from New York, Mr. Henry, was part of the coterie of transatlantic travelers. He was very fussy about wines, particularly dessert wines; he adored Cuban cigars and flirted with the pretty ladies. Mr. Henry ordered box lunches for us to enjoy on our train ride to Paris. He later came to our opera costume party in New York, transforming the fortunes of a lesbian actress friend of mine from Pittsburgh.

Meanwhile, Leila and I were dancing up a storm every night, drinking everything we could. In respect for the Taittinger baroness/proprietress aboard, we helped diminish the stock of her product, too. The night of the captain's dinner, Leila and I decided we would provide some entertainment, as none had been hired for the event. The captain "gave" us the orchestra for us to rehearse with on the upper deck, where the shuffleboard courts were located. We worked out a dance medley with tango, Charleston (Leila called it the "Charlie-stone") and the French sailors' rude dance, the ja-va. After rehearsal, I suggested we get into bathing suits and cool off with a swim in the outdoor pool. "Don't be stupido, I break zees dress and go like thees!" I stopped her from ripping her Dior and insisted on changing into appropriate attire. Leila was always willing to tear off a garment, break a necklace that was an encumbrance or throw a car into the Seine if it displeased her. I have never met anyone like her. It is improbable that anyone in the world today would be capable of her impetuous extravagances, or that anyone around would put up with such behavior. But then it was funny, extraordinary, astounding.

The purser had a cousin who managed the Brighton Hotel on the rue de Rivoli, across from the Tuileries. With his introduction, we enjoyed an apartment on a high floor of the hotel, with balconies overlooking the Louvre, the Seine and the Left Bank beyond.

The rue de Lappe still had *bals musette* at the back of seedy bars. Hookers, pimps and upstairs maids frequented the lower-class hangouts. "Don't dress up, as we are going slumming," Leila advised us on the phone. By now, I knew Leila's not dressing up would be trimmed in fur and pearls, so David and I adopted a middle-of-the-road attire for our Parisian slumming. As suspected, the charismatic Leila was in her white mink, designer dress and jewels. We walked on the cobblestoned rue de Lappe, following her into a smoky, disreputable establishment. Intrepidly, Leila strode into the middle of the tough clientele. Removing her mink, she tossed it across the sawdust floor and shouted "Ja-va! Une . . ." Others joined her calling out "Deux . . . Trois . . . Quatre" until the required number of requests indicated to the small band that enough people wanted to dance. We did our well-rehearsed sailors' dance, my hands clutching her ass, hers mine. We had a way of spinning our bodies around suddenly so that they collided in a rude frontal bump. The crowd loved it. David and Bill (who had retrieved her coat) lurked in the background, fearing for their safety. We had a ball!

Leila always led us on outlandish, larger-than-life adventures. At a Spanish nightclub on the Left Bank's rue Guénégaud, Leila and I each won the wine-drinking contest for women and men, making spectacles of ourselves. Later, when visiting Leila and Bill at their enormous apartment at the Palais des Pins in Cannes, we dined at a small bistro in Nice. Nice was still a small fishing town then. There were a couple of musicians in the bistro, but no dance floor. Bill induced the manager/owner to clear away some tables so that Leila and I could show off.

In the early 1960s, France completed her recovery from World War II. The School of Paris flowered, life was inexpensive, everything bountiful. David and I lived in a rarefied world of beauty, extravagance and fun. I remember our trip through the Loire valley. As cliché as it sounds, the chateaux were especially magical. Cows in the fields were plump, and fish plentiful in the streams. The food was exquisite, and the wines, of course, a grand complement to its taste.

Rome became our home base, with side trips to France, England, Greece, Turkey and wherever our hearts and inquisitive natures sent us. Thanks to my English friend (whom I had met on Vouliagmeni beach the previous trip), Catherine Hawkins at FAO in Rome, we located a sparsely furnished apartment near the Lungotevere Flaminio. Christmas was approaching, and we decided to adorn our simple apartment with our first Christmas tree. Catherine took us to a tree market outside the gates leading to the Piazza del Popolo. We placed the tree in the back seat of her Morris Minor convertible and sped up the broad avenue, with Catherine exclaiming, "I love to hear the wind in the pine trees, don't you?"

The American colony was full with the cast of *Cleopatra* in Rome for an extended shoot. Richard Burton and Elizabeth Taylor were the stars. Roddy McDowall, Rex Harrison and a large supporting cast settled in for the duration. Burton's secretary, Jim and Jim's lover became friendly with David and me. We socialized quite a bit and had a lovely time enjoying the Roman scene together. A wonderful benefit from this friendship was the continual availability of tickets to the opera, concerts and other events that Burton and his wife Sybil chose not to use. His secretary was not interested either, so he kindly passed them on to us.

The superdiva of the day, Joan Sutherland, with her husband Richard Bonynge, arrived in Rome. Bonynge was to conduct his wife's concert for the first time. David and I were thrilled at the opportunity to hear her in person; we knew all her recordings already. The Burtons were not able to use their tickets. Perhaps they preferred to stay at their villa on the Via Appia Antica with the kids, resting up from busy days on the lot of *Cleopatra*.

It was clearly our gain to be in the concert hall on the Via Nazionale for that momentous musical occasion. Sutherland appeared in an emerald green gown that had lots of tulle in a broad floor-length skirt. She swooped down the side aisle of musicians toward her downstage-center position, pulling down every music stand the unwary musicians had on the side of the aisle. Embarrassing as it was, it was also hilarious. To make matters worse, she managed to snare a few more music stands the

With Elizabeth in her dressing room for The Little Foxes.

musicians did not think to clutch when she exited for the first intermission. Roddy McDowall, sitting behind us along with other *Cleopatra* cast members, was convulsed with laughter. Sutherland's voice was sensational. At one point years later when (now "Dame") Joan and I were planning my exhibition about her career for the Library for the Performing Arts at Lincoln Center, I had the temerity to allude to the toppling music stands at this Rome concert. I thought she would chuckle and say something witty. My words fell on seemingly deaf ears. After a pause, she continued as though I had not said a word.

That was exactly the same response I got when I had the opportunity to thank Elizabeth Taylor for keeping Richard Burton busy so that I could be the recipient of all those choice tickets. Instead of her deep, infectious laughter, my comment was ignored. Perhaps it was not understood, but it certainly was dispensed with effectively. I discovered, perhaps inelegantly, that many people lack humor about themselves.

We looked up "poor Karen" and invited her to one of the Burton-no-show concerts. She drove us in a Volkswagen; en route singing hysterical parodies like Mozart's "Eine Kleine Wasser Closet." Her studio apartment on the Via Margutta was simple, light-filled and airy. David and I took her to dinner or lunch whenever possible, as we were under the illusion that she was a struggling artist. Her friends in New York always referred to her as "poor Karen," so we did our best to keep her amused, fed and entertained. Karen was a petite and bouncy girl with a tremendous sense of humor. She was fun and spontaneous. Catherine did not like Karen. Once, when leaving Karen's studio, she commented on the pressed flowers in a frame. Karen proudly announced that they were from Israel. Catherine, perhaps relapsing into early-learned anti-Semitic conditioning, sniffed, "When my parents and I visited there we called it Palestine." It was only the following year when we returned to New York, that we discovered Karen was from one of the wealthiest families in America. The Rosenwalds, from the Main Line outside Philadelphia, were great philanthropists, magnates of the Sears-Roebuck fortune. "Poor Karen" alone in Rome, a struggling artist, was not penniless at all.

Rex Harrison was in Rome, too, with the new woman in his life, Rachel Roberts. They attended the opera and many other events. I had enjoyed Harrison at the many performances of *My Fair Lady* I had attended on Broadway. His previous wife, Kay Kendall, was a terrific comedienne who died too young.

Vincent Price's *The Pit and the Pendulum* had just opened at the American Cinema. Sitting in front of us one afternoon was a young brunette. She looked familiar but it was not until that evening at Roloff Beny's Lungotevere penthouse that it dawned on me who she was. The star of the film, Barbara Steele appeared at the party wearing a skimpy black dress, sniffling from a cold. I remember thinking, Dressed like that it is no wonder she has a cold. It was the same girl who watched herself on the screen that afternoon in the American Cinema.

I know that any visitor to Rome today will think I am

describing another place, but it was so beautiful to come home after an event in Rome during the late evening. All the piazzas were illumined and the fountains splashed. There was little traffic and few pedestrians, only the occasional clip-clop of a horse-drawn carriage slowly wending its way, bearing its romantic passengers through lovely cobblestoned streets.

David and I earnestly attempted to visit the hundreds of sights of Rome. Guidebook in hand, we entered scores of churches to admire sculptures, paintings and architecture. Stories of Queen Christina of Sweden, the Borgias, the Farneses, Michelangelo and da Vinci gripped us. We had time to study, walk around, look and listen. Dutifully, we two young princes got measured for clothes on the Via Condotti and made the necessary arrangements for an audience with the Pope. John XXIII was affable, beloved by everyone. He was always having dinner with friends in Rome and was very visible at public events. One day, David and I went to ship a package from the American Express office near the Piazza de Spagna. It was the Day of the Ascension of the Virgin. Suddenly, all around us was a crowd of people cheering the Pope's open limousine. He stood with left arm raised, looking upward to his left. David had his Rolleiflex camera hanging from his shoulder. He adjusted the camera and took a few shots toward the Pope over the heads of the crowd. When the photos were developed, one looked as though "il Papa" was looking at an advertisement on a nearby post, which announced, "Fly El Al, Israel's Airline."

With his Truman connection, David made the arrangements for a Papal visit. I went to an office in the Vatican to pick up our invitation. "I'm here to get my invitation to meet the Heavenly Father," I announced. The kindly Irish clergyman looked at me in amusement and said, "Another Protestant. I believe you mean the Holy Father. It is too soon for you go meet your Maker." I returned to our apartment and mirthfully announced the error I had made, invitation in hand. Upon hearing that we were going to meet the Pope, our Italian landlady told us that she hoped he spoke English, as his Italian was terrible. Apparently he spoke with a heavy dialect, unintelligible to many Italians. The Italians love to joke about their "Papa." He may have the last word in Catholic ideology, but his countrymen (until the Pope was no longer Italian) made fair game of him in everyday gossip. I remember the talk in Rome about a later Pope who had late-night rendezvous with an actor of the same first name, who sneaked into the Vatican through the tunnel connecting with the Castel Sant'Angelo. The Romans were greatly entertained by that juicy hearsay.

David was very dogmatic on many things. One thing he impressed upon me was that when speaking to royalty and the Pope, you must not initiate the conversation and you must speak only on the subject they choose. And never, NEVER contradict. I wish I had remembered that some years later when I was alone with the Queen of Romania.

The day of the Vatican visit arrived. Carefully attired in our most solemn clothes and grateful that Leila was not with us, we made our way to the Vatican, stopping at a nearby shop to buy inexpensive holy medallions, which would be blessed simply by being in our pockets during the audience. We gave them judiciously to Catholic friends as mementos from the auspicious occasion. Bernini's graceful elliptical double colonnade ushered us into the enormous complex of the Vatican. We went upstairs to a marble hall past the splendid Swiss Guards. That led to another hall, which led to a small chamber where other visitors waited for audience.

Pope John XXIII entered, looking at once serious and pasty. Soon, his animation grew. He spoke faster and faster and his throat colored. "Who wants to speak English now?" he playfully requested, having finished a conversation in French. He began to have such fun that I think he forgot he was the Pope! Our audience was a delight, culminating in an invitation to view the burial place of St. Peter, amid the Etruscan burial chambers under the foundations of St. Peter's Cathedral. At that time, it was closed to the public. Since then, the reputed bones of St. Peter have been moved and the Etruscan remnants are open for viewing.

Ever mindful of our obligation to see and savor the highlights of Italy we set our sights for Florence, Milan, Verona and Venice. Venice was wintry and inhospitable. In the cold, damp fog, it seemed we were hustled by a gang of *facchini* (porters), each wanting us to go with them to the *pensione* of their choice. We arrived at night and St. Mark's Square was flooded. Planks were set up to enable people to traverse the square. It was eerie, forbidding, unwelcoming. The *facchino* bearing our luggage took us up and down dim alleys to a dubious *pensione*. Things looked much better in the daylight once we got used to the flooding and could pay attention to the wonderment of Venice.

Our adventure continued along the Adriatic in the direction of Greece and Turkey. We booked into a hotel outside Athens, which was on a hill overlooking an enormous plain. It was an attractive new hotel that shuttled its guests to and from Athens in a minibus. One day, on the minibus, I noticed a young woman sitting nearby reading a guidebook. We began to converse and formed a friendship that would bear unusual fruit. Diana was employed by British Air as a ground stewardess in London. She accepted an invitation to dinner at our hotel with alacrity; she would enjoy dinner with two young American men. Over dinner, she announced that she had an uncle who lived in New York City. Osborne Maitland Miller was a world-renowned cartographer, the head of the New York Geographical Society. As she had free transportation and liked to visit her father's twin, Diana called on New York every so often. She promised to look us up.

There was a royal wedding in Athens, which is why we could not get a room in Syntagma Square downtown. A prince from the Greek royal family was marrying a Spanish princess. As the wedding day approached, even our remote hotel was booked solid.

We had to leave Athens during the wedding. We took a Greek ship to Istanbul with stops in Crete, Rhodes, Santorini, and Pergamum to visit Ephesus. So much was yet to be excavated. Statues waiting to be plucked out of the ground were scattered around, half exposed. I wished I had my own truck and ship to take them with me!

Istanbul definitely frightened me, especially when we got lost in the *souks*, where no one seemed to speak English or understand my poor French. David and I barely made it back to the ship in time for sailing. Asia Minor was alien to me and not without challenges to my patience and understanding. Tales of Turkish ferocity and brutality told to me by Greek and Armenian friends colored my attitude, and I was wary. The mosques, with their minarets, were exotic; the Bosphorus bustling with activity was colorful, but my Western Christian upbringing put me on guard.

Our other casbah adventure happened during a brief interlude when we visited Morocco. Tangiers was especially interesting, with the guidance of a Dutch boy who traded our money on the black market. He showed us around and we enjoyed several days seeing the sights with lots of time poking around the *souks*. The maze and bustling activity was continually fascinating, tinged with intrigue and mystery. I wondered if I would be drugged and sold into white slavery. The young guide was engaging and attractive, but David and I were still so absorbed with each other that a *ménage à trois* was not in our thinking, although it may have been for the Dutch boy.

We had taken a ship over from Cadiz after a week in Madrid at the Palace and the Ritz, and some days in Valencia and Seville. We returned to Spain to visit the Alhambra Palace near Granada. I remember the terrible bus ride up hairpin curves to Granada, and my growing malaise. By the time we checked into the Alhambra Palace Hotel, I was definitely not well. Finally, a doctor was summoned and I was told to stay in bed for the next few days. I had a nice view of the valley from my bed; goat's bells tinkled and flowers sweetened the air but I was bedridden with a debilitating flu. Though I was within pearl-hurling distance of the Alhambra, I could not see it until the day of my departure. Visitors to the Alhambra were startled to see a figure promenading about the place in an Arab, silk, striped *djelaba* as though centuries had not passed by since the 1100s. I caught up on sightseeing that final day in a costume purchased in Tangiers earlier that week! While in Spain, we visited many antiquarians and stores selling reproductions of Spanish-style furniture. Selections were made and suppliers awaited our shipping instructions. It was to be a source for our New York shop's inventory, along with our Italian contacts.

Back in Rome, much news awaited us. We had read about the Burton-Taylor affair while in Greece, but specifics of "Burton plucking brains out of Taylor" were more fully detailed by our Roman friends. No wonder Richard Burton did not have time or inclination to go to concerts or the opera. Thanks again for the tickets, and thank you again Elizabeth for keeping him occupied. I do not recall anyone in Rome wondering why Elizabeth Taylor did not appear at any of these events. It never occurred to me to link her no-show with Burton's.

Other romantic news from Rome was about our friend Catherine, who was going to marry her Roman count, Mario Gambino. The wedding was to take place in England. David and I were on our way to England via France, where we were going to buy a Peugeot to take back home. It would accompany us to England for a break-in period and allow us enough usage to claim it as a used car for American customs. Catherine's parents were shocked when she announced that she was going to go on a Lorna Doone country tour with two American guys just weeks before her wedding. We had a delightful time visiting old houses along the Bristol Channel and exorcising ghosts over bottles of whatever. One morning, as Beethoven's "Pastorale" Symphony played on the car radio, we sat in the parking lot of an Elizabethan manor (apparently, the only one Queen Elizabeth I never slept in) as the pouring rain evaporated into brilliant spring sunshine as if cued by the music. The weather now inviting, we entered the gardens and manor house for a most pleasant tour.

Life was full of rich promise, mirth and goodwill. Horizons were ever-widening for young David and Eric. We bought paintings in Montmartre, icons and copper vessels in Greece, rugs in Venice, all to be transported via the *Vulcania*, which we would board in Venice. We ordered a case of champagne in advance with instructions to have it on ice for our arrival on board. We arranged to occupy Suite A in First Class with our new car in the hold. After a few sunny days in Venice, where we stayed on the Riva degli Schiavoni, David and I boarded the luxurious liner.

Suite A was the largest, most comfortably appointed suite on the ship. Two stewards and one maid awaited our arrival. They asked if everything was alright. Having had several "get me on my feet" libations before boarding, my shyer nature gave way to flamboyance. I looked around and startled them when I removed some pictures from the wall and told them to take up a couple of small area rugs. "We have our own," I grandly indicated by putting up our Parisian purchases and flinging down some recent acquisitions from a Venetian rug dealer. We drank some of the champagne and I flung my empty glass into the Adriatic as there were plenty more on the tray. Before we cleared the Giudecca, I had our steamer trunk opened, which had been shipped from Rome to the boat in Venice. The wardrobe I had worn from New York was hurled out the porthole like the champagne glass. Finery created for me in Italy would replace those rags—100 proof grand illusions!

Life on the *Vulcania* was the ultimate in self-indulgence. Our day began with breakfast in bed. A trio of stewards entered singing Italian songs, sometimes opera, perhaps with us joining in. Steak and champagne, an omelet with delicious brioche or baked pastry and some fruit started us off nicely. We would dress leisurely in smart, casual clothes and go to the pool to read, write letters or just sunbathe. Neither of us appeared in the dining room, a double-storied room with a stained-glass ceiling, *putti* in the upper corners and Renaissance-style painted rondels, until evening. The first day out from Venice, we had a chat with the "Capo" of the dining room. We requested a table for four but only the two of us were to be officially assigned to it. That way we could invite people we chose, a snobbish request that did not go unnoticed by our fellow travelers.

Early in the voyage, I met a nice girl while I was "slumming" in Tourist Class. I invited her to join me in First Class for dinner that evening. When she tried to gain admittance, the purser denied her entry. When I found out, I exploded in fury at him. If he was going to behave that way to my guest, I would not appear again in the First Class dining room. I proceeded to invite some very distinguished guests to join David and me in our private sitting room-*cum*-dining room in the suite. Waiters brought in food and we had a lovely dinner party. It caused consternation with the dining-room staff, however, as I was taking business away from them. If I continued my ban on the dining room by entertaining in my suite, they would lose tips. There were not many people on board so it would be ruinous to the waiters' income. My waiter asked me to go to the purser's office as soon as possible. I continued my leisurely poolside lunch and told him I would visit the purser later when it was more convenient. He was clearly upset that I did not immediately run at his summons, but I was adamant. When I did appear in the purser's office, he was very apologetic, oozing with ingratiating charm. There had been an unfortunate misunderstanding, which he hoped could be corrected. Yes, I told him it could be rectified. All he had to do was send his personal invitation to the young lady to join me for dinner together with his personal apology. He blanched at the apology part, but he agreed.

The staff was relieved to see the two young princes arrive for dinner in their formal best that evening. I had won a victory over the willful purser, and I gloated in it. The other passengers speculated on who we were. They assumed that we had been at the royal wedding in Greece, and they admired the beautiful silk outfits from the Via Condotti tailors. We were fairy-tale celebrities to them, which I took in prideful stride.

It was to be one of the last voyages of the grande dame *Vulcania*. Insurance was exorbitant for ships over a certain age. Jet planes cut into the more gracious transatlantic ship business. People were in a rush, they did not want to deal with steamer trunks or dressing for dinner, or pay the price for luxurious crossings. The southern route took ten days instead of the few hours hours it takes on a plane. On a sea voyage, the tips alone could have bought a plane ticket.

The things I remember and cherish most about that ship, after the comfort of Suite A and the magnificent dining room, were the oriental rugs in the hallway landings and the potted plants. There was an abundance of carved woodwork that one cannot easily find today, let alone replicate. The First Class bar was all carved wood. I believe Bob Hope purchased it when the ship was disassembled. The reason the ship managed to maintain its original fittings was that it had never been turned into a troop ship during World War II, as had other ocean liners. The crew purposely ran the ship aground before that could happen. The war was over or nearly over when the *Vulcania* was about to be disfigured for wartime use. Saved in the nick of time, she sailed intact with all her glorious appointments.

The boys arrived in New York with a lot of "stuff" and more on the way. First, we found an apartment in the right part of town: 72nd Street between Fifth and Madison Avenues. We rented a one-bedroom apartment on the top floor in the front of a town house. There was even an elevator. No more walk-ups for the grandiose grandees! After some preliminary casting about for a shop, it soon became clear that the cost of a decent store rental was more of a commitment than we felt secure in making. It dawned on us that our enthusiasm outweighed our knowledge, so the shop idea was discarded. Instead we used the things we had purchased to decorate our new apartment. The leftover supply of curiosities we used as gifts for weddings, birthdays and Christmas. We sold others for a small profit to friends for their own gift-giving or household use.

My next task was to find suitable, convenient employment. I wanted to walk to work, not commute on a smelly train or crowded bus. French and Company was elegant and to my taste, but there were no openings. Next door was the prestigious Parke-Bernet Auction Galleries. I tried there and met with the manager of the business office. Sandy Carroll and I hit it off immediately and she offered me a job in catalogue subscriptions and information. I would also be expected to help at the counter after a sale, arranging the billing to facilitate the discharge of purchased items. I found my heart's contentment there at the hectic, glamorous auction house, and slowly changed my job description to include special customer services, for which I got tips that exceeded my weekly salary. I created a couple of meaningful "firsts" in the auction world, while my imagination flowered.

A One-Man Show . . .

One subject, many artists, different times.

Eric, art dealer, portrait
by Charlotte Lichtblau, 1970

. . . to be continued

Chapter 7

GLAMOR AND GLITTER

Resplendent with art treasures, magnificent furniture and rare decorative objects, the venerable auction rooms of Parke-Bernet on Madison Avenue directly across from the Carlyle Hotel were perfect proving grounds for ambitious and avid Eric. Antiques and fine art stretched my mind in ways that continue to excite and challenge me. They fired my imagination and added to the basic knowledge gained both from school and my European trips. Added excitement was provided by the many illustrious people who passed through the rarefied halls. Aside from top museum people and notable dealers, social leaders and entertainment celebrities frequented Parke-Bernet. I remember Billy Rose, Eva Gabor, "The Hills are Alive" Maria von Trapp (the plump, dirndl-wearing Baroness was a disappointment compared with her Hollywood version, Julie Andrews), Andy Warhol, and the Metropolitan Museum crowd, including the student Philippe de Montebello, who became director in the 1980s.

Two unforgettable visitors were Jackie Kennedy and Greta Garbo. Curiously, they both came into the Galleries at the same time on a couple of occasions. If Garbo really wanted to be alone, it was good timing to arrive when Jackie was there. However, Garbo had ways of gaining attention if she felt too neglected; then she would go into the "I vant to be left alone" mode.

Dr. Max Jacobson, known as "Doctor Feelgood," had his office on the ground floor of my building on 72nd Street. President Kennedy often went there for shots. A couple of times I came upon Jackie walking toward the front door with two secret service men. She had the most unnerving way of looking me over, a bemused smile on her face. If she had been a young man, I would have thought I was being undressed by those inquisitive eyes.

The unctuous auction-room manager, who oversaw decor and the uniformed attendants, often took the VIPs around for private viewings. During one of those private tours with Garbo, who usually wore a blue raincoat with white bobby socks on her sneakered feet, he mentioned that my surname was the same as hers was originally: Gustafson. She observed me carefully and made a decision. She envisioned a way in which I could consider her my aunt, which in later years I put to good use. On two occasions, I left messages for "my aunt," who visited some of the same villas I was visiting. The first time was with the consultant to the stars, Gayelord Hauser, in his magnificent spread on the Letojanni beach below Taormina, Sicily. The next time was in Tunisia, at wine king Nicholas Feuillatte's seaside villa in Hamamet, Tunisia.

Garbo loved beautiful things, carefully collecting quality paintings and furniture for her residence near River House on the East Side, a few doors down from my *My Fair Lady*–days haunt at the East Gate. Naturally, she was drawn to the ever-changing exhibition of splendid objects, furniture and paintings at Parke-Bernet. I never intruded upon her, a discretion she relied on. I often saw her on the streets of New York, gazing in the windows of fabric shops or decorative arts' stores. She loved to walk, investigating everything. Her special lope, with raincoat and floppy hat, said "Garbo." Everyone said how lovely she was, but I think that is a prime example of how people delude themselves. They still saw her the way she was before retiring from the movies. In the many times I saw her close up, I was amazed how much like a road map her face looked. She was so wrinkled that even Tallulah Bankhead looked like a smooth beauty by comparison. Garbo reminded me of a large cat, her walk and unpredictability were feline.

Phillip van Rensselaer, Barbara Hutton's playboy, was a frequent visitor to the Galleries. Years later, I got to know him well enough for him to ask me whether I could find the time to help him type the manuscript of his new book, an exposé of the lives of the very rich and famous. I found him very attractive and charming, and could easily imagine why both women and men found him so desirable. He was always perfectly groomed, with a beautiful countenance that indicated years of pampering in a rich and pleasured past. Phillip's exploits were grist for the social columnists' gossip and conjecture mill.

Leslie Hyam, the president of Parke-Bernet, was a tall, distinguished English gentleman. He originally started the auction house as the American Galleries on 57th Street before moving up to the 70s on Madison and changing the name. He noticed my diligence and enthusiasm for the auction world. I often came in early to dispense with paperwork, so that I would be free to go up to the auction room to observe the sales. Sometimes, I bid on items for special customers. I was eager to learn the auction value of things firsthand, but I made sure the chores I was hired to do had been tended to first. Hence, when Mr. Hyam came in to begin his day, the "Out" box on my desk was already piled with work accomplished earlier that morning. It was evident that I had been in before the workday officially began. My desk was the first one in the business office, hence I enjoyed high visibility. The erudite, old-world dignity of Mr. Hyam lent great credibility to lofty Parke-Bernet. His executive vice-president was the straight-from-the-shoulder, well turned-out Mary Vandergrift. She took a liking to me, listening attentively to my ideas for the auction house.

In sharp contrast to those stellar executives was the carrot-haired Louis Marion, the vice-president. He was a rough customer who referred to me as "the Duke." Rumor had it his last name had been changed to Marion from a more ethnic name, perhaps Marioni. He must have been a ruthless businessman; his social graces were scant. When Leslie Hyam committed suicide, he left a note requesting that his English secretary be kept on and that I be made vice-president when Marion took over the presidency. I was called into the conference room to discuss my future at Parke-Bernet with Louis Marion and Mary Vandergrift. I was not supposed to know about the note or the fact that our president had committed suicide, so I made no reference to it when asked brusquely by Marion what I would like to do at the auction house. He suggested that I become an auctioneer like his son, John. I demurred, saying that I would be uncomfortable doing that. He exploded in anger, stating that he had begun in the mail room. "I am not you, Mr. Marion," I grandly rejoined, and shortly I took my leave, indicating with disappointment that if that was the best offer, I would resign and go elsewhere with my talents. I knew that Marion and I could never work harmoniously together, so why prolong the agony?

The funeral service for Leslie Hyam was at the Frank Campbell Funeral Home on 81st and Madison. His long-time girlfriend, a previous Miss Norway, sent a large horseshoe of white roses with a ribbon: "'Til we meet again." Gallery staff and clients gathered to pay their last respects. A jewelry dealer entered and Louis Marion accosted him near the coffin. Loudly, he argued about a valuable pearl he had been promised. Miss Vandergrift suggested to Louis that that was neither the right time nor place, while we shuddered, aghast at his lack of taste.

Mary Vandergrift tried her best to dissuade me from resigning with assurances that I was a "natural" in the auction world. She used my idea to augment auction activities with concerts and public-interest lectures, such as Desmond Guiness lecturing on Irish Georgian houses, when the auction room was "dark." It gave official invited status to the public, who were otherwise hesitant to enter the rarefied halls. For five dollars, the community could enjoy a cultural event. Admission acquainted them with the lay-out, restrooms, telephones and display rooms. It was a friendly way to share the treasures on view, and attending a sale might not then be as intimidating.

Another of my innovations, today indispenable, was the introduction of the telephone in the auction room for an entire sale, long-distance. It had never been done before. I thought of it while discussing an American painting sale with a client in New Orleans. He could not come up for the sale. I suggested that I would be in the auction room if he wanted to telephone me there and advise him as the sale was progressing. It was tougher than I thought it would be and I discouraged his buying a few paintings that got too pricey. Miss Vandergrift approved of my decision, saying that he was a contented customer for life thanks to my participation. My telephone call made international news, but before the sale Louis Marion demanded to be assured that it was not costing the Galleries a fortune. "Is the sucker paying for the call?" he demanded.

Because I had friendly relations with the top curators at the Metropolitan Museum's Painting Department, Marion asked me to give the VIPs a special tour when the Galleries were closed to the public. He asked that I eavesdrop, and tell him what inter-ested them, giving him any information I could cull from their visit. Clearly, "the Duke" had some value for this blustery charac-ter.

The most amazing Parke-Bernet story I witnessed firsthand involved the "two Marions." John Marion was auctioneer for a poorly attended morning sale. A couple of crystal chandeliers were on the block. No sooner had he announced them than his gavel descended. "Sold!" A priest had gotten them for a truly minimal price. I was puzzled, but later found out the convolu-tions of the tale. The priest was from Marion's parish in Westchester. The church's raffle of a Cadillac town car was impending. Surprise! The winner was none other than Louis

Marion! He wisely sold the car to Parke-Bernet for full value. I was working in the business office where the paperwork was put through. Parke-Bernet *gave* the expensive car to its president Louis Marion.

It was much better for me to leave that company for the abundant and growing world of New York that I had become more familiar with over the past five years. Nannette Cavanagh, my assistant, helped to organize a party for me to be held at Jaeger House on Lexington Avenue. Miss Vandergrift attended my farewell party, the largest given for a departing employee. Louis Marion was not invited. The one thing I should thank Marion for was his assigning the deputy-mayor of New York's daughter, Nannette Cavanagh, to me. Probably because I was "the Duke," he felt I was the logical person to handle a young postdebutante with no office skills but a sunny personality.

One of the first things Nannette did was to sit on an open inkpad in a Chanel suit, while I was explaining the basics of filing. She was a sweet, naive girl who developed a crush on her boss, me. She invited me to escort her to charity balls, great fun for me. Sometimes, we attended several events a week, increasing my social circulation tremendously. Often, we took the floral centerpieces for office decorations. The business office never looked more festive than when Nannette and I had been out on the town the night before.

Her aunt, Barbara Cavanagh, once Cary Grant's girlfriend, was now entangled with her brother's drinking partner and boss, the mayor of New York, Robert Wagner. After his wife died, Barbara and he got together and eventually married. It was not a bed of roses, more like wine and roses. I remember the heavy drinking when I visited the Cavanaghs on the North Shore of Long Island. Bobby Kennedy lived on the next property, and Jackie's frequent visits were noted with interest. Barbara pulled either a gun or a knife on Wagner and left for the divorce courts. She moved to Palm Beach to live with a female admirer.

*Nannette Cavanagh and I make opening
gala of Shepherd's disco on Park Avenue.*

Before all that, Nannette and I made the rounds with the
Mayor and Barbara. Once, leaving a reception at the Waldorf-
Astoria, Mayor Wagner asked us if he could drop us off anywhere
uptown on his way to Gracie Mansion. We were going to the
Junior League off Park Avenue in the low 80s, so we hopped in. I
called David before departure to alert him to be on the corner of
72nd Street and Park Avenue so that he could get a lift uptown
with us. I neglected to tell him we would be in the mayor's official
limousine with Hizzoner. What a look David had on his face as we
slowed down to pick him up and continue uptown!

Incidents like that were normal for me. After Pope John

XXIII had been on an official visit to New York, an acquaintance
of mine acquired the special limousine used for the event. He
invited me to join him for a cruise around Central Park. I telephoned from the deluxe vehicle to my favorite liquor store to
order a chilled bottle of champagne. The salesman, who had a
running account with me, was surprised on coming out of the
store to deliver the bubbly to find me luxuriating in the Pope's
car. Alcohol was a daily accompaniment to celebration, or any
reason whatsoever. I was seemingly indestructible, with a high
tolerance and a growing, insatiable thirst.

David and I were invited everywhere and we entertained
many colorful people as well. David loved to cook while I tended
carefully to the table. I planned seating and sent invitations. The
apartment was appointed with the treasures we had acquired on
our year's sojourn in Europe. We looked terrific together and
presented a charming household for invited guests.

When I was not being the official escort for the deputy
mayor of New York's daughter, I often escorted Alexandra Danilova. She was the second wife of George Balanchine, although
they never officially married. "I was, how you say? his common
wife," Choura would exclaim in her Russian-accented English.
Danilova was a perfect example of a well turned-out woman. She
was always elegant, full of verve, even when going to teach her
classes at the School of American Ballet. She arrived in mink,
whether at Carnegie Hall or upper-Broadway studios. Her signa-
ture scarf wrapped over tights was held in place by a costly jewel.
Perfume completed the effect. Ballerinas are not usually good
ballroom dancers. Danilova was the exception. I adored dancing
with her; we glided along the floor effortlessly. At the opening of
the State Theater at Lincoln Center, we were waltzing on the
travertine floor of the new theater's promenades. On either end
of the hall are enormous female statues by Elie Nadelman.
Choura glanced at them and referred to them as "Schmoos,"
which surprised me but so adequately describes the prominent

sculptures. Once, at a concert version of Bellini's *I Capuleti e i Montecchi* at Carnegie Hall, I turned to Danilova in the next seat. Referring to Giulietta Simionato's voice, I said that she sang like an angel. "She sings like a devil," Danilova corrected me. At Russian holidays, Danilova often had other Russian dancers to her apartment on 57th Street and Sixth Avenue. I met dancers from the Diaghilev period of her life: Igor Youskevitch and Leon Danielian, a favorite partner of hers.

I attached great importance to being desirable to famous people. It did not even matter to me if we ever went to bed. The invitation was most important. I hoped to achieve self-worth through those propositions. It was my ego that got fed instead, ego buoyed by alcoholic stimulants, my daily sustenence. I was desirable, and I was finally becoming "someone" on the international scene. "Our Gal Sunday" would have been proud of the boy from the Bronx.

The most memorable ballet dancer I met was Erik Bruhn. Regrettably, Rudolf Nureyev was usually around him. They shared a bed in talent agent Chris Allen's apartment in the next building from where David and I lived. After

The Prince of Dance: Erik Bruhn

several years together, life with David had became routine, lacking in stimulation. When I met Bruhn at a party on Gramercy Park, I was instantly enthralled. We seemed to have so much to talk about. We left the party to continue our conversation over dinner. I could not believe that I was alone with "the Prince of Dance." The blond god of the ballet world had to be one of the most elegant dancers ever. I worshipped him. Thoughts of David were put on the back burner. I knew he had his dalliances, even with friends I had introduced him to. These moments, this evening were mine to be treasured. Not caring where we dined, I suggested a hamburger joint Ethel Merman used to frequent on First Avenue in the low 50s. It was clear

Eric emerging

Erik was interested in continuing after dinner. Neither of us had a place we could go, as David was in one place and Rudy in the other, so I called a friend who lived near the restaurant and asked if I could bring someone up to his bedroom for a brief interlude. Never had I thought of doing such a thing, but when pressed, desperate measures are employed. "Sure, I'll be up all night working on a project," my friend told me. I am not sure if my friend ever realized who it was that I brought to his bed, as ballet was not an interest of his. We walked home to our respective apartments on 72nd Street as the sun rose. I remember the garbage trucks making their rounds in the still city streets. Our fingertips barely touched.

A few days later, I attended a black-tie opening of Tennessee Williams's *The Milk Train Doesn't Stop Here Anymore*, starring Tallulah Bankhead, Tab Hunter and my new friend Ruth Ford. Arriving in front of my building after the performance, I saw Erik with Rudy. I was glad I was so gorgeously turned out, so that I could hug Erik, kiss him on the cheek and turn coolly

toward Rudy to say "Good
evening," then dash inside my
building. Rudy was surprised
by my curtness, doubtless
demanding elucidation from
Erik. The grandiosity got
even grander shortly thereafter. One blizzardy night, I
managed to snare what
seemed the only taxi in the
neighborhood. David and I
were going to Central Park
West to have dinner with two
German lady friends. I saw
Erik across 72nd Street vainly
searching for a taxi. I had our
driver swerve up to him.

*Rudolph Nureyev and
Eleanor D'Antuono curtain calls
at Met for ABT's "Raymonda," mid-70s.*

Knowing he had a performance at the City Center in
Balanchine's *Swan Lake,* I offered him use of our cab. "Rudy is
with me," he indicated pointing around the corner. "That's okay,
come in here next to me," I invited. When Rudy tried to enter the
back seat, I pushed his world-famous buns out and told him to sit
with the driver. Imagine, ordering around *the* star of the ballet
world! Nureyev peered through the separating window trying
take part in our conversation, but I ignored him. David and I
were giving a "do" and I wanted Erik to come, which he did.

Years later, I attended a ballet performance at La Scala,
starring Nureyev and Carla Fracci. Nureyev used to eat garlic
before the performance to offend Fracci. He was so terrific and I
had been so beastly to him that I went backstage to make a gesture of peace. When everyone else had finished complimenting
him, he and I remained alone on the vast stage. I took his hand
and warmly congratulated him. He may not have even realized
that I was the rude queen from 72nd Street, but at least I felt I

had extended something positive and friendly toward him. The last time I saw Nureyev was at the April in Paris Ball at the Waldorf-Astoria, just before his death. AIDS had withered the once-mighty Tartar to a shadow of himself.

The last time I saw Erik Bruhn was at a bizarre party held in a town house in the East 60s. It was 1970 and the hippie movement had left deep scars in the social fabric of life in the Big Apple. It was "anything goes" after Warhol, pop art, op art and minimalism, which in my opinion contributed to the breakdown in artistic expression. Nudity and vulgarity were everywhere displayed shamelessly. There was even a "museum" of nudity on 96th Street near Park Avenue, run by a female midget and her hulky husband. They created an exhibition with live sculptures. A naked Christ was guarded by S & M leather motorcyclists. The exhibition was the centerpiece of a large party thrown in the East Side town house. Surfeited with drink, drugs and disco, the revelers danced all around the tableau vivant.

Earlier that week, I read in the obituaries of the *New York Times* that famous ballet dancer Erik "Brahn" died. I was shocked and outraged to discover that the *Times* had omitted many important facts. They even misspelled his surname, putting an "a" where the "u" should have been. I mourned my beloved Erik's demise with tears of deep sadness. When I expressed distress for the poor coverage of Erik's death to a close friend, I was informed that it was not *my* Erik Bruhn, but Erik Brahn from the Chicago Ballet. I was overjoyed to see Erik at the weird party. I hugged him, kissed him and welcomed him back to life. He told me that many of his friends had been as deceived as I was. I can only guess what went on upstairs. When he appeared I noticed that his hair was wet and his cologne freshly applied.

In 1962, the year after David and I returned from our European sojourn, we decided to summer in Fire Island Pines. The Parke-Bernet Galleries were closed for the summer. The employees had the option to take the summer off at half pay, or

Above, Alexandra Danilova ("Choura"),
Eric, and Ysabel.
Left, the Pre-Columbian chicken, at home.

continue a slowed-down routine. I opted for time off with half
pay to enjoy the natural wonders of Fire Island. David continued
his dull job at Diamond Match on Third Avenue, coming out on
weekends. There we met so many characters who were part of
our lives for years to come.

One in particular spectacularly changed my life enormously.
At a neighbor's cocktail party one evening, I was chatting with a
tall brunette. She said she had never been to Fire Island before,
and that she had come to the party with the couple standing outside the plate-glass window. The couple were embracing warmly,
which caused the woman talking with me to announce that it
looked as though they were "fucking." It was a startling thing to
say, the first of many incredible things to come from the mouth of
Ysabel. We hit it off quickly and the momentum gained as more
drinks were consumed. Ysabel suggested that I come over to her
place to have a special Bloody Mary the next morning. I appeared
and was startled to find that she had two maids in attendance: one
was to keep the other company! It was the early 1960s, the Pines

was still a modest though upmarket place to summer. It was before swimming pools and houseboys.

My Bloody Mary was mixed with beer, "hair of the dog that bit me," as we alcoholics are so fond of saying. It was an unusual combination but I drank it. Ysabel Aya explained that she was born in Colombia but had lived in New York for many years. Her accent was more English than Spanish and she was fluent in French as well as Italian. Furthermore, she was a neighbor. Her floor-through apartment was at Fifth Avenue and 76th Street, practically around the corner. We began what was to become a monumental relationship for the two of us, and I absorbed her enthusiastic, somewhat zany, expression of life.

There was a costume party that evening, which David and I were planning to attend as slaves. Nothing like showing off a young, bronzed body in a loincloth. We would light her way with our *flambeaux* if she would come with us. She readily agreed, leaving her sullen, disapproving older boyfriend at home with the two maids.

The mixture of characters increased as the weekend progressed. Our friends from France had returned. Leila and Bill Hart arrived with the two dogs. My friend Timothy Baum (from another ocean-liner trip) called at the last moment and arrived. He had managed to crease Noël Coward's Rolls-Royce in the parking lot in his hurry to make the ferry. Coward was a houseguest just down the beach, with Henry Fonda's ex-wife Susan, now married to the noted Shakespearean actor Michael ("Mendy") Wager.

Parties, hilarity, booze and sex. Strolling the boardwalks the morning after a large costume party, one noted an astounding amount of tell-tale debris: lost or discarded decorations, underwear, drinking cups and the like. The period of lavish costume parties soon came to a halt, but Ysabel appeared not to have realized it. She continued to live life as an ongoing fancy-dress party.

Soon I was absorbed into the pulse of Ysabel's fantastic lifestyle. Thursdays were "her" night to entertain at home on Fifth Avenue. Usually, she had places for seventeen seated dinner guests, but she always invited another mob of guests afterward for more drinks, and after-dinner entertainment. Her parties usually lasted until dawn. Once, Ysabel invited José Greco and some of his dancers to come for cocktails. They stayed until the wee hours of the morning. I told Greco I could teach him flamenco, if you can believe my nerve. He playfully said that he would be interested. I put him off by suggesting that my lessons would be too expensive and not to consider it. Dutch costume designer Freddy Wittop had been the top flamenco dancer before World War II, known as Federico Rey. When he was called into the American armed service, José Greco from Brooklyn moved in to take over.

Although David was abashed by Ysabel's outrageousness, I reveled in it. Her clothes were unusual, worn to show off her figure. She piled her hair high on her head in a loose chignon, wrapped and held in place by what she referred to as her "merkin." Her custom-made velvet dress might be very low cut in the back, which stimulated her to threaten to wear it the other way around next time, "tits out." On her travels she collected ethnic weavings, which she made into smart outfits. Usually, Ysabel wore one of her fabulous gold pre-Columbian pieces to finish the ensemble. Her stature and theatricality caused many strangers to believe she was an opera singer, Maria Callas–like in appearance. "Oh, yes, we know each other, but we would *never* appear on the same stage together!" she exclaimed grandly. Tone-deaf, "the diva" enjoyed her vicarious persona. She did love concerts, but did not care for the opera.

Sometimes, wanting to take a spontaneous stroll, we called each other, agreeing to meet halfway on Fifth Avenue. As I would approach her, I would note with shock that chic Ysabel was perusing the garbage cans on Fifth Avenue, oblivious to the stares of passersby. I learned that she was doing this to amuse me, so then I would do something unusual to compete. At times, I would walk quickly past her, ignoring her. We invented what we thought were cute pastimes and games. If we found a nice car with an unlocked door on Fifth Avenue, we got into it and had cigarettes, resting our legs out of the cold or rain. Then, we searched the car for anything of value or use, commenting rudely on the owner's lack of consideration in leaving a dirty ashtray and nothing of interest in the glove compartment. It was amazing that our childish pranks did not get us into trouble in the years to come.

David and I decided that Fire Island did not have the cachet of the Hamptons, so the next year we took a house in Amagansett. It was an extension of our life in New York, as many of the summer residents were playmates from the city.

Two guides from the United Nations were a fixture in our circle. The girls, chosen from all around the world, were ambassadors of good will from their native countries. They escorted visitors to the U.N., providing information about the vast organization. Off duty, they were the center of attention of many eligible men in New York. The girls were forever throwing parties to gather interesting men who would then show them around their territory in New York and environs. David and I met Allegra Kent Taylor from England and her roommate, Karen Gilmuyden, a Greek girl from Turkey. Their parties were always surprising. I never knew who I would meet there: a pretender to the Russian throne, A & P heir Huntington Hartford, stockbrokers, playboys—the gamut. Allegra, David, Karen and I made the most attractive foursome anyone could imagine. All doors were open and welcoming.

Balancing all that and escorting the deputy mayor's daughter, cavorting with Ysabel and participating with the Beautiful People's agenda was very demanding. Then, there were gay get-togethers with that ever-expanding circle. My over-sociability and bubbling success professionally and socially widened the rift with sullen, resentful David. Calls from his mysterious new "friend" and other embarrassing social intrusions deeply wounded and offended me. It seemed so graceless to be openly having an affair with someone else while living with me. I thought I showed a discretion in my personal life that would not have embarrassed David. The end was clearly coming.

Amagansett represented to us a big social step up from the Pines on Fire Island. The last time that we took the house in Amagansett, we planned a large dinner party. The legendary Libby Holman would be attending. Andy Warhol's first patroness, Ethel Scull, was there, mingling with the head of United Press International, Robert Gardiner (who spoke of still having decapitation rights on Gardiner's Island), a Spanish countess, an Italian *marchesa*, high-power music-world figures and a noted dancer from the New York City Ballet. My closest and dearest friends were on hand to witness the arrival of a short, red-haired decorator, unknown to everyone except David. I knew immediately who the intruder was, and I felt powerless to evict him. I tried to ignore the situation to avoid a disagreeable scene.

The original torch singer, Libby Holman, sat on my left in the dining room. The decorator was in another room or in the garden, presumably with David. Libby fingered her Dunhill lighter. She explained that Montgomery Clift had given it to her, and she had given him a similar one. We spoke briefly of him, as I had come across him on Fire Island a couple of years earlier. He had a glass house on the beach and could be seen peering at the oceanscape. Clift was ill, a recluse under the care of what appeared to be a nurse or companion. I remember thinking that I would never let my life get out of control as he had, nor would I ever sink into the depths of depravity and despair like this fallen movie idol. This would never happen to me. Libby put her hand on mine and looked me in the eye. "I don't know what's wrong, but don't worry. It will be OK!" She was ravaged from alcohol and long-term abuse of many other things, sun being the least of them. Her walnut skin was set off by a fluff of white hair. She did not know me very well; everyone else there did. Yet only Libby

*At home dress-ups. Above, Spanish party
with Greta Keller and Ruth Loveland.
Right, Opera characters played by
"Poor Karen" Rosenwald, Mr. Henry,
and Karen Gilmuyden.*

assuaged my bruised, battered feelings. Only Libby seemed to
pick up on my unspoken sadness and misery.

David went off with the decorator after dinner. Following
that event, we spent some very strained months together in the
New York apartment. In the almost seven years I had spent with
David, my life had taken many turns. The grand tour followed by
the Parke-Bernet experience bolstered my image as a young,
beautiful man in the world of movers and shakers. Entertaining
world figures became a way of life. Exuberance and the continuous flow of bubbles promised a future of more of the same,
maybe better. I felt that Cinderella had indeed achieved well-
deserved princesshood, but in this case it was princehood.
Cinderella is a man, after all. My fairy godmother had bestowed a
glass slipper upon David and me. It was a love that fit perfectly, at
first. In this case, it was impermanent.

"Poor Karen" returned from Rome. She telephoned me and
asked me if I would accompany her to a school chum's wedding

reception to be held on the St. Regis Roof. Shirley Chaplin was to marry *wunderkind* Broadway producer Hal Prince. There would be lots of dancing and champagne as well as luminaries from the performing arts. Karen did not like to dance, but she encouraged me to dance as much as I liked with the other guests. She was happy talking with chums while I "star fucked." I argued with Betty Comden, while twirling her around the floor, that she *had* to be married to Adolph Green. I told Lena Horne's daughter Gale that she should be on the stage because she was so terrific on the dance floor, then I found out she was the lead in a musical. Arlene Francis, of television's popular *What's My Line?*, asked me if I was in show business as we gracefully maneuvered a rumba. "No, that's 10 down, Arlene." And, so it went.

The culmination of the gala evening was the entrance of mink-clad Rita Hayworth with Gary Merrill (recently divorced from Bette Davis) and Zero Mostel. Unlike the other gowned women, Rita had on a plain brown, wool, in-town-for-shopping dress. Her only jewelry was a thick gold rope necklace. To my astonishment and delight, they sat at my table. Stimulated by countless glasses of champagne, I recklessly decided that it was the opportunity of a lifetime to give a spontaneous floor show with the goddess of cinematic dance for the pleasure of all the distinguished guests.

Politely and quietly I approached Rita Hayworth and asked her to dance. She looked over at Gary Merrill, who was busy discussing something with Zero Mostel. "It's OK. Let them talk while we enjoy a dance," I said assuringly as I led her to the dance floor, which was crowded. It was not long before I realized that my partner had also been drinking, she did not respond to my leads. Her distended belly pressed against my cummerbund, and we shuffled aimlessly. I burst forth with, "It is just as well that you are not going to be doing that Broadway play." Rita glared at me, demanding to know why. I looked at her cropped hair, an uninteresting red, and thought of the long-tressed Gilda who wowed

*Love goddess
in repose:
Rita Hayworth.*

us all in "Put the blame on Mame, boys!" The allure, the sex appeal and dynamic charm were nowhere in sight. "Because the play is not worthy of your talents," I stammered. Again, silence and shuffling. It was not the scenario I had envisioned. Remember how Mickey Rooney with Judy Garland at MGM just got up and did a terrific number? I really thought we could do the same thing. I gave up leading as it was to no avail. We were rudderless.

"I knew one of your husbands." "Whish one," she slurred vaguely. "Aly Kahn," I replied. "Oh, him," Rita said with feigned indifference, flapping her left wrist nonchalantly. Again silence. "We can sit down, if you don't want to dance," I offered. "But, I love to dance . . ." I asked her to show it by giving me a smile. A half-smile was produced. "Well, then frown." Hayworth gave me a clown's frown and then a truly broad smile. Around us, people were gawking and pointing. "A bunch of fucking bores," I heard myself exclaim. "Fuckin' bores," she repeated sloppily. "Let's knock them off the dance floor." We proceeded to bump into people, hips colliding with those around us. Noting who was abusing them, the guests left the floor until finally it was just Rita and me.

Lester Lanin had long seen me showing off on ballroom

floors. He watched us while leading the orchestra. Everyone else seemed to be looking at us as well. Unhappily, we had no routine to do, but the band played on. Gary Merrill saved us from further torment by approaching Rita and requesting that she sit down. The "show that never was" ended. Today, in sobriety, I remember the episode with embarrassment.

El Morocco, the famous nightclub, felt it needed a boost in its public profile. It threw an elegant shindig, admission by invitation only, which was taped for future television promotion. Celebrities and New York glitterati filled the tables, sipping free champagne, dining on gratis gourmet feasts. Hope Hampton came in her ubiquitous chinchilla and her bleached-blond pageboy. "Bobo" Rockefeller donned the same Norell sequinned, ostrich-trimmed gown she wore everywhere. Everyone dressed to the hilt for the cameras' sake. One would have thought it was a glamorous turnout for an evening at El Morocco. The strange thing was that it was in the afternoon. We departed at the end of the "soirée" while it was still light out. We were so involved with the party that really began at lunchtime that it seemed like eve-

Nannette's Stork Club birthday celebration for Eric.

ning. People were just returning from their offices as we left what appeared to be an all-night bash. Another publicity job.

Nannette gave me a birthday party at The Stork Club, which her public relations man fed to the press. When David and I went skiing (neither of us skied) for a weekend in Vermont, the papers lying by the fireplace in the lodge's sitting room had pictures of me "frugging" with Francine "Le Frak." It was another publicity device created by the society public relations firm I had been briefly affiliated with after Parke-Bernet. David wet his feet in their offices, too. They handled the debut of the young Lefrak girl, which involved cleverly bending rules, altering facts, so that a nice Jewish girl could make the grade in Old World waspdom. Lefrak became Le Frak to carry through the French implication of "Francine." Known to the firm as a "player," I was used as a debutante's validation in the photo.

The most spectacular event I participated in during my stint with the society publicist was working on the world premiere of *Lord Jim*, starring Peter O'Toole. Tension-filled weeks of planning for the Times Square gala with a supper dance following at the old Astor Hotel brought many more celebrities into my life. Joan Crawford headed the committee to generate interest and support for the event. Crawford was an amazing woman, with great drive and true star quality. She was a crack professional. Standing next to me at a mutual friend's bar before a committee meeting, I did not even notice her in her daytime *mufti*. If television personality John Daly had not greeted her, I would have paid no attention to the short woman in the nondescript suit. She had the penthouse of the building she owned on the corner of Fifth Avenue and 70th Street, where we were invited to meet in the all-white, shoes-off living room.

On glittering opening night, however, it was a different story completely. Mobs of movie fans pushed against police barracades. Limousines pulled up to the theater to unload their elegant passengers. When a celebrity alighted, he or she was announced for the benefit of the waiting public and press. I was stationed close to the curb and was able to monitor the proceedings. Scotch heightened my excitement as the celebrities arrived. All went smoothly until a particular limousine arrived. It did not pull up to the curb as the others had. Rather, it stayed about ten feet from the sidewalk. No one emerged. After what seemed a very long time, a face appeared in the window. It was Joan Crawford. Slowly the window was lowered. She waved but made no effort to get out. It was not until the entire crowd was aware of who was in the car that the door slowly opened. She stood beside the door, leaning slightly back so that the heavy beading of her jacket assumed a dramatic line. She raised her arm in greeting. Flashbulbs popped and the crowd's cheering grew into a frenzy. Until then, she made no effort to begin her entrance toward the theater. Now, with an added ten feet of entrance, she moved forward. She raised her arm to wave to "a friend" at a distance just inside the door of the theater. What a pro! The device of choosing someone to aim toward as a means of gracefully propelling forward amid the crowd's approbation was a lesson in showmanship for me. A friend of mine was in the car behind Crawford's. Later, he told me that the aging actress he was with thought the crowd had recognized *her*. She was so pleased they remembered her, but she soon realized the roar was for Crawford.

If I had had a lot to drink, Judy Garland and Peter O'Toole were no slouches either. As I was officially handling aspects of public relations for the event, O'Toole asked me to introduce him to Judy Garland. It seemed a great photo opportunity, and I thought afterward that I should have gotten into a photo with them, too. She was with an Indian prince that evening, very much in her cups, or rather her dinner plate. I had quite a time getting her to stand up and meet with the star of the film. The pictures were taken of the two of them together, although I am not sure if either of them remembered it. MGM spent a lot of money to keep O'Toole's indiscretions in the Plaza Hotel's men's room out

Tennessee Williams with Dr. Ruth Loveland and Walter Stane.

of the press. He seemed a very likable guy, but when he shook hands with me it was like squeezing a damp sponge. His drinking put me into the amateur class.

I do not remember everything from that evening, but I do have some photo mementos. One is of a charming, sweetly smiling Tennessee Williams. We met several times at social functions, either in mutual friends' homes or at an event such as the *Lord Jim* opening. He was always friendly, cordial, unassuming. Once, Danilova met him at our friends' cocktail party. The prima ballerina kneeled in front of him and kissed his hand in respect.

The social public relations firm specialized in a service called "Entrée Unlimited" for out-of-towners who wanted to "make the scene" in New York. It also serviced wannabes with money who needed publicity in the media to exalt their existence. Over lunch with Cliff Robertson and his bride-to-be, Dina Merrill, at the World's Fair, Merrill queried me about the organization. "Don't the same people just meet each other?" she wisely asked. It seemed like what Elsa Maxwell had made into her livelihood in the not too distant past, when she introduce the Duke and Duchess of Windsor to avid nouveau-riche Americans visiting the Riviera or Venice, pocketing the profits after splitting them with the royal couple, always strapped for ready cash.

More cash was something I could appreciate. Even more so could my playboy acquaintance from Parke-Bernet days. When fair-haired Phillip van Rensselaer resurfaced in New York I was delighted to see him. Phillip was forever hocking the costly cufflinks given to him by Barbara Hutton. Now, he was going to take them out of hock with the advance he was getting on his new book. He wondered if I would assist him retyping portions of it and finishing up the book for publication. I was pleased he needed my help and agreed to work with him on *The House with the Golden Door.*

Quickly, I began to suggest changes, expand his descriptions. We explored the heroine's sexual exploits more fully. Phillip filled my glass with iced vodka and my imagination took off. I was more than typing his book, I was co-authoring it. It was delicious fun, especially the flow of iced vodka. The publisher was a subsidiary of the staid Random House. The book, in its early stages, was given back with the directive to include at least 100 more pages of sex! Kay-Kay, who later became Cherry Towers, got fucked in every orifice by everyone in every position. More vodka and more porn. When I was not busy typing, Phillip took me to lunch, often with his brother Charles, who was then writing the Cholly Knickerbocker gossip column in the newspaper. I got current high-society shenanigans from both of the horses' mouths.

When I left the auction world, headstrong for further flowering, I briefly contemplated offering myself to the Metropolitan Museum of Art. I gained an interview in the inner office of the director. Ted Rorimer was off-putting. He interviewed me, his boots up on the desk. My well-hidden shyness surfaced, and I mumbled my way out of the situation.

Carlin Gasteyer, administrator of the Museum of the City of

New York, was different. I felt comfortable with her and I became her assistant, if only for a brief time. She claimed that I brought a bit of "Camelot" to the dusty, staid environment. After the hectic, fast-paced auction-house life, I was bored by the snail-paced existence of the museum. When I was not on the phone to friends, I snoozed at my desk, my workload quickly dispatched. I invented things to do, such as dry flowers upside down in my file cabinet with camphor. Nannette came to visit me with a huge bouquet that became my first experiment.

Tim Baum, whom I had met crossing on the *Liberté* (and to whom I will always be "Bosie") worked at the Galérie Moderne at Brentano's on Fifth Avenue. Jeanine Walkenberg created the original art gallery, which featured contemporary School of Paris painters. I met her through Tim and saw her when she came to Parke-Bernet. Jeanine was a survivor of Auschwitz. Some of her fingers were lost in experimentation there. She was prone to headaches, the lasting result of Nazi beatings; they eventually killed her, in the form of brain cancer. One of the great human beings I ever met, she quite naturally shared her love and appreciation for art. After a long period of trying to interest me in joining forces with her at Brentano's, I decided to go into the commercial art gallery world. Museum life seemed as dry as the flowers hanging upside down in my file cabinet.

As a further inducement to join the gallery staff, Jeanine worked out a plan with the president of Brentano's to hire me for two jobs, hence two paychecks each week. As the gallery paid small salaries, I was to be consultant for the chain of stores as well. That meant setting up inventories in newly created spaces in store locations in Boston, Washington, D.C., Hartford, and so forth. It allowed me to be on the road, do my own thing and have diversity in my job. I was not stuck in the gallery, keeping shop hours.

When the old Metropolitan Opera house was to be demolished and the company moved to the newly created Lincoln Center, I was saddened. So many youthful evenings had been spent in that historic and glamorous old house. I wanted to make a tribute to the Old Gal but what could I put on the gallery walls that would be appropriate? The obvious bridge was my great-great aunt Christina Nilsson, who had opened the house, and Birgit Nilsson (no relation) was to sing the final performance. I thought about the costume and scenery sketches that were used to create the productions. Who owned them? Would it be interesting to accumulate a collection of them for exhibition, and perhaps try to sell them? I called the set designers' union for information on the whereabouts of Metropolitan Opera designers, past and present. They gave me a few names and numbers. The costume and set designers were amazed that someone was interested in putting on an exhibition-for-sale of their work. Usually, they gave them away to the stars or crew, filed them in portfolios in the back of closets or threw them away! Sell them? How could one put a price on them? They helped me get in touch with other designers, who in turn put me in touch with more theatrical artists. I spent time visiting their studios and homes and gathered a very nice tribute to the Old Met, which went up in the Galérie Moderne in April 1966, the month the Old Met closed.

Having learned a few tricks from my brief public relations stints, I managed to have a few actresses of yesteryear, such as Anita Louise, at the opening, together with the usual climbers, for photo opportunities. I realized I had stumbled onto one of the last of the collectibles: original costume and set designs. They were the right size for modern apartments, had artistic merit and sentimental value and were decorative and inexpensive.

The first design I sold was to a young man who often came into the gallery to browse. He lived in Brooklyn Heights and was in love with the theater. It was the first design he ever bought and it started him on a long career of collecting. His collection is now one of the largest private ones in America and his reputation is firmly established. Later, with his encouragement, I created many more exhibitions and museum collections. Paul Stiga and I remain good friends.

Gian-Carlo Menotti asked me to come visit him at his East 62nd Street residence as a result of the exhibition. He was concerned about the quality of his Festival of Two Worlds in Spoleto, Italy. I was asked to consider mounting an exhibition there the next June and July (1967) to add cachet to the Festival. It sounded wonderful and I was agreeable to his offer of sponsorship and support, even though I wondered about leaving my position and the other logistics of opening a show of designs in Italy. We parted amicably for the first, and last, time.

Another exhibition I created at the gallery included a collection of amusing small sculptures created by the cartoonist Rube Goldberg. Later, with a friend, I transported the exhibition to Hartford by truck. I talked the president into having Fred Winship from UPI come up, for publicity value. My lively coterie kept the event from being completely dull. Without the loyal support of his New York friends, Rube Goldberg's sculpture was too expensive to fly in Hartford, cute as the pieces were. But, what a nice party we had!

An exhibition that Jeanine and I mounted at the Galérie Moderne consisted of the contents of a private collection from a Connecticut estate. I used my Parke-Bernet experience to evaluate, catalogue and promote the extraordinary array of blue-chip art. Edward Albee, a frequent visitor, came often for a private viewing of a Degas drawing of a male nude. Jerome Robbins, who purchased a rare Korean screen from us, often contemplated the collection. It was a perfect example of Jeanine's vision to offer first-class original art in a fine bookstore.

One of the Beautiful People on the New York scene was the tall, blond Czech, Yveta Love. We developed a brother-sister relationship and shared her husband, unbeknownst to her. Her father was a distinguished Czech man of letters, who gave his daughter a large collection of Czech master paintings for her airy

Park Avenue apartment. One of the contemporary painters Yveta wanted to help had a brief one-man show at the Galérie Moderne. The opening had a sprinkling of VIPs, but sales were light. Yveta and her husband invited me and the very determined Ethel Scull to dinner. Ethel pushed for La Grenouille, where she often lunched with Ruth Ford (Mrs. Zachary Scott) and others. Ethel ordered caviar and champagne, which I knew almost put Love into hate. Never known for her good taste, Ethel obliviously took her due and was never invited anywhere again by the Loves.

Ethel and Bob Scull had achieved a great deal of publicity. Their taxi fleet brought them spending money, which they invested in pop art. Warhol did her portrait; George Segal did her in plaster; they lent and gave Rauschenbergs and Oldenburgs to museum collections. They were bucking to be chosen for the board of the Metropolitan Museum, and they tried hard to capture publicity at every turn.

I helped David into a public relations job, which was a welcome release from his sales position. The social public relations firm that I had been with was glad to get a good-looking man with strong family connections. What I had learned he picked up and took farther with ruthless determination. One of the firm's clients was opening a disco near Bridgehampton. The Barge was to have a spectacular opening, with lotus-eaters in search of fresh pleasure, a few even arriving by helicopter. I was one of the three chosen for the ride. The attractive Prince of Hesse was to join me, Ethel Scull being the third passenger. The helicopter was late arriving at the Barge to pick us up, so the Prince left.

A long black limousine pulled up with Andy Warhol and his entourage. He was chosen for publicity value to join us now that royalty had fled their grasp. Andy wanted to bring one of his groupies but was firmly dissuaded. There was only room for three. Ethel sat sniffing with displeasure between us, complaining to me about Andy having to be with us. Warhol had a reputation for crashing parties with his gang of unwashed characters and his antisocial behavior. As it was tight company, he heard every unkind word we had to say about him. Having had a few "pick-me-ups" while waiting to depart, I announced to Ethel that I felt like pushing the puffy pink-and-white asshole out the door. We were out over the ocean when I reached across Andy's lap to put my hand on the door handle. "No, don't . . . it's too good for him," Ethel sniffed. "The cameras are on us and his death would be recorded for posterity. It is much too good for him." I agreed and sat back, prepared to descend earthward, anticipating the party ahead. We exited the helicopter to a battery of exploding flash-bulbs and television cameras. Andy rushed out first through the crowd, not to be seen by us anymore.

I took Ethel to the opening of a beach club that month, escorted her to the Paper Ball (ladies wore evening gowns made of paper) at the Wadsworth Atheneum in Hartford and got her included in the Barge folderol. Thus, I found it particularly unkind and self-absorbed of her to refer to me in the profile done about her in *The New Yorker* as "some boy from Brentano's who looked jet set." She did not even give me a name. It seemed ungrateful, even graceless and left me with feelings of having been used and abused.

A variety of interesting characters wafted in and out of the Galérie Moderne. A dark young man from Philadelphia often came in to pick my brains about running an art gallery. Andrew Crispo was destined to get a gallery on 57th Street bearing his name, and notoriety resulting from his compulsive death-dealing S & M capers. Am I glad I never took him up on his invitation for a *ménage à trois* with his friend, Arthur! Having my wrists tied to the bedpost was a notion that I gladly turned down.

Definitely off-center was balletomane-artist Edward Gorey, who came in often. And the artist-designer Pavel Tschelitchew had lovers and lovers of lovers who permeated Brentano's. We managed to get drawings and watercolors done by the deceased master from one of his long-ago lovers who had fallen on hard times. The manager of the store's partner had been a major fixture in the artist's life. Henri Ford's actress sister, Ruth, had modeled for him and owned some major works of his.

Ysabel was friendly with many prominent artists. Joan Miró, when in New York, came to visit her at the floor-through Fifth Avenue apartment. Knowing he liked to work with ink and brushes, she always had them available, along with paper on which he could create. After many drinks, he painted four abstracts and gave the series to her. Miró was joined by Alexander ("Sandy") Calder and José Maria Sert one evening over libations with Ysabel. Before going home, each of them took turns decorating the inside of her gentlemen's coat closet with original black-chalk art work. She went to sleep in the evening content at having been given a valuable work of art by the distinguished painters. When she awoke late in the morning, she discovered to her horror that the maid, who usually had to be prodded into cleaning chores, had carefully scrubbed clean the creation. She did not know modern art and had painstakingly erased the "mess" from the night before.

Another artist friend was Salvador Dalí and his shrewd wife, Gala. We partied with them on numerous occasions and Dalí also often came without her; apparently, Gala charged him for each appearance she had to make. The scale varied and was dependent on how boring or interesting the event promised to be. The last time I spoke with Dalí, he was Gala-less at the Italian Consul General's party on Park Avenue and 69th Street. The Consul General was a close friend of mine, whose assistance with connections in Rome proved invaluable, enabling me to find a way of realizing Gian-Carlo Menotti's invitation to have an exhibition in Spoleto the following summer.

Meanwhile, I attended rehearsals at both the Metropolitan Opera and the New York City Opera in their new Lincoln Center homes. It may have been my bearing or alcohol-supported attitude, but I always walked with a strong sense of belonging into

With young Maria, Dalí, his Gala, and Ysabel.

both opera houses without a ticket, nodding to those backstage, entering the house from there. Nodding also to ushers, I took seats reserved for company members and enjoyed the proceedings. I was always received with polite deference. Once, I greeted the telephone operators backstage at the Met and proceeded through the connecting door to the auditorium. It was a closed rehearsal, so that I thought my chances were slimmer than usual. Sure enough, an usher guarding the door stopped me and announced that no one was to be admitted into the closed rehearsal. I returned to the backstage entrance hall where the receptionist-telephone operators sat. One of them said to me, "He didn't let you in? Didn't he know who you are? Wait, let me get him on the phone." I do not know who she thought I was and did not hear what she said to the door guardian, but I was requested to return. He opened the door to the forbidden rehearsal with great politeness and reverence. I never figured out who I looked like. Even during the final days of the old Met, Rudolf Bing always greeted me warmly. When entering the Met's backstage elevator, I usually got cheerful "hellos" and once even a comment on the wonderful performance last evening. Who knows? I still had to work out who I was, too!

One of the avenues I explored before going to work at Brentano's was at joining another auction house. The only other one of significance (hence worth my effort) was Christie's, which had offices just across Madison Avenue, near my apartment. Thomas Peers was then a big gun there. I had met him at a number of parties and found him strange but attractive. One day, he invited me to his apartment for drinks to discuss my future plans. His telephone rang constantly and I gathered he was having a get-together there that evening. Tom was wearing a belt that had loops almost completely around it. I asked him why the belt would have all those loops and was informed that it was for when it was used as a collar around someone's neck. He had other equipment downstairs for use later that night. If I wanted to come, I would have to agree to participate. I was stunned, stam-

Indestructible heldentenor in grandiose setting (Red Rocks, CO).

mering definite reluctance. After the Spoleto Festival, I bumped into him leaving a sleazy hotel in London. It was a place where he claimed no one heard the cries!

Life was invigorated by the opening of Lincoln Center. UPI's chief, Fred Winship, took me as his "date" to the opening of the new Metropolitan Opera. The entire plaza was jammed with people observing the dazzling opening-night audience. Only a narrow walkway between the mobs permitted entry to the new house, done up in Chagall murals and Austrian chandeliers. I remember being impressed that I had a $500 ticket given to me for the event, a lot of money in 1966. Champagne flowed and I even took some to my seat. There was a dinner with obelisk centerpieces. I took mine home and had an artist paint it for me. The air was festive and everyone was kissy-huggy, even in the men's rooms.

I found a black silk collapsible top hat at the end of the evening. At a lunch later that week, my host, Jonathan Talbot, complained of losing his top hat at the Met. In this small world, I was able to return it to him with alacrity. He taught me a lot about pretense and the colorful gift of gab. I had heard that when he was much younger, he "put out" for Tabasco-rich Henry McIlhenny of Rittenhouse Square, Philadelphia and wisely invested his earnings from "bending over." To hear him talk, his father was a horticulturist. From his presentation, one would never guess that his father ran a florist shop in the train station. Jonathan knew how to charm dowagers, and Ninn Ryan was his favorite. The daughter of Otto Kahn, she occupied a prominent niche in the New York and Newport social worlds. My friend invited me to his rented cottage in Newport and we made the rounds of the more famous hostesses. David joined us for the terribly grand weekend. One season of social revels easily blended into the next; a change of clothes to suit a change of weather.

The new Whitney Museum opened on Madison Avenue

with three special by-invitation-only parties. I attended all three with different friends. Its new location was close to home and so much larger than the space it had occupied just north of the Museum of Modern Art. The Huntington Hartford Museum on Columbus Circle opened shortly thereafter with Lady Bird Johnson in attendance, together with the ever-familiar faces of Ruth Ford, Oliver Smith and such. Life was a nonstop, full speed ahead merry-go-round with libations plentiful. Happily, I enjoyed enormous fortitude and felt indestructible.

The last holiday David and I were to take was to St. Croix, with a Canadian girl and a young, attractive and intriguing married couple. Paul Stooshnof was a gorgeous blond art dealer who claimed Russian descent; Christine was a sturdy swinger on both sides of the fence. It was a sunny but bland time. I finished the trip on my own in Puerto Rico. I ran into a well-known decorator on Condado Beach who was going to visit the coffee heir Bert Martinson on the other side of the island. I knew Bert from various New York social events, especially the New York City Opera. I liked Bert, so I tagged along in the car with a couple of other guys. It was the last time I saw Bert before he died.

Returning to the troubled homestead on 72nd Street, David and I prepared for the visit of his mother from Denver. It was rare for her to make such a trip, so we wanted it to be very special. We invited good friends over to meet her. Included were his cousin Margaret and her husband Clifton Daniel. Unbeknownst to me, for the second time David's decorator was to make an appearance at one of our parties. Again humiliated, I complained to David while he was carving the roast. He meaningfully brandished the carving knife with fury in my direction, commanding my silence and indicating that he would harm me if I got in the way. That truly was the end. In tears, I rushed up the street to Ysabel's apartment for consolation after our party. She was outraged. "You can't leave him! Where else will I get fed so well?"

A One-Man Show . . .

One subject, many artists, different times.

Eric as Gustav III, portrait by David Ewing, 1979

. . . to be continued

Chapter 8

DESIGNS FOR LIVING

The Festival of Two Worlds, held annually in the charming Umbrian town of Spoleto, Italy, in July 1997 featured my gallery of original costume and scenic designs. A combination of events permitted me to accept the invitation of the festival's creator, Gian-Carlo Menotti.

In February 1967, I had met with two Englishmen at the Plaza Hotel to discuss a possible partnership with them in a gallery devoted exclusively to theater designs. They had such a gallery in London named after themselves, the Wright-Hepburn Gallery, and they wanted to expand, with a New York–based partner. It sounded intriguing, but I was wary of leaving Brentano's. I easily related to the younger partner, David Hepburn, an attractive dancer, but Peter Wright seemed remote and dubious despite his firmly reassuring manner. They expressed relief that I was not a cretin like the others they had considered. I was flattered, yet I felt the need for caution. What would happen if I accepted Menotti's offer to show in Spoleto, using their inventory as a trial run? They leapt at the notion. If all worked well that summer, we would negotiate opening together in New York in the fall. They sent their assistant, Terry, along to help run the shop and keep an eye on inventory and sales.

One of the clients from Entrée Unlimited was determined to "make the scene." I suggested that a sojourn in Italy might be an agreeable way to reach her aspirations. Nell Webster was delighted at the prospect of acting as my hostess to the international clientele in the Spoleto gallery. She wanted "nothing" out of the deal. The pert redhead and I met the Englishmen in London to work out last-minute details.

His Excellency Vittorio de Montezemolo, the Italian Consul General in New York, asked to take me to the airport. The pre-departure party was at Ysabel's. Upon leaving David that spring, I had taken a studio apartment in a brownstone on Lexington Avenue just north of Lena Horne's daughter Gale and movie producer Sidney Lumet. I rented it to the poet Ned O'Gorman while I was in Europe, to gain some extra cash.

We held a large cocktail party in the London gallery, to which darling Allegra from the U.N. days appeared. "Uncle Monkey's" niece Diana, who had picked me up in Athens years before, was there as well. The star of the London Festival Ballet, John Gilpin, attended with his wife. I had not seen him since the ballet party given on my roof terrace on East 76th Street a dozen years earlier, when he had arrived with "Pat" Dolin, former ballet star and his then-current lover.

Gloria Burns, a minor player on the Park Avenue social scene (about whom notoriously wicked people whispered things about her blackmailing her first husband into paying a huge alimony for her silence to the I.R.S. about hidden assets, and her suffocating her second husband to inherit a fortune), had introduced me to an unctuous, wealthy American man living in London. Full of licentious suggestion, he had urged me to call him when I was in London. His Mayfair flat had a pleasant terrace on which he suggested throwing a cocktail party. I thought dinner at the new and very "in" Hungry Horse Restaurant on the Fulham Road would be appropriate for afterward. Many gin martinis later, I suggested it was time to depart from Mayfair for the Fulham Road. Gilpin had a green sportscar that conveniently fit only two. I volunteered to go with him. His wife could join the others in taxis. John had as great a love for drink as I did. We stopped by his club in Chelsea, which was, after all, on the way. Patsy Jellicoe, an English countess with whom I had had a very wet champagne lunch the day before, held court, along with one of the Guinesses. Upstairs by the billiard table there was the beautiful Terence Stamp of *Billy Budd* fame. We decided it was okay to have yet another drink, as everyone would be having one at the restaurant while waiting. Eventually, after it seemed too late to intrude on their dinner, John and I weaved our way to the Fulham Road. The restaurant was closed and I badly needed to relieve myself of some of those martinis. I discreetly (so I thought) pissed in a decorative flower planter in the entranceway.

In the morning, I contritely went to Mayfair with flowers for my host, who had kindly picked up the tab for the dinner that I gave but at which I never appeared. I paid him and thanked him but he did not seem greatly mollified. Everyone thought John and I were killed or maimed in a car accident. Otherwise, why had we not called the restaurant? It was difficult to explain my gin-filled brain, nor was I willing to confess to my personal pleasure at being alone with the fascinating ballet star.

Thanks to connections from the Italian Consul General, getting portfolios of original artwork through customs was easy. Bluff and blustery temper, egged on by massive alcoholic consumption on the plane, helped me accomplish my mission. Red tape was dispensed with by invoking powerful names in an authoritative tone. I threatened to call them directly if we were not cleared immediately. Italy is one of the only places where that kind of showmanship works. The three of us were ready to set up shop in the enchanting hill town of Spoleto. Menotti promised to help me in every way possible. He got us a small, well-placed gallery space on the ground floor on the Via del Duomo, near the famous piazza. A three-bedroom apartment was secured, a short walking distance from the gallery. We set about hanging the art on the rush-covered walls.

People from all over the world who came for the concerts

and other attractions in the Piazza del Duomo sauntered over the narrow cobblestone street past our gallery. Periodically, the cheerful theater design gallery gave open-house drink parties as promotional vehicles. The press came to photograph us with Ingrid Bergman, the Stuttgart Ballet dancers, sexy Menotti protegé conductor Thomas Schippers and other notables from international society.

Peter Wright convinced me to have all our monies banked in England to avoid Italian taxes and complications. My friends from the United States came and brought others who bought. Strangers, too, came in and bought. Cheerfully, I sent it all along with Peter when he came briefly for a look, and then with Terry when he took the unsold designs back to England.

I had a delicious whirl of a time entertaining and being wooed. There was time for opera, concert, theater and ballet at the two theaters in Spoleto and the other spaces used for improvised performances. It was gratifying to lunch or dine with the performers on an ongoing basis. It was a privilege to share private moments of their lives and then later experience their performances.

On the piazza was the Caio Mellisso, a baroque theater Queen Christina had attended on her way to Rome, having abdicated the Swedish throne in the seventeenth century. Noonday concerts were held with lots of drinks at round tables on the cobblestones in front of the theater. Another, larger theater was closer to central Spoleto and much newer. Grand opera and ballet were performed there. Every day, performances in both theaters and in other places such as churches and outdoor spaces lent liveliness and excitement to the atmosphere. I enjoyed many lunches in various trattorias or villas on Monteluco or the lake. Dinners at nearby inns in the countryside and late-night cabarets with singers, dancers, actors and pleasure-seekers quickly passed the time at the Spoleto Festival. Young and vigorous, I did not spend much time sleeping, although I did enjoy "bedtime." My playmates varied from shy boys from Spoleto or from nearby towns to Roman aristocrats and distinguished soloists making Spoleto appearances. Terry was a homebody with no adventures; Nell wanted to run and play but did not get the invitation. I was the insatiable bon vivant with an incredible appetite for drink, food, adventure and men.

One day, while visiting a ruined church on a mountainside, I insisted that my Roman count make love to me on the altar. At a lake outing, I ravished a Dutch impresario in a flat-bottomed rowboat not too far from the rest of our party. Alcohol gave me a rush of daring and flamboyance to live the 1960s with a barrier-free attitude, encouraged by the spirit of the times. Although beautifully turned out in my Italian silk suits, always properly kissing the marchesa's or principessa's hand and discoursing charmingly with impeccable manners over dinner, I had hot blood pulsating profanely through my entire being, seeking expression. It was a time when all my years of inhibition and insecurity could be junked in the glamorous pursuit of free, available love and adoration in gorgeous settings that heightened the intensity. Wine, brandy and distilled spirits encouraged me to break down barriers and reach for whatever titillated me at the moment. The gallery did very well and I enjoyed an unending round of festivities, all within the colorful panorama only Italy could provide. The arts were all around me and I was entrenched both in them and the artists as well as the monied people who made it all happen. The landscape and the beauties of the Italian villas, palaces and hilltowns were my perfect playground.

It was time to think about going home via London to work out details with my new partners and settle accounts. First, I promised myself a brief vacation in Sicily, where I was to meet a very rich American admirer. My only contact there was through the Princess Maita Niscemi whose palazzo, La Favorita, was the backdrop for *The Leopard*, a film based on the novel about her relatives. In the eighteenthh century, Marie Antoinette's sister was Queen of the Two Sicilies. She lived in the palace next door, Villa Valguarnera.

When I got to Palermo, I called the palace. Maita had been called away, I was told by her sister Mimi, whom I did not know. However, I had met her husband-to-be, Prince Romanov, at a bathhouse in New York! Mimi told me that my American friend had cabled a message to me care of La Favorita, stating that he would not be able to meet me in Sicily after all. With that disappointing news, I decided to take a train out of Palermo to what was said to be a seaside town of great charm and antiquity, Cefalù.

While waiting in my compartment for the train to depart, a burly peasant entered, placed a valise on the luggage rack, then smiled and said farewell to the attractive, slim man who entered after him. Enchanted and intrigued by the young man, who got up to have a cigarette in the hallway, I went out for a cigarette as well. In my best Italian, I asked him for a match. He looked at me with twinkling eyes, cheerfully asking me if I spoke English, as he did not understand Italian. Seeing how I could easily accommodate, I informed him with delight and relief that I was an American on holiday. He was from Zambia but had been living in Sicily. He utterly charmed me with his forthright friendliness. David Scott Melville lived in a small villa above Taormina, where he raised white fan-tailed pigeons, played his guitar and sketched the extraordinary landscape reigned over by the ever-fuming, lava-belching Mount Etna. He explained that the husky young man who had seen him off was the houseboy of the Anglican priest who lived in Taormina but who currently had duties in Palermo. David had been visiting the priest and now was homeward bound to tend his pigeons. By this time, the train was pulling into the Cefalù station. Impulsively, I invited him to come with me for a visit to Cefalù. I offered him my hotel room if he would invite me to Taormina. David had never been to the interesting old town, and he grabbed his bag, descending with me for a couple of blissful days on the shore of the Mediterranean. I was in love with another David!

Our days were passion-filled, both for each other and for the glorious beauty of Sicily. From his perch above Taormina, we descended the steep hill to Letojanni, where the beach extends for mile after beautiful mile with clear, blue-green water lapping the shore. Sometimes, we hiked over to the ruins of the Greek town Naxos, where we rummaged through Hellenic potsherds before splashing in the cool, clear sea. We picked figs off the trees and stopped at local fish places to eat fresh-caught delicacies. Our high spirits were infectious, and we became the center of the Anglican church's knot of expatriates, many of them elderly gay men who delighted in our enthusiastic presence.

With the resolve to return somehow or to have David come to New York, it was time to get to London and meet with Wright-Hepburn. As soon as I deplaned, I knew something was amiss. Expecting only one of them, they both stood waiting for me. Instead of going to their flat, where I was supposed to spend the night, they had booked me into an Earl's Court hotel. We went to an undistinguished restaurant, where a silent David listened to a strained Peter inform me that they had changed their mind about my being a partner. Furthermore, the money they owed me was not forthcoming, excuses were made. I had given notice to Brentano's while in Italy "on vacation." There was no job to go back to in New York. I had no money left after my amorous Sicilian holiday, as I expected to get money in England. I had nothing but David the Second. With all the reserve and calm I could muster, I spoke calmly about their decision. Inside me a voice inside screamed "Unfair!" but outside I appeared indifferent. I raised no protest, feigning delight in being able to rejoin my new lover. After creating the Spoleto gallery and putting all that work into it, I was outraged to be bilked in that fashion. Adding insult to injury, I was informed that little Nell, who had wanted "nothing" from the venture, was to become their partner. She had private funds and now had some experience from the Spoleto gallery.

My unflappable exterior was greatly disturbing to Peter, the mastermind of the dishonest plot. He expected that I would make a scene and carry on in queenly outrage. When I did not, it upset him. He removed himself to the men's room where he regurgitated, David later informed me. I have marveled at myself in similar situations in which my exterior becomes cool, almost detached, while the sudden catastrophe is roiling internal turmoil. They deposited me in a less-than-distinguished hotel with promises that we would meet in the gallery the next day.

My hotel was paid for and I further requested that they cash a check of mine for $200, which was all I had in my New York account. Reluctantly, I was given the cash with which to purchase a return ticket to Sicily. One of the first things I did was to write Nell about the monies owed me. Since she had come along for the ride and been supportive of the venture from the start, I thought she should claim the money, at least. There was no reason for Peter Wright to pocket my portion of the profits.

Shortly after returning to Taormina, a blue envelope from the Carlton Hotel in Cannes arrived from Nell. I knew she was meeting Peter there. I opened the envelope with great anticipation. "Bon voyage on your road to oblivion," the letter stated. How utterly naive I had been. Nell was not innocently roped into partnership with the shady character; she was one of the manipulators intending to knock me out of the box! The mean sentiment of her note from the plush Riviera hotel had a strong effect on me. As I sat on a hillside above Taormina, surveying the volcano and blue sea, I realized I had no pocket money and I was on the verge of a nervous breakdown. Abused and bruised, I pondered the harsh finger of fate. But I had David, the lovely fan-tailed pigeons, the scenery and the wonderfully healing clear sea to bathe in daily.

David was surprised to see me again in Taormina. As soon as

it sank in that the prince departing was now a pauper returning there were subtle changes in his attitude. I tried to ignore them, but they should have given me a clue to the man who was now in my life.

Daily walks through farmland produced the occasional fig or tomato. Mussels gathered from rocky promontories along the beach were steamed open, mixed with pasta for dinner. We visited Professor Kreitner and his wife, two German Jewish refugees who had settled in South Africa, where they amassed a fascinating African art collection. They had moved to Sicily in retirement. I watered their rose bushes and pruned their garden. The old doctor could not work on them himself because of a weak heart. They were adorable, like an aunt and uncle to me.

David had a German lover who worked in a hotel on Sardinia. Once in a while, he would send some money for David to buy provisions both for the pigeons and himself. David did not write him about me, for obvious reasons. I told myself that David would never treat me the way he did his unsuspecting German. I was different. What we had was more meaningful and durable. Finally, when I recovered from the shock I had gotten in London and then from Nell's letter, I began to gain strength from our healthy hikes and swims in the sea.

One fine day, David and I packed a bottle of water and a sandwich for an outing along the long stretch of beach at Letojanni. Walking along the seaside, I noticed a boat with about six attractive men in it just offshore. They were close enough for me to recognize. One was a young actor, John Phillip Law, I knew from New York who had just made a hit in the film *Barbarossa.* I knew he had been launched by Frances Carpenter, the wife of a DuPont. She had once picked me up hitchhiking on the Montauk Highway and taken me and a woman to a terrific lunch at Herb McCarthy's in Southampton. Frances had a lesbian connection with Pat Hemingway, who owned restaurants in both Bridgehampton and New York. Rita Hayworth had been part of the Bridgehampton ménage, as had John Phillip Law. We saw each other at parties given by a New York psychoanalyst, Ruth Loveland, and her retired, gay ballet-dancer husband, Walter Stane.

A surprised John waved back to me as the boat approached the shore. In the boat were men I had seen at the Spoleto Festival: actors Ramolo Valli and Jean-Claude Brialy. Waiting on the shore just in front of David and me was a distinguished older gentleman. I knew Gayelord Hauser had an opulent villa on the beach there and that Rita Hayworth had recently visited him. The motley group amicably chatted on the beach. Hauser invited us to join his male guests. We accepted, hiding our small sack of paltry edibles. The gardens of the villa were lovely and lush. Hauser had a longstanding reputation as an adviser to the stars on nutrition, health and beauty. He grew his own olives for olive oil, and lemons and other delicious comestibles for his sumptuous table. As he was known to entertain the most interesting people on the international scene, I was pleased to be there. It was also a treat to have such classy food served to me on lovely majolica plates after those weeks of deprivation!

Brownie, Hauser's sedate, mild-mannered life-mate, told me about Hauser's curious history. As a lad in his teens in a German hospital, he heard a group of visiting Japanese doctors talk about his case. The German doctors declared that his disease was incurable. To their surprise the Japanese visitors exclaimed that they could cure it by putting the patient on a diet of fresh lemons. Hauser put himself on the diet, cured himself and went on to be a leading spokesperson for nutrition. His inspiring story of adversity turning into something positive, even lucrative, revealed to me how extravagantly out-of-control I was. Luxuriating in the comfortable hospitality of a world personality with distinguished guests, I lapped up too many preprandial drinks and way too much wine during lunch. Contrary to our host, I disputed the virtues of olive oil over vegetable oil with him. I was so full of myself and my unquestionable knowledge about everything that our host got up and left the table, never to return. At departure time, I wished a fond farewell to Brownie, with best regards to Gayelord. Garbo was due to arrive in a few weeks. I made sure that they promised to send regards to "my aunt."

Alcohol bolstered my confidence, always too much. It loosened my tongue, again too much. With alcohol racing through my system, I threw caution to the winds and tilted flamboyantly at windmills of my own making.

When the time was ripe and I had enough postage for letters to two friends in New York, I wrote, offering to sell certain art works from my New York apartment. The psychoanalyst and her gay husband in the city purchased my Cocteau drawing; the Consul General bought an ink drawing of a jockey mounting a steed, which he had long admired. Eventually, there was enough money for me to invite David to America. We returned via London, where I saw Allegra, Diana and other friends and told them of the deception and my Sicilian adventure. We were New York–bound with hearts full of renewed courage and determination.

Piecing together a new life in New York with David II in tow began with a sojourn in the large East Side apartment of Silvia Gronich, a stylish matron who had worked for me at the Galérie Moderne at Brentano's. I continued to sublet my own apartment for pocket money. Silvia enjoyed having younger people around, especially as her daughter took a strong shine to David. I have little doubt that they shared intimacies when no one was observing them. The hospitality at Silvia's gave me a respite from the harsh world so that I could seek means of support.

One day, walking on East 81st Street just off Fifth Avenue in front of Philip Roth's residence, I heard my name called from French windows in a town house across the street. It was Dickie Ransohoff, a soulful bohemian writer I had met in Spoleto. What fun to see her again! I went up to her small, elegantly appointed apartment. She knew of an art gallery that was searching for a director. There was a hitch, however. It was a cooperative gallery, which could not afford a salary but did promise a nice commission on all sales. A cooperative gallery does not have the same cachet in the art world as a commercial gallery. As each member is theoretically a co-owner, prestige diminishes in the estimation of the critics and general public. It is more estimable to be invited to show one's own work than to present it oneself.

The space was wonderful—some work had to be done to make it more attractive—and the location was superb: West 56th Street off Fifth Avenue, two floors up from the street with a manually operated, not automatic, elevator. Usually, visitors walked up the two flights of steps. As I liked the artists I met and thought some of the work had promise, it seemed an interesting challenge. The back room was quite large, with a fireplace and skylight. Next to it was a large walk-in closet and a washroom with toilet. The notion of living in the back room and using the closet to hold my refrigerator and hot plate encouraged me to accept the position. I could always heat hot water for washing and shaving, and there were many friends' bathrooms in which to do my serious cleanups. With the understanding that I would have a controlling say on who joined the roster of artists and who remained when their contracts were up, together with getting approval to live on the premises from the artists' council as well as permission to use the back room for theater design exhibitions (with an occasional big show up front), I became the official director of the Capricorn Gallery.

Eric was back in the running! Not only was I director of a New York gallery, but also I was going to open The American Center for Theater Designs two weeks earlier than the New York design gallery of the English cads. The race was on for the most prestigious list of participating designers.

One of the founders of the gallery was the lover of the famous lighting designer Jean Rosenthal. Jean did the lighting for major Broadway shows as well as opera and ballet. She was the doyenne of lighting in America, consequently she knew everyone, especially theater designers. Oliver Smith came to me through Jean's good offices. Not only was Oliver one of the top designers in the country, he was also on the board of the American Ballet Theatre. He even gave Jackie Kennedy watercolor lessons. Oliver's participation led other "greats" such as Freddy Wittop, Miles White, José Varona, Ming Cho Lee and many other designers into my gallery. A couple of designers had left the competition to join me because their designs sometimes disappeared in the other gallery, or they were presented with enormous framing bills that were clearly out-of-line. Cecil Beaton and Oliver Messell (Lord Snowdon's uncle) threatened them with lawsuits. The air was full of deception and suspicion. I fought hard to keep my reputation separate from theirs, but the public persisted in confusing one design gallery with the other.

It pleased me that I was the first to show original costume and scenic designs on a continuous basis in the United States. Later, I helped Sotheby Parke-Bernet organize their first theater design auction. My reputation in the field developed, and I became the authority on theater design, officially permitted to perform appraisals. Soon, I helped to form major museum collections.

Enthused with energy and success, I decided to take an exhibition of theater designs to Santa Fe the summer of 1968, to help celebrate the opening of the new Santa Fe Opera House. The summer season in New York was so slow that most galleries closed until fall. It was a perfect opportunity for me to spread my wings even farther and network in a new, promising market.

David was delighted by the prospect of moving to the "wild" West, which he had only heard about through Westerns. He was glad to give up living in the back room of the gallery, even though he sometimes stayed at Silvia's and, briefly, when Ysabel was in town, on Fifth Avenue. More overt than Silvia's daughter, Ysabel made no bones about dragging the lithe David into her bedchamber. David acquiesced obediently, causing me no small amount of dismay. However, I knew it was only a momentary thing and that he would come back to the guest room after Ysabel's experimentation.

Halloween, I took David to Provincetown to visit various friends. We stayed at Larry Jones' Locker and got all costumed with Larry's new friend, Jerry, from Boston. David was "Prince Charming" and he managed to charm many guys, too many, I thought. He attracted lots of attention with his charming manner and British-African accent, flashing eyes, easy smile and Mediterranean tan. I felt I had to keep close watch over him.

Since David did not have a green card, Ysabel suggested he think about marrying an American girl. What about Silvia's daughter, Susan? Other people had been known to get green cards that way. David was indignant. He exclaimed that he would never marry a Jew. Ysabel rose to her feet. She declared that her father (the General of the Colombian army) was a rabbi. That astonished us. "And furthermore, my grandfather was a grand-rabbi! Get out of my house, at once!" she demanded. Meekly and in great confusion David exited to Silvia and Susan's apartment. I roared with laughter at her outrageous claims but admired her intolerance of bigotry.

David had few prospects of employment in New York. He helped me a little at the gallery, but he needed something more substantial. That winter, he accepted employment with my friends Woody and Helena, helping them to maneuver their boat from Cape Cod through the inland waterway to Ft. Lauderdale. I was concerned about the handsome gay co-pilot aboard, and for good reason. David proved adaptable to the wild, alcoholic trip and nearly caused our total breakup. In anger over his obvious infidelity, I refused to express mail his forgotten passport until he repaid me the money I had spent bringing him to America. My feeling of being used and abused replayed from the previous

David as well as the Spoleto venture. When would I ever learn? My expectations and demands were not in tune with life on life's terms. My bringing David to America was not altruistic. It was another misguided attempt to create my own sense of reality, distorted as it was. When the trip was over, David returned to me repentant, assuring me that our life could pick up again, so, westward ho!

Unframed designs were packed in plywood crates I made specially for bus cartage across the country. Upon arrival in Santa Fe, I presented myself to Margaret Jamison of the Jamison Gallery, located just across from La Fonda Hotel. Because her eyes were hypersensitive, she always wore dark glasses. A mop of reddish-blond curls adorned her pale painted face. Her manner was open, friendly and provocative. Margaret spoke to me plainly. No, she would not mount an exhibition of the designs in her gallery, but she recommended two friends who had a smaller gallery and frame shop next to the oldest house tourist attraction just off the Old Santa Fe Trail. Bernie and Bill (Margaret's sometime lover as well as life-partner of the older Bernie) enthusiastically took in David and me. We were invited to stay until we got situated, and they encouraged my exhibition in their gallery.

Opera singers and others affiliated with the opera took efficiency apartments at a complex on the hill just outside of town on the way to the opera house. We, too, rented one of the apartments. One day, sunning by the pool, I heard a dark-haired man talking about me in Italian to his young friend. I assumed he did not imagine that I understood what he was saying, but I did. Wearing only a small white bathing suit, I must have pleased him. He fantasized that when I was immersed in the pool, my body would greatly raise the pool's temperature. I did not stir and made believe that his words were unnoticed. Soon, I could not resist getting up and diving into the pool. Other erotic comments were made but I appeared to pay no attention.

That evening, I was sitting with a soprano at *Madama But-*

terfly. Near us was the Italian-speaker, his friend and the noted set designer Rouben Ter-Arutunian. Rouben had opted to show in New York with the "other" gallery so I did not include his work in my Santa Fe exhibition, which greatly upset him. During intermission, Rouben stopped the soprano and me on the aisle. He introduced the Italian-speaking man to me. It was none other than Hans Werner Henze, the acclaimed composer whose work was about to have its world premiere in Santa Fe that week. Rouben proposed that we all go to the Opera Club and talk, over a drink. In flawless Italian, looking Henze in the eye, I exclaimed that I could not possibly do that, perhaps another time. Henze realized that I understood all his comments at the pool and was startled, greatly amusing me as I grandly swept up the aisle.

In the same swimming pool some days later, I heard some agitating news. I had gone to an opera party at an apartment in the complex. David was invited to go somewhere else with one of our best gallery clients. Lou Hurr, a young banker from Canada, had purchased some choice designs from me and requested that David go with him. I was going to the other party, so I agreed with David that he should have a good time with Lou. One of the stage directors invited me for a swim. Bliss Hebert was well loved as a director and friend at the opera. He wanted to make sure that I knew something, but he made the revelation oblique. Bliss made believe he was unaware of my relationship with David. He asked whether I knew that Lou was having an affair with some young fellow from Africa. Dumbfounded, I sputtered that the "fellow" was my lover. I clutched the side of the pool under the starlit New Mexican sky, fighting back tears of hurt and frustration. Bliss was on the verge of breaking up with his longtime partner. He had his eye on me and told me the story about Lou and David as a means of speeding along my breakup. Bernie and the younger, blond Bill took me aside in their frame shop adjoining the gallery the next day. I told them the news. They confirmed it, as they thought it unfair of David and Lou to string me along by not telling me of the affair blossoming behind my back.

Just as with the first David, it seemed everyone in town was aware of my cuckolding before I was. For David's birthday in August, I had promised to take him rafting down the Colorado River on an eight-day trip. Once the truth was out, we agreed the trip would be our final time together. River-running through the Grand Canyon was not as popular then as now. The Kennedys had made an abbreviated trip, which captured the attention of the public. My sense of romance and adventure was stirred by the prospect. We appeared at the appointed dock, joining about a dozen other intrepid adventurers. We used two large rubber rafts and had two young, hearty and relentlessly straight boatmen. It took a day or two before we fully realized, while sitting around the campfire, that our group was not getting accurate information about what we were seeing. One boatman would say one thing, another something else. We could not even count on them telling us the correct time. They seemed to be pulling a private joke at our expense. To aggravate matters, they were lazy about getting the rafts ready each morning. Sometimes, they let the rafts get caught too far up on shore, when the waters from the dam receded during the night. All of us had to help unload everything and haul the rafts to the water's edge, then reload. It was an onerous chore, especially as we had paid a goodly price to be taken care of, not to be enslaved by crazed boatmen.

The boatmen ate the best food, too. They growled when it was time to feed us. Often, they tossed the frying pan into the sand in front of us, saying, "Here, eat this shit!" The group was afraid to complain as the boatmen were usually high on drugs and/or alcohol, and we were dependent on them to get out of the canyon. Two young lesbians bonded with me, in defiance of the guys. One of the guys tried to make out with the prettier of the girls, who clearly rejected him. He got the picture, growing irritated, resentful and insulting toward her and toward me. David played up to the boatmen rather than lend us much-needed support.

A couple of accidents caused the group to thin and to become more wary. The trip grew into a nightmare. The boatmen threatened to beat me up. David told them I was crazy; the girls came to my defense and stuck close to me. I had thought to cut the ropes to the rafts so that helicopters would spot them during the morning surveillance, but I did not have the courage. Instead the group pleaded with them to take us back a day early, which they did. Running the river, especially on drugs and alcohol, was a nerve-wracking job. The boatmen finished one run and then they would start another immediately. Little wonder they got drunk and were so hostile. On shore, they tried to attack me. The girls made a stink, shouting and running to the phone to call the police. David did nothing. Each passenger had the names and addresses of the others. We agreed to write the owner of the rafting company, Orin Hatch. Each of us would send copies of all correspondence to the group members. The girl the boatmen wanted to molest was the daughter of one of Arizona's top lawyers. He would prosecute if necessary, but he died of a heart attack before anything happened. Hatch wrote each of us that he was surprised at our complaint. He explained that no one else on the trip complained, even though each of us had the others' letters of complaint. Eventually, the errant river-runners were taken off the run for another, less demanding trip; our lawyer had died; and we all went our separate ways with a hair-raising story.

David lived in style at Lou's house on the Old Santa Fe Trail. Aviaries were built to house exotic birds purchased for him; there was a large pool, and fireplaces and wall spaces to perfect his Southwest painting skills, which would come in handy later when "Louise Whore" (as Helena was to call Louis Hurr) scurried away in bankruptcy. Soldier-of-fortune David started bed-hopping from Santa Fe to Taos and back again to keep cigarettes and food available. He was quite adept.

My final days in Santa Fe were spent horseback riding with Winnabelle Beasley at her ranch in Tesuque. Often Margaret Jamison and Bill (sometimes with Bernie) joined me. From time to time, kids from the opera went on a riding picnic. Once, an attractive demure young singer came along with us. Frederica ("Flicka") von Stade was on the threshold of international fame. Knowing the indifference that Winnie had to general hygiene, we all brought our own provisions. After shoveling horse manure or feeding mice to her pet snakes, Winnie would prepare some dish or other for us without thinking to wash her hands. Sometimes, those treats were leftovers that had long outlived their shelf life from a gathering in the past. Dear, eccentric Winnie often stopped on the trail to pick up a potsherd or Indian arrowhead, otherwise settling for a black snake, which she coiled around her neck for the ride back home. It startled visitors in her sitting room when Winnie, wide-eyed with excitement, would exclaim "So *that's* where you are Josephine, I've been looking for you!" Under the guest's chair was the escaped snake, coiled in sleep.

The fall season in New York found me gearing up for an interesting series of exhibitions at Capricorn and an unending series of events at "955," where Ysabel and I entertained. The Whitney Museum of American Art opened on Madison Avenue around the corner from Ysabel's apartment. I invited one of Capricorn's artists, Nathalie Marshall (Van Buren), to attend the opening night of the Georgia O'Keeffe retrospective held on my birthday, October 7, 1970. Nathalie painted with a spirituality akin to O'Keeffe's, holding O'Keeffe in highest regard as artist and woman. We carefully examined the exhibition but did not see the great lady herself. Nathalie, who lived in Connecticut, had three teenagers at home to worry about and wanted to leave. Exiting the elevator on the ground floor of the Whitney, I spied O'Keeffe coming in the revolving doors. "Nathalie, there she is!" I exclaimed, excitedly pointing through the crowd. Many people noticed the living legend as she made her way across the lobby.

She did not turn left or right to acknowledge the well-wishers but walked resolutely closer and closer to me. Like an ocean liner cutting through the water, O'Keeffe approached me, hand extended. "You are a friend of mine, aren't you?" the great lady said. I sputtered something about being an admirer and fan, then presented an overwhelmed Nathalie. We were both thrilled to the bottoms of our souls (and soles), while the vast crowd wondered how we got to be so special with Georgia O'Keeffe.

At a Whitney Biennial I attended with the artist Rita Simon, a group of women's libbers flagrantly demanded more representation, more voice, more

The great Georgia(O'Keeffe) with artist Paul Sarkisian.

everything. Much to everyone's annoyance, they had whistles that kept piercing and aggravating the din at the show. It was the first time the museum used all its floors for a show, so that spectators could go up and down the stairwells from gallery to bar and back. Artwork hung from every conceivable surface, including the stairwells. As Rita and I made our way down a stairwell, I protested the trash ("art") on view. I disdainfully indicated a green marble bench strewn with drinking cups in various stages of consumption, some with cigarette butts floating in them. "That is as much art as what we see in the galleries!" I proclaimed. She agreed. The creative urge overcame me. I took the NO SMOKING sign out of its holder and turned it over. With a felt-tip pen I wrote:

AFTER THE PARTY
mixed media
1968
Glorietta Trash

I replaced the placard adjacent and above the littered bench and continued in high spirits. Rita laughed as well. One of the women's lib artists with a whistle around her neck greeted me and said that I looked very happy. "I am. I just looked at the installation of one of my California artists.

Rita Simon and Eric making a museum opening scene.

Glorietta Trash is her name and her work is in the stairwell. Go see it. She is one of the better women artists in America." "Yeah, I like her work," Rita chimed in, "and she's an interesting person, but I could never show with her. Our work just doesn't go together." No one liked to be ignorant or not in on what was going on in the art scene, and they were reluctant to admit they had never heard of Glorietta Trash. If Eric and Rita were so enthusiastic and knowledgeable about her, they had better catch up. In the days following, it seemed that Glorietta Trash was the good, if not best friend of most of our friends. They heard so much about her from me and from Rita that soon she was common property. I wrote an op-ed piece to Charlotte Curtis at the *Times* titled "Trash at the Whitney," which was returned with a curt note saying they had already done something on the Biennial. It was exhausting to continually breathe life into the fictitious character, so poor Glorietta Trash came to an ignominious end.

Sic transit glorietta.

A One-Man Show . . .

One subject, many artists, different times.

Eric as the Sphinx, *Sands of Time*
by Rita Simon, 1982

. . . to be continued

Chapter 9

INTERNATIONAL ROMP REDUX

"If pretty young girls are queens in the game, pretty single men are even higher prizes," blared the *Boston Sunday Globe*'s feature story in November 25, 1967, issue about "New York's New Guard." It continued, "Robert Eric Gustafson, around 30, whose blond hair is brushed in continental waves and whose dress combines British and Italian tailoring, does not work at present though he has been involved with art galleries. 'Every night I go to three cocktail parties, then a dinner, then theater or the opera, a ball or party in a home, then out to breakfast. I try to stay home one night a week,' he says, 'but then I have people in.' Gustafson has been married, and believes marriage passé. 'Most people who are married don't see much of each other, not because the relationship is unsound but because the life is unsound. The life is so fast. So many things one must see and do. . .' His eyes move to a brunette across the room, standing, her shoulders slightly forward, in the society slouch. His eyes return, and he says, with a lift of the eyebrows, 'It's a jungle . . . But I love it.'" It amused me to give such an obnoxiously superficial tongue-in-cheek comment to the press. Call it arrogance or belligerence that masked my vulnerability and insecurity. A large photo of me leaning blasé toward blond-tressed Yveta Love accompanied the story. I remember how outraged my aunt in Lynn, Massachusetts, was when she read it. Actually, I think she was secretly thrilled that her nephew had achieved such notoriety in the Boston papers.

My family was perplexed by all the publicity I was getting. *Town and Country* did a fashion spread on me in the Capricorn Gallery. Occasional pictures or references to me appeared in social columns about glittering events and notables. I was enchanted and hungry for more, as it seemed justification for my haphazard existence. It promised that I was on my way to "arrival." I dreamed of the day I would not feel like an outsider, as I had since puberty. I yearned for recognition, love. In addition to my deep reverence for art, creating a viable art gallery gave me entree into the scintillating world of artists, stars and rich, cultivated personages. Being with, and eventually one of, the movers and shakers was my goal.

I had my European explorations and my work in the prestigious auction house and then the social public relations firm. The Galérie Moderne enabled me to continue my journey, culminating in Spoleto. At the Capricorn Gallery, I developed a reputation, owing to lively exhibitions of theater designs in the adjunct American Center for Theater Designs. Nostalgia and glamor surround theater designs. Costume and scenic designs for opera, ballet or theater bring to life memories of our experiences in those performing arts. They embody history. They have particular meaning for me because so much of my youth was spent in the lonely indulgence of opera and ballet, for which many of the designs were executed. I loved dealing with the artworks, placing "the last of the collectibles" in good homes. Revenues from sales supported the cooperative gallery and afforded me the income to maintain myself more comfortably. I wondered why no one else in the country had thought to exhibit and sell those treasures on an ongoing basis.

I continued to go to Metropolitan Opera rehearsals, always the highlight of my week. Whether with Yveta or alone, I always enjoyed preferential treatment by the staff. As usual, they assumed I was one of the artists when I took a "reserved for artists" seat in the best part of the orchestra. The French actor and director Jean-Louis Barrault staged a new *Carmen*. I remembered learning about him in theater classes at Queens College. Who could forget that rare moment in *Les Enfants du Paradis* when Bip tries to cry out to his beloved to capture her attention in the Mardi Gras mob but gets a choking mouthful of confetti thrown at him, losing the precious moment? Barrault was a hero high in my pantheon of theatrical greats. It was exciting to be invited to meet him over dinner at Yveta's. He was not traveling with his actress wife, Madeleine Renaud.

He had met Yveta at the opera. Enchanted with her Czech beauty and charm, he accepted her dinner invitation and predinner sauna. He had never had a sauna, and he was intrigued. Yveta had a small sunken pool adjacent to the sauna in her apartment. Usually, it was filled with ice-cold water to give a real contrast to the extra-hot sauna, as well as being good for circulation, that was the theory. I did it often, enjoying it enormously. I planned to take a sauna with the French star before the dinner. Alas, Barrault canceled the sauna but did appear for dinner.

The curious, if not shocking thing about his coming to dinner was that I was the only one there who really knew who he was! Hence, it was up to me to engage him in appropriate conversation. I had to lend Yveta my copy of Eric Bentley's *In Search of Theatre*, which talks about his career. She was delighted to rub shoulders with celebrities, especially from opera or ballet, but she did not do her homework. Barrault arrived bearing one of her silk shoes full of fresh flowers. He had surreptitiously taken the shoe at their last meeting, now returning it in bloom as a tribute to the lady. She and I concurred that it should be used as the centerpiece of the dining table.

Before dinner, about eight of us gathered in the small, upholstered bar of the apartment to smoke marijuana. That was another first for our visiting Bip. After all, it *was* the late 1960s, so it seemed mandatory to indulge in the pastime of that era. I remember the small, enclosed room filling with smoke. I was lying on the floor enjoying the enormous flower that grew out of the top of my head. It was so heavy that it seemed easier to lie back on the floor, letting the flower grow with each puff. At one point, I opened my eyes and saw the magnificent mime doing a Bip routine. No one else seemed to notice, as they were off on their own trip. It gave me great pleasure and a sense of the extraordinary to have the great Jean-Louis Barrault miming just there near my feet.

Promoting my exhibitions made dealings with the press immensely important. Freddy Winship of UPI was a longtime friend and admirer of mine. That contact diminished with his marriage to Joanne, a child actress married twice before, with a relentless passion for fashion and social prestige. We did not like or trust each other. Bill Como, the editor of *Dance* magazine and the new *After Dark* magazine became a friend. He often published news of my theater design exhibitions in his magazines. Bob Jacobson, editor of *Opera News*, befriended me too. We sometimes went to Boston, Washington, D.C., or Philadelphia to cover opera performances. Bob and I went to the Met on numerous occasions where I met the many luminaries who craved his attentions. On quieter evenings, I made ratatouille at his apartment. Bob inscribed his book *Reverberations* to me: "For Eric who reverberates more than anyone I know . . ." When I left New York, our paths separated. He later died of AIDS and is missed greatly.

The Max Reinhardt Collection is housed at the University of New York at Binghamton. From time to time, heads of the theater department came to the Capricorn in search of theater designs for their collection. In the autumn of 1968, a Reinhardt symposium was held on campus. Notables from the theater who took part in the symposium included the indestructible, glamorous Stella Adler, who had appeared in Reinhardt's immortal 1930s classic *A Midsummer Night's Dream,* Walter Abels, Francis Lederer, director Bobby Lewis and designers Ming Cho Lee and

Ben Edwards. A stellar list! Somewhat looped for courage, in order to attempt equal footing with the legendary personages I maneuvered myself between Stella Adler and Bobby Lewis at dinner. My intrusions were provocative, tinged with aggressive bad taste. But the two pros overlooked my blustering with indulgence and good manners.

Networking, whether at theater symposiums or festivals, was vital to my development as a man of-the-world in the arts. Ever-widening circles were the result of my intrepid efforts. Ever-growing consumption of alcohol, too. Alcohol had always been in my life, but with progression I used it more heavily and persistently. Ysabel taught me to drink in the morning without guilt. I relied on alcohol to sustain me during times of stress or celebration. A glass in the hand was an all-day natural, with the time in between drinks diminishing as the time flew by.

Freddy Winship introduced me to a cheerful, slightly chubby woman, Marguerita de Lema. She had a condo on Condado Beach in Puerto Rico and invited me there for New Year's. While on the beach the afternoon of New Year's Eve, I met a most appealing young American man who thought it splendid to come back with me to spend the evening. I presented him to Marguerita with the idea that he would stay with me. The hostess consented, but urged us to hurry as the distinquished guests would be arriving shortly. Both of us needed to wash off the beach sand, so we jumped into the only guest shower together. An English girl staying there had the same need, so she jumped in with us before we could express any opinion for or against. All of us had consumed punch heavily laced with strong rum while preparing it for our hostess. It was the most giddy, erotic shower in my experience.

The guy and I appeared spruced up for the party; the girl appeared in her frilly mini-nighty, intended to pass as a party dress. Surprising but cute, she attractively greeted the startled guests—the Spanish were so proper and dignified. We were glowing with rum and naughtiness. Conversation was slow and stilted. I decided to put on dance music and then asked the English girl to do an "interpretive dance" with me. Inspired by 100-proof rum, I lifted her into the air. My hands around her waist caused her mini to rise. Although I could not see it, her crotch was eye level with the astonished, bolt upright guests. I slowly danced her past all eyes. Her exposed pussy caused a general gasp among the guests. The final outrage was perpetrated when I spun my partner around and let her slide prone across the floor. Her mini gathered around her neck. It was then that I realized she was not wearing underwear. Spread-eagled on the dance floor as though posing for porno, the girl was engulfed in an atmosphere of stony silence. Guests gathered themselves for a hasty retreat while I helped my partner to her feet for a consoling spot of punch.

Our hostess rose, tears welling in her eyes. She wailed, "How could you?" After the guests departed with perfunctory farewells, the three of us had another drink, this time straight rum. Sheepish grins abounded as we tried to console our hostess through her locked bedroom door. She sobbed despairingly.

It was a good thing I was leaving for St. Thomas the next morning to enjoy the invitation of the cabaret entertainer Hugh Shannon to stay with him at The Mill, where he was appearing. Dropping my bags, I hugged him hello and farewell, and was off to the beach. Still chuckling about the outrageous floor show the previous evening, I settled onto Morningstar Beach to quietly take the sun and enjoy the blue-green waters of the Caribbean. The shadow of another David passed over my sun-worshipping body on Morningstar Beach. The handsome David the Third enchanted and overwhelmed me. Sexy, intelligent and an Anglican priest! So much was compressed into that one night and morning. David III was short-lived. After a visit to Boston soon afterward, it was clear that our island romance was only that—a brief, nice memory. Again, the slipper did not quite fit.

On the plane to Puerto Rico I savored the "Sadie Thompson feeling" of having fallen in with a preacher! Perhaps it was the ceaseless rain that recalled Sadie as well. I could never decide how I would play her—as Joan Crawford would? Or maybe Rita Hayworth? The stopover at the San Juan airport for the connecting flight to New York permitted me enough time to taxi to La Mallorquina Annex for yet another drink. I was positively glowing with sun, a great toss in the sack with yet another David and the drama with which I enriched my farewell to the islands. I must have transmitted the glow effectively because I noticed that I had lots of male attention in the gay bar. There were no standoffish attitudes toward *me* that night. I felt like a magnet, but it was tiring. I slipped out the back door and headed for the flight home. I shall never forget the sensation of attracting so many guys. I remember Leonard Bernstein and the young Prince Charles as having that magnetism. If only I could recreate it for myself again when I needed it.

The 1960s, beginning with the flower children as well as the Stonewall incident, are often spoken of with such reverence that I wonder about my own sensibilities. Yes, the flower children were charming and seemingly sweet, but they devolved into extravagant derelicts with spaced-out mentalities and messy, irresponsible lifestyles. I made believe I was a hippie when an occasion presented itself, but I lived in Ysabel's large apartment on Fifth Avenue overlooking Central Park, in the very best part of town. My clothes resembled hippie costumes but they were custom-tailored impersonations, clean and darling. Drugs meant very little to me; they simply got in the way of my drinking, which I greatly preferred. I playacted hippiness but had no quarrel with the establishment. To the contrary, the establishment supported my lifestyle and I enjoyed my dips into the best it had to offer. I have always admired good manners and dressing well. With reverence for the Muses, I always dress nicely for the opera or concert: no blue jeans for me, thank you! I have made efforts to try to

look as attractive as possible for the enjoyment of others as much
as myself. Drugs destroyed much beauty in the world, leaving
scars and shambles in it wake. I have often wondered how much
more beauty I myself might either have created or appreciated
had I been undimmed by alcohol all those years.

I know that the Stonewall riot of gays against the police is a
symbol of gay power, but I have never felt that the quality of my
life improved as a result of it. Perhaps I did not feel the intense
pressure to live covertly, as do so many gays, because I lived in a
milieu of artists. Life in New York, London or Paris had to be different from that of a young homosexual seeking identity and com-
panionship in Nebraska in the 1950s or 1960s or even later. My
recollection of life from my twenties onward was not one of terrible oppression. Even though I was not officially "out," I had many
gay friends with whom I met openly at bars and restaurants
before Stonewall. There was a mode of behavior and signs that
others of similar inclinations could pick up on, which made cruis-
ing exhilarating. Discernment had to be part of the game, however. There was an abundance of queenly glamor and pizazz fed
by images of Bette Davis, Mae West and Joan Crawford, musical
theater and opera. My role models were colorful, lavish, witty,
beautiful. What could top *Tosca* or *Mame*? I reached for the stars.
"Drama queen" describes me pretty well during those years of
masquerading as a Fifth Avenue hippie or as a well-turned-out
jet-setter. I was delirious with activity and booze. I had increased
income from the gallery, permitting more travel, more extravagance.

Clayton Cole, an ex-Hollywood dancer with a trust fund,
became a drinking partner and confidant. We often dined at
Max's Kansas City where we ran into the Warhol crowd and the
rock stars Jimi Hendrix and Janis Joplin. Each of the musicians
died shortly after our paths crossed. Clayton blamed me for their
untimely demises. He invented the notion that I was a jinx for
rock stars. Having smashed enough guitars for the evening,

Hendrix would prowl around the East Side in his limo looking for action, often parking ominously close to Clayton's apartment. We stayed clear of any involvement.

Helena was now ensconced in Ft. Lauderdale awaiting her lover Woodie's divorce from Madeleine in Massachusetts. The wife wanted a million dollars more when she heard that her best friend Helena wanted to marry Woodie. My alcoholic friends decided to create a smokescreen to save the million by having Helena get married (only temporarily) to someone else. I was the someone else. Despite my rational logic that Madeleine would never believe Helena was really preoccupied with the likes of me, they insisted on playing the scenario through. A silver Rolls-Royce hired for the occasion drove Helena and me from Ft. Lauderdale to Palm Beach. We were "married" there and we celebrated *à deux* over supper at our Colony Club dwelling (separate rooms, how romantic). Helena and I telephoned friends from our supper table in the swank restaurant (very Hollywood), announcing the news. Helena was certain the gossip would reach Madeleine quickly. After dinner, Helena straightened her blond wig and joined me in the Rolls to go to a local gay bar in West Palm Beach. The driver was also a bodyguard for her, as she had had terrible mishaps wearing major jewelry to a gay bar in Chicago. After a brief time, she left to retire alone. I took a new friend back to my "marriage" bed. Following a sumptuous breakfast, my prince-for-a-night and I caressed farewell and I drove back to Ft. Lauderdale with Helena to return the rented Rolls. Woodie was grateful for my time and effort. He handed me an envelope containing many hundred dollar bills, and a solid gold pocket watch with solid gold chain. Madeleine did not buy the ruse. She got her money. Helena and Woodie were married and soon divorced. Madeleine remarried Woodie. I do not know what happened to her Brazilian lover.

Ft. Lauderdale was not far from Miami, so I planned to join Santa Fe Opera's director Bliss Hebert at the Miami Airport for a weekend in Puerto Rico. First, I put four of the hundred dollar bills in an envelope and sent them to my painter friend Nathalie. I knew she had financial worries and was coping with putting three teenagers through school. This bought me at dealer price one of her loveliest paintings for my growing collection. I had a less than thrilling time with Bliss on our erotic holiday, though I tried to make it work. "Sisyphus of the Bedchamber" might sum up that effort. There was no question of the slipper not fitting. Another drink and another day later, I was back in the daily activities of the gallery and cavorting in Gotham by night.

Phillip van Rensselaer introduced me to Greta Keller, the Austrian cabaret singer who claimed to have taught Marlene Dietrich to sing. We liked each other immediately and managed to keep in touch both in New York and Vienna. From time to time, she asked me to escort her to an event where her girlfriend would not be appropriate as her date. Her studio pied-à-terre in the East 50s was between those of Van Johnson and Hermione Gingold. "The boy next door" who June Allyson swooned over in the wartime films goosed me at an Election Day party on Park Avenue. The true-blue all-American boy was gay, or at least curious! Life seemed a merry romp, made more so by this unexpected goose.

Summer sojourns in Europe grew lengthier each year. I was able to conduct gallery business while broadening my continental social ties. I was invited to visit Bianca, Princess Lowenstein, and her American husband in London. Would I bring along a sculpted bust that she did, which was in her New York apartment, when I came to stay with them on the Chelsea Embankment? Sylvia Tysik (from *West Side Story* and *Sail Away*) was now married to a Belgian count, Hughes van der Stegen, and living in Chelsea. Her first-born, Serge, was in his bassinet when I came to visit with Allegra from down the street. It was a cozy London visit, but I needed to keep moving to fulfill my ambitious itinerary. My first Berlin visit was next. Tenor Lorin Driscoll, whom I knew from Santa Fe Opera days, was a principal with the Berlin Opera. He had a house in Grunewald with his ballet-dancer lover. Lorin took me to see the Berlin Wall, a grim, menacing spectacle, subsequently torn down in 1989 to great cries of celebration, a measure of the world's changing tolerances.

I met a young Swedish man crazy for opera. Björn Bexelius was pleased to meet me. When he heard that I was going to Sweden, he invited me to share midsummer's evening with him and his family on a lake north of Stockholm. His father was adviser to the king (the present king's grandfather). I had the impression that he was someone worthwhile cultivating, so I asked him to join me afterward for a brief trip north to investigate a small village that I had read celebrated pagan midsummer rituals. He agreed to meet me at the Grand Hotel in Stockholm a couple of weeks later.

With that pleasant prospect on the calendar, I set off for Hamburg, where I knew one of my favorite designers was at work at the Opera. José Varona was designing a new production. Someone recommended that I meet a young impresario in Hamburg. At his apartment I met the young, soon-to-be-discovered Tatiana Troyanos, with the prerequisite small dog on her diva arm. Everyone was pleased to entertain me because of my connections with scenic and costume designs. I was comfortable on my pedestal and I made good use of it.

I breezed through Copenhagen before Sweden. David the First contacted the top furrier there, implying that I was a VIP who got loads of press in the USA. He recommended that wearing one of their coats would reflect well on the queen's furrier. I was outfitted with a pin-seal coat that I got at cost. Another elegant notch, and I believed I wore it well. In Copenhagen, I met a young sculptor who had been featured by Bill Como in *After Dark*. He took a flirtatious interest in me, as I was the director of a New York gallery. We made plans to hook up again in New York later that year. I visited artist Bjørn Winblad's studio before departing for midsummer's night in the land of my ancestors.

I prepared with great care to go to the country house of the adviser to the king of Sweden. Swedes are notoriously snobbish, so I carefully decided on a plan of action. My name betrayed a humble Swedish background, but I had three aces up my sleeve. First, my great-great aunt, Christina Nilsson, was a heroine in Swedish history. As a great opera singer, she was revered both for her talent and her kindness and generosity. Christina was the prototype for Christine in *Phantom of the Opera*, a star at the Paris Opera as well as other international houses. Thus began my claim to fame. Greta Garbo was Gustafson before she changed her name and she said I could claim her as my aunt—my second ace. Last, but not least, I counted on personal charm to ease acceptance by my august hosts. I did not know what form it would take but had some confidence I could pull it off.

Björn and his sister picked me up at the Grand Hotel, as planned. Elsa made it clear she would compete with her brother for my attentions. I was careful not to encourage her, however. I was content with Björn's company and did not want to wander into her uncharted waters. I stayed in a small, comfortable guesthouse in the garden adjacent to the main house. The cordial, very correct doctor and his handsome wife warmly invited me to join the family and an old family retainer at a table set under the trees overlooking the peaceful lake. They mentioned having just returned from Italy, which explained the rich tan that Mrs. Bexelius sported. Having established my first two aces, I searched for the definition of my last winning card. Conversation was mild-mannered and warm. The atmosphere had the nineteenth century bucolic charm of a Bergman movie. A Scandinavian smorgasbord under the trees on a warm early summer's night with the sun never setting. The lake shimmered and invited . . . I found it!

"After dinner, let's have a sea battle," I exclaimed. "I will be one captain and have this lovely princess (indicating Mama) in captivity. And you (pointing to the king's adviser, my host) will be a slave!" Everyone was startled, but intrigued by my madness. "Yes, a sea battle. One team can use a canoe and rowboat; the other team can use the other canoe and kayak," I suggested. The second youngest daughter tied a napkin over one eye and declared herself the captain of the other boats, calling herself Lord Nelson. They never dreamed of having a sea battle on their lake but the fantasy captured them. We rushed through dinner, making plans and finalizing teams. My hostess was thrilled to be a princess in captivity and my host was astonished but amused at becoming a slave. After changing into bathing suits, except for the youngest daughter (nude), we went to "sea." We splashed about on the lake amid crashing oars and overturned vessels. The sauna warmed up the soaked crews and we retired to our rooms to slip into dry clothing. Then, we had coffee and chocolates in the drawing room. The ladies returned combed and made up, in pretty long dresses. Only their wet hair betrayed that they had been up to something before partaking of polite Mozart and coffee. Although it seemed as if nothing had happened earlier that evening, I knew it had. I had opened the imaginations of my Swedish hosts, if only for a brief time. Despite it never being mentioned again, when I saw Björn at future meetings he indicated that his family had inquired about the fellow who had created the sea battle for them.

That was the first time I experienced the midnight sun. The night never got dark. At three in the morning, I could have read a newspaper in the half-light. The only thing that changed during the "night" was that the night birds stopped singing at one point. There was a lull, with perhaps a mosquito buzzing hungrily or the call of a moose. Then, the morning birds began. It was an enchanting experience. Björn sneaked over to share my first midnight sun with me. When he returned to the main house, it was light enough for me to notice Elsa's curtains moving. She, too, took notice of our midsummer's night.

Leksand is the tiny town on the Baltic where Swedes go to have a rollicking midsummer's night party. By the time Björn and I arrived, the place was strewn with after-party debris. It reminded me of the Fire Island boardwalks after a costume party. We made love on the shore of the Baltic and our naked, perspiring bodies were assailed everywhere by enormous mosquitoes. Annoying as it was, it did not deter the youthful lust so essential to the spirit of midsummer.

The night before my departure for Rome, where I was to meet with Ysabel to go to Tunisia, my new Swedish friends prepared a farewell feast at the Stockholm apartment of a beautiful young Huguenot. She was intrigued by my relationship to Christina Nilsson and proposed that we all go out after supper to the park on an island where the diva's bronze statue stood. A taxi was summoned after calling the police to determine the exact location of the statue. The lovely hostess grabbed two especially fine bottles of wine from her collection for the special occasion as well as two candlesticks and a bouquet of flowers. Our driver looked sternly at the two bottles of wine, as driving with open bottles was frowned upon. But when he heard where we were going, he became enthusiastic. Sure, he knew where the statue was, because he had proposed to his wife under the same statue. That I was a relative of the opera star made him proud to be part of the undertaking.

En route, the taxi passed the villa of an ancient countess. Björn asked the driver to stop. He got out and went to the countess's flagpole. The Swedish flag had not been taken down, so he lowered and folded it, placing it carefully on her doorstep. We proceeded, only to find that the statue was not where the police or our driver expected to find it. He used the car phone to call the police again. Years of pigeons sitting on the statue necessitated that it undergo a deep cleaning, and it was being restored.

"How about putting the flowers on Jenny Lind's statue?" some-one rudely suggested. No, the competition was not going to be adorned with those flowers. We lit our candles, although the mid-night sun did not require them, and drank our wine on a park bench, with a toast to the great and wonderful Christina Nilsson.

I boarded a plane for Rome, anticipating new chapters of "Travels with Ysabel." Driving from Leonardo da Vinci Airport to the center of Rome, I felt like a homing pigeon returning to its nest. I located Prince Lanza's gate on the Via Margutta with no difficulty. As I parked the car around 11:00 p.m., I spotted Ysabel opening the gate to depart for supper. I called to her, then joined her for a meal at La Etruscana nearby. She chastised me for miss-ing the party given in our honor that had just broken up. Angelo Lanza and his girlfriend would be joining us in a moment. Where had I been? I had never received her cable, not surprising as Ysabel was often vague about addresses and had probably sent it to the wrong country. But, there I was and there she was—statu-esque and vivacious. I loved being with her and I worshipped her spontaneous, sometimes erratic charisma. Ysabel listened to my meanderings about London, Berlin, Hamburg, Copenhagen and Sweden with great interest and always with provocative com-ments.

Life seemed rosy now that I had the exuberant company of Ysabel and our many negronis (our recipe called for gin, Campari and little or no dark vermouth). Through Dickie, we rented a sparsely furnished farmhouse in a field of poppies on the outskirts of Spoleto. It did not have hot water which did not matter as everything else was so cheerful. "I want me coffee," Ysabel would implore upon awaking. "Me coffee!" The kitchen was devoid of food as well as coffee but there was a generous supply of gin, vodka, Campari and a handful of oranges and lemons. The refrig-erator contained nothing but ice. Carefully, I put some ice in a glass, poured Campari and gin over it, and topped it with a slice of orange or lemon. There, coffee was made! Thirstily, Ysabel

soon called for more coffee. Our usual waiter in the Piazza del
Duomo in town brought "La Principessa" and me more negronis
before the noon concert. After the concert, the checkers game of
who would lunch with whom, and where, was anxiously played.

Herbert von Karajan's assistant, Peter Busse, appeared next
to me at the box office while I picked up my opera tickets. They
had no seat available for him. When I learned who he was, I took
him to one of the public relations women who dominated the festival. Karajan's top assistant must *not* go wanting for a seat. Peter
was grateful for my intervention and agreed to come with Ysabel
and me to our country lair. Before allowing Peter and me to
spend time alone in a quickly improvised bedroom in the barren
kitchen, Ysabel wanted to inspect his "goods" herself, on the outlandish pretext that she needed to warm her hands. We laughed
at her approbation of my newly acquired prince. The next morning, I made "coffee" for us all, except that Peter chose not to
indulge, but settled for ice water.

We piled into our little, battered car and lurched off for the
noon concert. The car suffered greatly in scrapes with the iron
railings and stone walls where I tried to park. Negronis under-
mined caution when I was in a hurry to park, often illegally. In
those days, parking tickets to foreigners meant nothing. I would
have a mountain of them if I had saved all the ones we got those
few days in Spoleto!

Peter and Dickie joined Ysabel and me after the concert at
a bucolic restaurant on a small lake near Spoleto. Swans glided on
the water, enchanting the Sunday lunch crowd of families and a
motley group of tourists and locals. Having exchanged lascivious
glances with Peter over our meal, I announced after the bill was
paid, "Andiamo a letto, subito!" All four of us hastened to our
feet, pushing over our rush chairs. Those about us were startled
and amused to watch the foursome hurry to the exit with the
express purpose of going to bed in a hurry!

As we approached Spoleto, I let the two ladies out of the car

Tunisian idyll.

to fend for themselves, while Peter and I disappeared behind a dense thicket, blanket under arm. Carnal pleasure was not limited to the permissiveness of Swedish midsummer nights, and besides, the Italian hillside was mosquito-free.

Before our departure from Spoleto, Menotti invited Ysabel and me to a postperformance supper at the palace where he lived. Doubtless sensing that Ysabel had money, he was not going to ignore the potential of another patroness for the festival. In conversation, she pleasantly asked after his mother. "She used to cook for us in Colombia," she informed him. I almost choked on my food. Menotti probably had a similar response but kept an even countenance. He was not amused at the prospect of having it known that his mother had been a servant in her native Colombia before her migration.

Willem de Kooning wandered vaguely about the festival under close scrutiny from the staff. Ysabel and I decided to have an afternoon cocktail get-together at our adorable country house surrounded by its fields of poppies. The painter and I talked quietly in front of the Duomo one sparkling morning. As I invited him to join us, his guardian appeared to whisk him off to safety. He was "on the wagon" and they wanted to keep him that way in Spoleto. The opera star Justino Diaz and his ballerina wife Anna Aragno joined others at our bucolic drinking party. I felt sympathetic toward de Kooning and was glad that I, at least, could handle *my* drinking.

The Duke of Marlborough's daughter, Sarah Spencer Churchill, had recently married someone both Ysabel and I

knew, Guy Borgos. Some years earlier, I had been to the engagement party for her brother to an American girl, Gillian Fuller. A
photo of me dancing at that festive event appeared in *Vogue*.
They joined us in Spoleto and again in Siena, and we made a jaunt
to Perugia, Assisi and Arezzo. Many white truffle and laughter-
filled lunches and dinners later, Ysabel and I were prepared to
continent-hop.

In New York that spring, I had met a couple of delightful
Tunisian men. One had a family-owned hotel in Tunisia, near the
ruins of Carthage. The other had many friends and relatives in
colorful Sidi bou Said. Both of them knew Minister of Culture,
Dris Guiga, and his wife, Shasha (of Algerian birth). Being the
cousin of President Bourguiba, Dris had a comfortable career
until Bourguiba's demise as head of the government. Dris and
Shasha welcomed us into the international community at Hamamet warmly and enthusiastically. Life on the flowering seaside in
Hamamet was truly paradisical. Every day was sunlit and full of
pleasure and colorful people. Evenings were like sumptuous cos-
tume-banquets. It cost little to live so well. Everyone was highly
accommodating and I felt thoroughly smug with the circumstances.

Countess Cavalli had alighted for the season. She had a
large Berber tent erected on the beach for her private use. Every
day, Carla and her daughter Marina lunched with selected
acquaintances in the shade of the tent. Carla was attractive, with
a vibrant personality. Her longtime protector was heir to the
Cinzano vermouth fortune, and she enjoyed spending money lavishly. In contrast to Carla's incessant need to be glittering and
social, Marina was far more reserved and quiet. I liked them both,
but found Marina more endearing. She was trapped in marriage
to Gianni Agnelli's cousin and colleague at Fiat, the marchese
Ferrero de Ventimiglia. Marina's husband was never around,
seeming to prefer the busy life in Turin to the playground in
Tunisia. Marina had a young son who also remained in Turin. She

seemed relieved to be away from there, though at times her mother's sociability exhausted her. Marina and I would sometimes sneak out onto the moonlit waters in a small boat in search of her "golden fish," which protected her. She believed in feeding it real oriental pearls from her valuable necklace, which seemed very extravagant to me. Marina mumbled something about Lloyds of London recovering the loss, so it did not matter. Occasionally, we heard Carla's laughter piercing the lovely night air from the shore.

For Carla's birthday (no one ventured to guess which one), another huge dinner and dance in costume was held. Her tent housed the musicians and many of the revelers. To outdo every other party, Carla had three orchestras. One played traditional Tunisian music, another traditional Western music (foxtrots, rumbas and such), and the third played rock. As a surprise for her mother, Marina organized a fireworks display. Carla hated it because of the noise; everyone else thought it magnificent. I remember Carla, clad in tomato-red chiffon, bedecked in diamonds and rubies, standing on the edge of the dance floor on the beach. She gazed into the distance, where French wine king Nicholas Feuillatte had his fabulous villa. A caravan of camels approached. "Slaves" bearing torches lit the way along the seashore. As they got closer, Nicholas was spotted, dressed as a sheik. His houseguest, a noted Dior model, was on another camel, decked out as a veiled desert princess. Patrick, his young French lover, displayed his muscular body as one of the torchbearers. I do not remember if the Comédie Française *sociétaire* Denise Noël was part of the retinue or not, but it was a dramatic entrance in the midst of a long night of pleasure.

Dawn exposed an amazing amount of debris and passed-out lotus-eaters. Glaring morning sunshine interrupted my sleep. I woke with a start. In my slumber, I brushed my lips across what I thought was Ysabel's arm. How hairy that arm seemed. When I opened my eyes, it was the arm of the American attaché to Tuni-

sia. I had taken quite a shine to Stephen Lawrence and agreed to
go home with him to a charming place he had in the *souks*. What
I had not thought about the night before was how I was to find my
way through the conservative casbah in the bright light of day
dressed in only a gold bikini, a gold Buccellati bracelet that
Marina had lent me and a scarlet royal Moroccan robe bordered
in gold. It frightened me to pass through the narrow streets
dressed like that, but I had to. Reaching the beach, I rolled up the
robe with bracelet inside it and ran home to Ysabel to tell her
about her "hairy arm."

On July 20, 1969, the American astronauts first walked on
the moon. We were in Tunisia. Ysabel and I were invited to view
the momentous event on a television at Nicholas's villa. I wore a
balloon-sleeved blue shirt with white stars, which caused the
Arabs to cheer, "Vive l'Amérique!" Everyone was jubilant, even in
remote Hamamet, garden paradise by the sea.

Ysabel had plans to visit Spain. I would stay on a bit longer
before returning to spend a few weeks in Italy. Karim, a charming
but pathetic Arab boy, had latched on to both of us. His father
had been assassinated by the current regime and the family lived
in greatly diminished state in the *souks* of Tunis. Karim and I had
an agreeable relationship. There was plenty of smoke but no lasting fire. Tears streaming down our cheeks, we waved farewell to
our Princess as her plane flew off to Spain. I kept our accommodations in Hamamet and invited a film director and television
personality from Cologne to share the place with me. I had met
Freddie Biolek in Spoleto and ran into him again in Tunisia. He
was directing a German-French film in Hamamet, starring Jean-
Claude Pascal. I was pleased to have the company of a distinguished actor-director and he was glad to have free and
convenient accommodations. Sex never entered into it, especially
as I thought he was straight.

Actors have often expressed disgust at the way I manage to
get invited to participate in films and plays, in which they have to

fight for a chance to appear. My houseguest-director asked me to be in his film. I was to play a sybarite at a Tunisian party. It did not take any method acting at all! I borrowed a white silk *djellabah* from Marina, along with her Buccellati bracelet. I had lots of Berber silver necklaces, some of which belonged to Ysabel. A bunch of white jasmine behind my ear completed the picture. Instead of wearing the *djellabah* in the ordinary fashion, with my neck coming through the front top opening, I wore it with one shoulder coming through. It was loosely draped to reveal a tan, taut body. A belt of Berber silver kept it from falling off my exposed body. My hair was sun and salt-water bleached, falling in dramatic curls around my tanned, smiling face. As I entered the set, a heavily made-up Jean-Claude Pascal fixed his eyes on me. The old actor had a costume that covered his weathered body from neck to toe. We were in painful contrast and I could see the involuntarily jealous look in his eyes. "*Tant pis*," I thought. "I guess he thinks he's the star of this film," I arrogantly commented to myself, making my way to the cast bar for a double scotch. As no one seemed to be able to do a Tunisian dance, Shasha reminded whoever was casting that I could easily portray the party boy, dancing with Berber silver in one hand to mark the beat and jasmine in the other. And so it was that I gained the spotlight in that number.

At one of my frequent visits to the cast bar, I ran into the English girl who was my heartthrob's official girlfriend. Wanting the American attaché completely to myself, I wished her far, far away. She told me she was looking for a job. With the American moon walk on everyone's mind, I responded in malicious earnest, "Oh, I know of one. Ysabel and I are thinking of opening a whorehouse on the moon. You could work there!" I dramatically swept away to prepare for my dance number and thought I was so clever in that nonsensical ploy.

My plane ticket to Italy permitted me a visit to Sicily en route. Philip, the Anglican priest, had arranged for me to stay at an English friend's guesthouse just off the Corso in Taormina.

The English woman who owned and ran the Fortuna explained that no unregistered visitors were allowed. Anyone breaking the rule would be expelled. I settled in and made my rounds of the familiar places and beaches. I got to know Josette Stielle. The Belgian "poor man's Rita Hayworth" spent most of her time in Taormina to escape from Brussels and her dull husband. He thought she was there as a curative. Josette was amazing, insatiable and sex-absorbed, full of fun and adventure. I laughed at her

unabashed escapades with Sicilian men. We enjoyed many lunches and drinks on the Corso, then back to my strict *pensione*. As I felt both lonely and above rules, I invited a German boy back for an evening. Although my room was near the front door and the hour of departure was just before dawn, I was caught and expelled. Barely able to afford it, I moved to a more expensive hotel room until my departure.

Dancing in A Night in Tunisia.

An Italian art collector who lived in New York and was friendly with the Capricorn Gallery met me in Milan to arrange my stay at an artist's *"fattoria"* on the canal Leonardo da Vinci had designed some four hundred years before. The sprawling farmhouse had basic comforts, providing a good place for me to rest before the new season in New York. Danieli Oppi and his wife, Franca, were cheerful and goodhearted. We had fun concocting delicious dishes in the kitchen and washing them down with lots of local wine. Danieli tried to emulate Salvador Dalí in looks and behavior. They took care of me to the best of their ability for those weeks. I do not remember whether our mutual friend helped them financially or if I offered a modest sum to be their houseguest. Before my return to the USA, I agreed that Danieli could become a Capricorn artist.

The new Capricorn Gallery season had some setbacks and challenges. The landlord did not want the gallery to remain in that space at that rent. Often, basic services were nonexistent. Despite the extensive repairs we made to the gallery, it was always an uphill battle to render the place presentable to the visiting public from whom sales were derived. I found excellent space on Lexington Avenue near the YMHA. The price was right and the exhibition possibilities terrific. The board of the Capricorn Gallery was in agreement to move, but at the last minute there was a snag: I had decided not to bring Jean Rosenthal's lighting system with me; her girlfriend was up in arms and reversed her vote. A woman who was closely aligned with her in sentiment changed her vote, too. A major battle was looming on the immediate horizon.

Another contretemps was about to happen that autumn of 1969. On my birthday, a Dutch girl from the United Nations had a Spanish party. I had run into her in Positano that summer and she invited me to come for this fiesta in her East Side apartment in October. Mya had had a romance with Cliff Robertson. She knew I had been acquainted with Cliff and his wife-to-be, Dina Merrill, and asked about them each time I saw her. In keeping with the Spanish motif of the party, I wore an Andulsian outfit, complete with flat-brimmed hat given me by Ysabel. She claimed that Tio Pepe of the eponymous sherry had given her the sterling silver tassels that ran down the pants leg. I brought a Spanish girl named Maria with me. She also worked at the UN and lived in the building next to Mya.

At the party, a garrulous Iranian man kept annoying us. He

made noise while the musicians were playing and constantly flirted with Maria. At one point, I told him to fuck off. He became enraged each time he saw me. He made many trips into the bathroom, where I suspect he took drugs. Finally, the hostess suggested I leave quietly. I had taken Maria home and come back to the party for a much-needed nightcap. When I did make my final exit, a Greek girl gave me a farewell at the door. The Iranian looked over and realized I was going. He lunged for the door but was stopped by the hostess. I rang for the elevator, which seemed a long time coming. At the street I tried to flag down a taxi. The Iranian was at the entranceway, he brushed past the doorman, two of his friends following. I thought how silly it was to run away in a taxi when I could just speak reasonably with the overwrought young man. I let the taxi pass. Before a word could be uttered, the two accomplices grabbed me by the arms and pushed me in the gutter. The Iranian leaned over me and struck me several times across the face with his fist. A ring on one finger narrowly missed taking out one of my eyes but created a deep gash over it. Blood gushed down my pleated dinner shirt. The Iranian departed but one of the accomplices returned momentarily to say how sorry he was.

I stumbled back past the blind doorman up to the hostess's apartment. The Greek girl opened Mya's door and screamed. I got lots of gentle, sympathetic attention from the guests at the party. Lying on the bed with ice-packed towels over the eye, the bleeding finally stopped. Mya claimed not to know the identity of the Iranian, which was strange, as he had been her lover not too long ago. A guy who did not live far from my Lexington Avenue apartment saw me safely home. I was in shock but did not know if I had a concussion. After much probing, I discovered the villain to be a close relative of the Shah of Iran, a student at an upstate college. The two guys with him were his bodyguards. It was not until he had left the country that his identity was divulged.

That night, alone with my orange cat, Tyrone, an amazing

phenomenon took place. There was a sleeping loft that I did not use. Just below it was a shelf on which I kept books and a piece of delicate pottery that Janine Wolkenberg had given me years before. I had put it there to keep it out of harm's way as it was high up, above the closet doors. An oversized volume on Henry Moore leaned against the wall behind it. Below both was a floor lamp, its small, round table attached. As I fell into deep sleep after my traumatic evening, a loud crash woke me. Tyrone jumped too. The Moore book had crashed to the floor below, knocking over the lamp. To my utter astonishment, the sculpture that sat in front of it did not fall straight downward, as gravity would demand. Rather, it made an arc over to the side of the bed where I was sleeping. Being fragile, it should have smashed into many pieces. Instead, only one small armature cracked off. It seemed as though I had taken that artwork off the shelf and lain it near me on the floor. My troubled mind had exerted enough energy to bring something that I loved close to me in that stressful time.

Two harridans on the board of the Capricorn Gallery decided that the knock on my head was what caused me stubbornly to insist on moving the gallery to Lexington Avenue. They conveniently forgot that they had previously agreed to the move. As I had signed the lease and wanted desperately to get away from the 56th Street location, I officially broke with Capricorn. Taking the best artists with me and following sage advice from Oliver Smith to do my own thing and let "the girls" do theirs, I bravely opened the Compass Gallery. It showed theater designs as well as contemporary art. The second floor was to accommodate my living arrangements as well as an extension of the ground-floor gallery.

Rita Simon, my longtime artist friend, took over my Lexington apartment, which was only next door. My expenses were reduced by the move but were still sizable, as I no longer had the cooperative setup to count on for income to defray gallery costs.

Rita helped me create a couple of highly attractive theme exhibitions to open the Compass Gallery, generating much press and favorably received by public and artists alike. As usual, I was operating near the edge, an edge even closer than ever before, both financially and emotionally.

My flamboyance grew, perhaps to cover my precarious state. On Mondays, since the gallery was officially closed, I capriciously invited people to party on the floor above. A large terrace was contiguous to the back side of the gallery. The revelers would spill out there on nice days. That block of Park Avenue apartments could easily view the terrace. Prince Egon von Fürstenberg was one of the voyeurs.

With Clayton and Ysabel urging me on, we spontaneously held a sacrificial wedding of a "virgin." Ysabel had a young woman from South America visiting whom she thought "needed a good fuck." A young, attractive actor whom we called "Sweet Tom" made a great stud for the event. Naturally, we all dressed up in whatever weird costume could be found in my closets to imitate what pagans in ritual might wear. While my phonograph played strange, fitting music, we chanted, libations in hand, and paraded around the gallery, out to the terrace and back again with ritualistic aplomb. When our jugs of wine ran low, I asked Clayton to go down and get more at a nearby liquor store. Without changing out of his flowing orange robe, the balding, bespectacled "priest" blessed babies he passed en route to the liquor store. We watched the hilarious sight from the plate-glass gallery window while passersby gaped at our exotic regalia. Libations refilled, we continued our rite. Everyone gathered at the foot of my couch, opened into a double bed to receive the sacrificial virgin. She hesitantly allowed herself to be placed prone on the altar-bed. However, when "Sweet Tom" arrived, his robe about to be removed from his gorgeous body, the virgin seemed ready to fly away, trepidation written on her face. Norma Maynard, my French-American friend, stepped up and nudged the "virgin" away. She "sacrificed" herself, lying there naked and receptive to the penetration of our actor friend, who was *not* acting. The raw sex proceeded accompanied by our avid attention and vicarious pleasure. An Armenian woman was heard to mumble, "Disgraceful . . . disgusting," but no one paid any attention to the spoilsport. Ysabel cried, "Bis . . . bis . . ." after their climax. "Do it again," she encouraged.

That kind of scene was the epitome of the late 1960s and early 1970s, the sort of happening that encouraged the licentious von Furstenberg to snoop around for his own pleasure. One night, I saw him pick up a friend of mine in our local gay bar. The next morning, I called the friend to inquire how he liked doing it with a prince. He was puzzled, as he had no idea who his partner for the evening had been. Egon was highly attractive but did not fit into the brief Compass Gallery scene.

With the best intentions and an increasing burden of debts, I faced the inevitable. I had freed myself from the entanglement of the Capricorn Gallery but I now had to cut myself free from the burden of trying to run a New York gallery. I closed the Compass Gallery, salvaging what I could and selling off whatever was possible. I moved my possessions to my parents' home.

Pooling my resources, I was going to run for the colorful shelter of Europe, which had been such a retreat in the past. In May 1970, I flew to London to visit Bianca von Lowenstein. She was planning a trip on the Continent, so she brought me to the building next door to meet the bleached-blond Irishwoman whose building it was. Actually, it was a low-profile brothel right on the Embankment Gardens, but she took in the occasional paying guest. After Bianca and her husband departed, I moved into a comfortable room overlooking the Royal Hospital Gardens. The location was great and the price affordable. The underside of the operation was barely noticeable, even from the inside. I enjoyed telling my grand Mayfair friends that I lived in a brothel. My "forever-39-year-old" actress friend LoRaine Hulbert had a chum who lived on the other side of Bianca's place. Katya Douglas was intrigued to know about her neighbors through my revelation.

For a week in Paris, I visited with Norma, the "sacrificial" princess, Jean-Charles (a playmate from New York who had moved back to Paris and often offered his apartment for my use), and Ysabel's sister Cecilia, whom I had never met. She showed me off at Fouquet's sidewalk cafe one late afternoon in early June. It gave me insight into the Parisian gossip and intrigue mentality. Alice Babber, a New York painter acquaintance invited me to her Paris *vernissage*. She was staying at the Île-St.-Louis apartment of writer James Jones.

A player in the ever-changing art world, even without a gallery, I continued on to Austria to join one of my favorite Capricorn artists, Lotte Lichtblau. She had taken a portion of a huge farmhouse in Alt Aussee, where painting, reading and observing the Lauser mountain were our only concerns. Time spent with Lotte has always enriched me. Her generosity in sharing her spirit, intellect and emotions opened vistas of understanding that continue to add depth to my life through elucidating talks about art, religion and humanity.

A brief visit to Salzburg and Peter Busse was disappointing because Peter was late in arriving and had agendas other than mine. However, he put me in touch with Peter Hauser in Vienna, where I met with music critic Gerhard Mayer. I enjoyed the networking and relied on it as a survival skill. Much of these activities were to bear fruit in the future.

Josette had introduced me to a butch, moody guy when I was in Sicily. Nino Peluso invited me to visit him whenever I was in Milan. Josette and I called him "Titano," which pleased him, even if we meant it as a joke. Nino took himself very seriously and would have enjoyed being a Titan, so we made him one. Actually, if he had assumed a more assured air without brooding, with his build he had the makings of a Titan. Titano greeted my return to Milan with the news that we were going to Venice with his friend

Maria Luisa Belgiojoso. I was delighted to meet the cultivated, modest young woman and interested to learn about her family's colorful heritage. There was the type of person who made Milan so very special to me. Rome was so flagrantly vulgar, Milan so cultivated.

As the Biennale was being held in Venice, I stayed on. I met a young Venetian artist who welcomed me to his studio dwelling. Gianni was eager to be involved with the Biennale, to which I had my press card from *Arts Magazine* in New York. Hope springs eternal in the artist's heart when it comes to the possibility of a New York show. He tagged along with me to exhibitions and the many parties held all over Venice.

Sitting quietly on a park bench with her sculptor husband, Louis Shanker, Libby Holman sat unnoticed by the Biennale crowds. "Libby," I called to her with delight. They agreed that they would enjoy attending various parties with me later in the day. She had been so kind to me at the dinner table that night in the Hamptons, when David the First cruelly foisted his new lover into the party. The torch singer's infamy about the mysterious shooting of her Reynolds tobacco-heir husband always lingered about her. We met at the Swiss consulate's party and proceeded to the French consulate for more libations. Then we walked over to the Hennessy party. So many people crushed into the house, but Libby managed to get a place on a sofa near the bar. There were no more glasses left so I grabbed a bottle for her and one for me. We were in pig heaven! Having imbibed quite a few before getting to that roaring party, we were flying high. But that was the point, wasn't it? We were only doing the natural thing. I remember Shanker, Gianni and I helping Libby into a water taxi. We agreed to meet again in the morning in her suite at the Grand Hotel.

Hennessy had painted some capes, one of which I had gotten my hands on. Not wishing to relinquish it, I rolled it up and took it along with me in the water taxi that took Gianni and me out to Murano. The "Barefoot Contessa" was having a dance in her palace there. When the Venetian boy and I entered the party, I realized I had forgotten the cape in the water taxi. Later, wishing to dance, I put my box of Dunhills down on a red plush, gilded ballroom chair. In the box was the Dunhill lighter "David the Cruel" had given to me as recompense for falling off the Matterhorn while skiing some years earlier. Upon return, the box was gone. Whoever wanted the cigarettes got a valuable lighter, too. Never mind. I had another much-needed drink before returning to the mainland.

The next morning, Libby and I emptied her refrigerator of its alcoholic contents, speculating about how she cut her leg the night before. She had a simple solution to opening bottles without a bottle opener. Placing the bottle top in the notch where the tongue of the lock sits when the room door is closed, Libby gave a strong jerk. Off came the cap, sometimes with splinters of wood, too. "I've ruined more doors that way," she told me.

Titano awaited my return to Milan. We had a strange relationship. I thought he was straight, yet we slept together naked in the same bed. He always gave me a kiss and a hug goodnight. How civilized those Italians could be, I determined. It was only later, when I met one of his friends, that the truth came out. I enjoyed an afternoon of sex with his friend while Titano was at the office. It was then that the friend confessed that he often came to the very same bed with Titano. They had had a relationship for a few years. After a brief visit to the Spoleto Festival, Titano bade me farewell and sent greetings to Josette, whom I was about to visit in her new villa in Taormina. Her husband had finally given her enough money to buy the villa rather than renting an apartment for several months each year. However, frills were not included. Clever and wanton Josette used her "beautiful body" and wiles to achieve a completed villa. She found the best-looking iron worker to do her windows and doors at cost. "*Banco de Sicilia*" is how she referred to her iron protection. A telephone was installed quickly thanks to her seduction of the young technician. And so it went. Everyone had a good time and the house was equipped to her satisfaction.

Allegra wanted to visit with a beau from London after hearing my glowing tribute to the beauties of Taormina. She agreed to rent Josette's villa for a modest sum while Josette and I went to Tunisia for a holiday. Josette wanted to emulate Ysabel's visit with me, after my tales of Hamamet adventures. And so it came to pass that I was about to embark on a return to Arabian days and nights along the North African shores on the Mediterranean. The repercussions would be thrilling, bittersweet and long lasting.

A One-Man
Show . . .

One subject, many artists, different times.

Eric with bust of Apollo,
portrait by William Feilding, 1986

. . . to be continued

Chapter 10

Following the Italian Army is Hell

Fragrances of jasmine and orange blossoms wafted from the garden of the Hotel Sindbad through gently rustling palm trees. The warm blue-green sea and the receptivity of the Arabs to our every whim increased the romance of Hamamet. Domed, arcaded houses added to the distinct charm of the quiet North African village.

Josette and I were received like old friends by Shasha and her coterie, still holding court at the Sindbad. They missed Ysabel and eyed Josette with amused reservation. Shortly after arrival, Josette and I attended a program of Berber dancing below the ramparts of the *souks*. Nearby, in the crowd of gawking tourists, stood a short, slim young man in a flamboyantly flowered shirt, shorts and sandals. He stared at me with unabashed interest and we struck up a conversation. He was Italian, visiting Hamamet for a couple of weeks with his good friend Verdi Visconti, who I quickly surmised was a niece of the famous filmmaker and granddaughter of the fashion designer Schiaparelli. The young man was twenty-year-old Giorgio, the son of the duke Sanfelice di Bagnoli, and was in his final year at university in Rome. We rapidly developed a sexual affair, although I was reluctant to get involved so quickly. I remember sitting on the beach with "Giorgetto" explaining that there was fifteen years' age difference between us as well as an ocean. He was determined, and he asked me to suspend my doubts.

Josette was pleased that I had found a *duchino*; she was in search of an Arab prince. Soon, she located a very handsome youth who seemed pleased to service the exotic Belgian with the villa in Sicily. For him, adventure was an assured benefit from the relationship. Giorgetto wanted to stop at Josette's villa on his way back to Rome. As a joke, all of us bought matching Tunisian-print outfits in purple and white. The men wore drawstring trousers with thin white Tunisian pullovers; Josette had a matching printed *djellabah*. We were prepared to stroll the Corso in Taormina, catch every eye and make tongues wag.

Ever needy, I forced myself to believe that all obstacles threatening the success of my relationship with Giorgetto would be overcome by love, so I fell hopelessly in love with the young duke. He did everything to support my illusion. I was delirious with passion and dreams of the future. Sun-drenched days and sex-filled nights passed too quickly. We found an abandoned puppy on the beach. We called it the Arab word for love and decided to keep it. Fed warm milk from an eyedropper, the struggling pup was sneaked through customs after we disembarked from the steamer in Palermo. Josette made odd squeals covering those of the unhappy puppy as we passed the border inspectors.

As expected, the citizens of Taormina were amazed, if not appalled, by the four of us strutting the Corso arm-in-arm. Josette announced that Eric had found a duke and she a prince. The time arrived for the ersatz prince to return to Tunis, never to be heard from again. Giorgetto and I proceeded to Rome for a few last days before I had to go back to the United States. I was heartsick to leave, but I promised to find a way to return soon to be with my darling *duchino*.

My return flight was from London that 29th day of September. It was a fine, if sad day. Daydreaming while looking out the window, I was aware of fuel being jettisoned out of the wing on my side of the plane. How odd to drop fuel over Ireland so soon after takeoff. I got up to change to a seat near an attractive young man I had noticed upon boarding. As we chatted, I noticed that the captain came into the cabin, taking my former seat and looking out the window. Soon, a somber announcement over the public address system urged us not to panic, but the plane was jettisoning its fuel in order to make a forced landing back at Heathrow. The

My young duke joins me in Taormina, Sicily.

hydraulic system was failing; it was not certain if the gear and brakes were operative. The airport was closed and fire and ambulance crews were on the runway. Passengers reacted in various ways. The queen next to me started tying his camera equipment around his ankles so that it would not be lost in a crash landing. I sternly told him not to do that as I might get tangled in the straps trying to escape. Some people held hands or hugged each other as though it was the last time. Others were in tears. A steward had to be removed from the cabin, having lost his cool. There was a darling, petite stewardess pertly giving directions on how to hold the pillows over our heads. She went through the drill with a light manner as though rehearsing a Broadway musical. "Now let's try it from the beginning, once again," she chirped. I admired her. I knew that I was helpless and resolved to let fate play its hand. I appeared cool as a cucumber.

Before the plane touched down at Heathrow, I saw the fire-trucks and red-crossed ambulances waiting. Impact, wheels screeched, yet the brakes held! Naturally, my first concern was to retrieve the duty-free liquor in the overhead compartment of my original seat. I opened it and passed it to my fellow passengers. Suddenly, I realized that the elderly should be tended to first when we got out of the plane. We were all in shock, needing something more beneficial than a swig of liquor. I created a wheelchair race to help take our minds off the ordeal. All of us had contemplated our impending death—serious business. A wheelchair race from plane to terminal seemed the perfect relief from the strain. The madness was met with delight by my fellow passengers, and away we went into Heathrow, wheelchairs full-tilt. After refreshments and assurances that the plane was fixed, we went back on the same plane like so many sheep. It seemed odd that we would return so obediently to the disastrous plane without a murmur of protest.

Then it was determined that the plane was not fixed after all. We would have to spend the night at a hotel in London. Things began to get hazy after that. I remember being annoyed at the long wait on the chartered bus into London. Spurred on by alcohol, I tried to start the bus and drive it into town myself. Airport police intervened. In the morning, I woke up on the floor of the hotel room, my clothes in disarray. Who knows what happened that night? I remembered nothing after the bus ride.

I freshened up and appeared for our predeparture break-fast, befuddled and tired. A pretty girl from Los Angeles was at my table. I called her "the Actress" because of her looks and because of her proximity to Hollywood. We decided that it was a pity to return to the States after our trying ordeal. After checking with TWA, they agreed to cover our hotel costs in London for three days and deliver us to the airport as recompense for the distress we had suffered.

While the other sheep returned to Heathrow, "the Actress"

and I took a cab over to the Embankment Gardens for a three-day holiday. I took her to the Irish madam's place, where we were given madam's own suite to use at TWA's expense. Champagne all around, and with neighbor Katya and friends Allegra and LoRaine we celebrated our salvation. The final touch to this episode was the return trip. The airline had a limousine pick us up at the Chelsea brothel and deposit us at Heathrow three days after our "crash landing."

At the airport, I was recognized at the check-in counter as the guy who had started the wheelchair races. We were given an upgrade to First Class and each presented with a large tin of beluga caviar as a special gift. Upon entering the cabin, I said something to the stewardess about my friend "the Actress" having to get back to California. A man who had been examining papers when we entered looked up at us. Later, when I awoke from a nap, the actress and the man were having a glass of champagne. She explained to me later that he was Ray Stark, Barbra Streisand's producer and son-in-law of the legendary Fanny Brice. He had heard me say she was an actress and was taken by her looks. Over champagne, he offered her a movie part. She declined, saying that she was better equipped to be a secretary than a film actress!

My life in New York was fraught with new uncertainty. Without a gallery, I had to freelance as best I could, selling theater designs privately or appraising them. As I had no apartment in the city, I stayed with friends, "Uncle Monkey" being one of them. His large apartment near Columbia University was always available, but not as convenient to midtown cavorting as others. A friend who was on a trip loaned me his apartment on 55th Street near Sixth Avenue. Renata Tebaldi lived on the same floor down the hall and we happened on each other once in a while. How elegant she was, with correct manners. I loved to hear her vocalizing while I waited for the elevator.

One evening, Yveta asked me to escort her to a dinner party

given by mutual friends who lived across from Carnegie Hall. Her firm condition for my going to the gathering was that I not drink any alcohol before coming to fetch her. Some very high-power people were going to be there and she did not want me to appear intoxicated.

Earlier, I had been to lunch at a Beekman Place apartment with a young woman who had worked for me at Capricorn Gallery. She told me the unsettling story of her two young children taking her plastic bag of marijuana to the police. The cops demanded to know where the kids got the pot. Frightened, they claimed to have found it in an alley near their home. They confessed to their mother. Terrified that the cops might come to search her apartment, she put the remaining pot into a batch of brownies she was preparing, à la Alice B. Toklas. After lunch, she asked me if I would like to sample one of the brownies. Warning me that they were powerful, she suggested I eat only one.

We went to see Andy Warhol's new film, *Trash,* with Holly Woodlawn in the leading role. The brownies were taken along to munch during the movie. Never having ingested pot before and feeling no reaction to the first brownie, I had another, then another. The camera panned slowly over the bare buns of Joe Dallesandro, revealing a mole on one cheek. Hands with red-painted fingernails clutched his cheeks. The camera moved for a frontal view. Kneeling in front of Joe, Holly fervently gave him a blowjob. It was an attention getter, for sure. I hooted with laughter. I found the whole thing hilarious and roared with laughter. What was the matter with everyone else? No one seemed to find the scenes as uproariously funny as I did. It still did not dawn on me that the brownies were doing their mischievous work. When the lights came up, I rose to leave. I could not get up. What was going on? My brownie baker helped me to my feet. She asked if I was okay, reminding me of the potency of the brownies. I stumbled to the street and bid her farewell. I had to get changed for the dinner party.

Bloomingdale's was across the street and I cut through on my way west to the apartment. How fascinating everything was in the store! Captivated, I lingered over everything. Once in a while, I would remind myself to keep going. I had to change clothes. It seemed an eternity before I regained my friend's apartment. Time itself had changed. Everything was different. I could not manage anything easily. It was hard work just getting into my dinner clothes. Finally, I was on my way, but not free of the marijuana's effect. When I had smoked it in the past, I could get in and out of the effect with little effort. There was no getting out of its grip that night. Obviously, ingesting it was a different matter.

From Sixth Avenue, I went over to Madison Avenue on foot. I could not afford a taxi all the way to 90th and Park, and I thought walking might be the best way to get out of my drugged state. The only problem was in determining which way was uptown and which downtown, and I am a native New Yorker! Well, if I walked one block up I would know whether I was going up or down. So I tried that, but I forgot what the previous block's number was by the time I got to the next street. I prayed I would not run into someone I knew, as I was thoroughly disoriented. Of course, twice I was greeted by friends. I brushed them off politely, as though in a terrible rush. I got the impression that they were puzzled. I was puzzled. I hated the predicament, but finally reached Yveta's door. "Oh, no!" she cried. I must have looked terrible. "You *promised* me you would not drink before coming here." I assured her I had not, I had merely ingested marijuana brownies! I was ordered into the sauna and then the ice tub. While Yveta was in the sauna, I sneaked to the bar for something sweet. I had a craving for crème de menthe, gulping some down. Then back to the sauna.

We arrived at the party. When the host asked me what I would like to drink, I replied, "Nothing, thank you." The host knew me too well. He insisted. "Give him a club soda," Yveta advised. Among those I met were David Sarnoff, the president of NBC; the developer of space equipment that had brought our men to the moon; Herbert Bayard Swope, the newspaper publisher and Maggie Hayes, his retired actress wife who was going to open a jewelry line in Rome. I was utterly quiet during their conversation. They got the notion that I was very intelligent, as I seemed to agree with them. The favorable impression I made on the guests led me to believe that I should learn to shut up more often at social functions. Two employment offers for Rome resulted from the dinner. The actress wanted me to consider representing her interests in the jewelry venture; the space electronics manufacturer needed an intelligent contact for his business. I went to a party spaced-out and got such responses!

I pursued neither offer, as I could not conceive of playing either role. I was going back for Giorgetto, who had just told me that he was entering his military service in the Italian cavalry division. Every male in his family joined that branch. He was on excellent terms with the commandante, a good friend of his father. It was understood that although he was only a private, he could change location according to the season. Winters, he would go to Caserta, outside Naples, where his family had an ancient palace. Later, he would be on the Adriatic near their country villa and vineyard.

The camp in Caserta did not have hot water available to the lowly privates. Giorgetto rented a studio in town to be able to enjoy hot showers. He invited me to live in there while he did his initial military service. I packed a steamer trunk with items I thought I would use in my new life: a box of silver left over from my brief marriage, an eighteenth-century Spanish bedcover David and I had bought in Madrid, and other vital, potentially useful items of sentimental value. I mounted an exhibition of my own collection of theater designs at Queens College in October. Then, waltzing with Beverly Sills at the post-opening-night New York City Opera dinner dance marked one of the last social events in my soon-to-be-finished New York life. I was facing tomorrow in a foreign land as an expatriate, not the tourist of other times. It was scary but very dramatic, and I prepared myself with many libations.

Loaded with dozens of Christmas presents for Giorgetto, I boarded Air India's flight to London and on to Rome to catch the train to Caserta via Naples. My beloved Italian soldier boy had planned time off so we could spend Christmas on Capri, culminating in a fireworks display in the garden of the Countess Sorignano, who had invited us for New Year's Eve festivities.

I was glad that I had taken my three furs with me. It was cold and rainy on Capri. We rented an apartment in the house of Thomas Mann's daughter, who looked like a stereotypical Italian widow from central casting in her ubiquitous black. The window of the tiny kitchen looked out over the famous Faraglioni. It was a romantic location, but rain drenched everything. Pin seal fur from Denmark, Swedish raccoon purchased from Clayton Cole for a song, and the muskrat vest that Norma had given me managed to keep us warm. Every day, I admired the phallic rock formation washed by the waves. Even when it rained, Capri was a place for lovers. I enjoyed cooking pasta, but Giorgetto thought it ridiculous to stay in that tiny kitchen (even if the view was world famous) when we could be in the piazzetta or any other location of which Capri boasts. My sense of economy and need to feel I was doing something caused me to focus on the kitchen as a source of our meals. Advice to honeymooners: do *not* linger in the kitchen!

After the fireworks on New Year's Eve, Giorgetto wanted to visit a local nightspot. Inside, we bumped into his previous lover and some other friends of his. I wanted to get away from the noise and those people. He recommended that I return to our lair, promising to come shortly. I was wearing the elegant Spanish cape Ysabel had gotten for me, excellent protection from the rain but a bit dramatic for Capri. Spying a dry doorway across from the disco, I decided to bundle up and wait for my pal. I was hurt and jealous that he chose to stay on with others on New Year's Eve. It was a bit of a wait but he emerged with a young lady whom he had promised to see home. Noticing me, he crossed the street and told me I was crazy to be huddled in the doorway that way. He would return in a moment and we would go back to our nest together. I resented having to wait for him at all. Control was an issue long-instilled in me by Mother as a futile attempt at keeping a relationship going.

Life in Caserta consisted of aloneness and waiting. Each morning after dressing, I went to the nicest bar in town and ordered a gin and Campari, a brioche and a double coffee with steamed milk. No one ever asked me what I was doing there, day after day. Perhaps everyone knew. I was the only American in town off-season. I would have thought they would speculate on what I did with myself each day. I, too, wondered what I would do with myself day after day.

A couple of hundred years ago, the King of the Two Sicilies had had a summer palace there, his retreat from stifling Naples, conceived as a smaller Versailles. After visiting it and the gardens on numerous occasions, I ventured to Naples. One day I went to the museum at Capodimonte, another to a matinee at the opera (Wagner in Italian). I searched for culturally challenging things to fill my time while waiting, which stretched into an eternity. Thrilling were the moments when I heard soldier boots clicking on the marble stairway outside and the door sprang open. I never knew when he would be free or for how long, but when he was there it seemed worth the wait. He was full of stories of the soldier's life in the Italian army. On maneuvers one day, a few soldiers stopped marching to pick some flowers; another time, he returned to base before midnight to find two guards doing a Viennese waltz to a cassette player. No wonder the Italians never won a war!

Instances accumulated which indicated a real gulf between

the two of us, as I had always suspected. His grand nobility gave him attitudes I found heavy-handed. Giorgetto was taught to believe that Jews, even those who had been living for generations in Italy, were not Italians. "They are Jews," he would argue when I chastised the Italians for having rounded them up for Nazi extermination. We had just seen *The Garden of the Finzi-Continis*.

It was clear that Giorgetto was indeed much younger than I, with different needs. He came from a background of self-absorbed nobility—another sensibility. I was glad I had not unpacked my steamer trunk, as I realized that my experiment of moving to Italy with Giorgetto was a failure. The trunk was sent back, and I jetted home. It did not mean that all was over between us, at least to me. Practicality indicated I get on my feet on home turf, and we would stay in communication to try to work something out. *"La lontananza sai e come il vento . . ."* the popular song claimed in Italy that season. Distance, like the wind, extinguishes the small flames but fans the big ones.

"Uncle Monkey" with Manx.

Ysabel's apartment was rented out while she was in Europe. I went to stay at "Uncle Monkey's." Long since retired as director of the New York Geographical Society, he suffered from age and too much solitude. His World War I wounds aged him greatly, making his seventy years seem more like eighty. Taking to vodka on a serious scale did not help his balance or his health either. Outwardly, he seemed the height of Scottish respectability. He was educated, distinguished in his field and a courtly gentleman.

Behind the mask of respectability, he was closeted, reveling in the company of young gays. He was intrigued with my lifestyle, encouraging me to bring friends home for dinner and drinks. I added spark to a life that had become narrow and lackluster. People first meeting "Uncle Monkey" always asked how such a refined gentleman had gotten the unusual nickname. His eyes twinkled as he smiled and explained. When he was young and in the church choir, he would screw up his face when singing, looking just like a monkey. Later, when his twin brother had a daughter, Diana could not say "Uncle Maitland." "Uncle Monkey" resulted. So, the affectionate appellation continued into the New World and the gay community of New York.

We sat over multiple vodkas, and I told him about the wonders of Italy and my yearnings for Giorgetto. Uncle Monkey had been on expeditions to the Arctic Circle as part of his geographic professional life; he had seen the horrors of the First World War in France, and been in various part of the globe. Never had he gone to Italy, a place that enchanted his imagination. Fired by my descriptions, he suggested that we both go to Italy. Like a fairy godmother, he provided me with another great opportunity. He invited me to show him Rome, Florence, Venice and the Italian Alps, where Giorgetto was now stationed. It was a pleasure to show the elderly gentleman Rome and Florence as I knew them. He was so intelligent and receptive. At Venice, I was close to being reunited with my Italian soldier, five hours north by train in Bolzano. We left for Bolzano with plans to return to Venice after our visit in the Italian Alps. We found a charming old-world hotel in Bolzano, with a fast-running stream that could be heard from Uncle Monkey's window. He was content with the comforts of the place and its lovely garden.

Giorgetto came from the nearby army camp that evening to meet Uncle Monkey and go out with me after dinner. My enthusiasm and excitement were dashed that evening by his reluctance to do more than talk. I suppose soldiers are not permitted into hotel rooms when in uniform, but it seemed there was more to it. In fury, I sent him back to the base. Entering the hotel, I asked the desk clerk to get me a double scotch on the rocks, which I took up to our suite. Scotch was a good answer to everything. Uncle Monkey took one look at me and asked what was the matter. "We are leaving in the morning for Venice," I informed him. "Oh, no, I love this place," he pleaded in vain, but acquiesced to my demand. We set off for Venice, where I hoped to lick my wounds amid its glories. Giorgetto discovered that I had retreated to Venice, bombarding me with telephone calls and telegrams that awaited us upon return to our hotel on Riva degli Schiavoni. I told Uncle Monkey that I had to respond to the *duchino*'s messages by returning, yet again, to the mountains. He took it in resigned stride. We agreed that the hot train ride would be too tiring for him, especially for such a brief visit. I would go in the early morning and return that night. I was clutching at straws, but insisted on making the effort.

It was to be a surprise for Giorgetto. The surprise was on me, as it turned out. Telephoning the army base upon arrival in Bolzano, I was informed that Sanfelice was on a day's leave, they thought in the nearby village of Tirolo with his comrades. I reached Tirolo and started searching for Giorgetto. In a restaurant that had a back garden, tables were set up in a quadrangle. There was my soldier boy with three comrades. I took a table across the quadrangle from him, but in full view. As I passed his table, I gave our familiar call of p-s-s-t, which we had used in the past to get each other's attention. Sitting down, I noticed his surprised, befuddled look. He made his way over to me, saying how startled he was that I was there. I asked him what he had told his friends across the way before coming over to greet me. "Oh, I told them you were a friend of my mother's," he admitted. That sealed our break. Full of exuberance and thrilled to see him again, I was hurt that he did not seem to have the same enthusiasm. After my sacrifice to be with him, after his promises that our relationship

"A friend of his mother!": Break up in Tirolo.

Allegra Kent Taylor with "Uncle Monkey."

was bound in love, he would not even acknowledge me as his lover, or even a good friend. I was "a friend of his mother's." Again the glass slipper was a misfit! Perhaps overreacting but hurt and humiliated, I returned to Uncle Monkey in Venice. We capped our Italian holiday with a few days in Capri at a small hotel not far from my nest above the Faraglioni. The weather was sunny and warm, but the air was laden with ghosts.

"Madame" awaited us at the Riverside Hotel on the Chelsea Embankment in London. It had been a long time since Uncle Monkey had spent any time in London. He usually just passed through en route to family in Scotland. He shared his memories of World War I. Uncle Monkey had been operated on in the makeshift hospital that was the converted mansion of Edward VII's red-peruked mistress. She had donned a nurse's uniform to attend the indigent gentlemen officers who were taken into what had been her London town house. Ether was administered to those needing operations. Knowing that often a patient was operated on before the ether fully took effect, he asked the royal doxy to hold his hand until it went limp. She did, to his eternal gratitude.

It amused Uncle Monkey to occupy a room in a brothel, however low profile. My usual friends gathered: Katya, LoRaine, Allegra and Maureen. London in May was a dream, the entire city in bloom under a pleasant, sunny sky. What a fascinating trip it had been for Uncle Monkey; what another disjointed adventure for me.

A One-Man Show . . .

One subject, many artists, different times.

Eric and Fred, portrait by
Joan Hierholtzer Bennett, 1996

. . . to be continued

Chapter 11

Out and About

No amount of morning vodka or scotch at night eased the sadness and remorse I felt back in New York. On the telephone with Margaret Jamison in Santa Fe one evening, I received an invitation that I could not refuse: Would I please come to Santa Fe to take over directorship of the Jamison Gallery? Margaret had long admired my astuteness in matters pertaining to art as well as my business acumen. We enjoyed each other's company, making merry drinking partners. She was tired of trying to cope with running her prestigious gallery. Together, owner and director might make the thing sing.

A mariachi band welcomed me officially to Santa Fe; at Margaret's large home a "simple" luncheon—for forty or so. I adored the grandiose scale. I was invited to stay in her enormous house until I located a place of my own. The house had been a country club. Years ago, Margaret had had the olympic-size swimming pool filled in and covered with lawn. The main room had a gigantic custom-made oriental rug in the center. There were three different pianos in the room. Entertainment was ongoing and lavish, which pleased me greatly. Sometimes, after coming home from the club at La Fonda, where Margaret was often requested to sing the blues, we had a nightcap together and she played one of the pianos, singing soulful songs of lost love. Her company was endearing and poignant, especially after yet another nightcap. Aside from reorganizing her gallery, I escorted

225

Margaret and I at home in Santa Fe.

her when her sometime lover Bill was otherwise engaged. The Jamison Gallery was internationally known for dealing in works by top-quality school of Taos and Santa Fe artists. Clients came from all over the world to acquire those masterpieces. Relying on the blue-chip art kept in the back room or closets, Margaret sometimes ventured very cautiously into more contemporary art.

Fascinated by the lore of the Southwest, I investigated Taos when time permitted. I came upon the Navajo Gallery and its young, enticing director, Edmund Gaultney from Georgia. Ed introduced me to his boss, the Navajo artist R.C. Gorman. All of us drank heavily and acted out grandiose fantasies. R.C. created a "nude" portrait of me, which was used as the frontispiece to the dessert section of his *Nudes and Foods*. Margaret and I discussed having R.C.'s first Santa Fe exhibition at the Jamison Galleries. It was before he made his break into worldwide recognition. That was the wedge that permitted other contemporary artists to find distinguished exhibition sites in Santa Fe, which was very stodgy about art in those days. There was not the profusion of galleries in the early 1970s that exists today. The bill of fare was cowboy and Indian art or blue-chip Southwestern works by Reynolds, Russell, Berninghaus, Blumenschein, Couse, Sharp and the other big-name painters that exceptional galleries like the Jamison traded in.

I wanted to bring contemporary artists who lived locally into public attention. I began to write articles for magazines and newspapers about the "new" Southwest art scene. I fervently believed that what was happening in Santa Fe and Taos was more vibrant than what comprised the New York scene. The "barely" Indian Fritz Scholder had a successful exhibition that same year at Jamison. My publicity about "the *wunderkind* of the Southwest" was so successful that he began to believe it himself. That caused great consternation for me, as we had two egos running headlong into each other.

My enthusiasm about Santa Fe and Taos fired the imagination of Ysabel enough for her to agree to come out for a visit. Renting a charming house on the Camino de las Animas, I settled in with possessions of my own. I borrowed Margaret's station wagon and drove East to pick up books, records, clothing and art work that had been stored in my family's home in Westchester. It was quite a sight to see the wagon loaded beyond belief for its westward journey. From Ysabel's Fifth Avenue window, the top looked like the tarpaulin was strapped down with bra straps. The flesh-colored ribbons that my mother supplied were strong and serviceable, however.

To add to the load, Titano had arrived from Italy for his first American visit. He was thrilled to drive out West to the land of cowboys and Indians, but had no comprehension of the vast distance. To compound matters, our Italian visitor requested that we not speak Italian because he wanted to learn English. Ysabel and I proved to be extraordinary mentors. We began by teaching our Milanese guest local customs of the highway. Each state that we passed through was to be respected with a libation. Stopping at the nearest rest area after each border, we would pull out the vodka bottle and toast the state. According to the size of the state, we carefully drank an appropriate amount. Delaware was a one shot state; Texas required at least four belts.

His annoying lack of conversation caused us to dub him "Loquacious." A trait that I admired in Ysabel was her ability to create lively conversation. When driving, especially long distances, I was grateful for her companionable talk. Titano was a drag. We decided to liven up our journey by teaching him English but with a Swedish accent. He never seemed to catch on to our mirthful deception. The fast-food restaurant Stuckey's became a singsong Stoo-key's and Oklahoma took on a melodic, if idiotic Ooo-kla-hooma, with inflections rising and lowering dramatically. Titano realized by arrival in Santa Fe that the U.S. of A. was a much larger country than he imagined it to be. We three

Ysabel Aya by R.C. Gorman:
Left, before 100 proof martinis, right, after 100 proof martinis.

emerged from the cramped front seat like apes, hunched over and tired.

The next evening, Margaret asked to have Titano escort her to a party given by some Hollywood people. They were amazed to hear our Italian relate in his startling Swedish accent the places he had seen cross-country.

R.C. Gorman suggested that I bring "the Princess" to lunch in Taos. Ysabel, Titano and I drove along the Rio Grande to quaint Taos for a very unusual afternoon with the Navajo artist and his entourage. His official hostess then was Cynthia Bissell who provided us with many 100-proof martinis in her home near R.C.'s Ledoux Street home and gallery. Before Virginia Dooley presented us with the tasty lunch she had prepared, R.C. did a profile portrait of Ysabel, with whom he was entranced. After lunch he did another full front portrait, which clearly indicated the strong effect of the libations.

Irritating us from the start of our feast were the two southern "belles" from Georgia, who insisted on continually photographing us for posterity, then, continuing in Andy Warhol fashion, requesting us to speak pearls of wisdom into a microphone of the tape recorder. They were sweet guys, but sophomoric. It was announced that over lunch the mike was going to circulate around the table. We were each going to relate our most memorable pee for the tape recording. Waiting until our illustrious host, R.C., began his recitation, I quietly got up. Unzipping my fly, I proceeded to pee into the nearby half-empty zucchini bowl. Miss Sopapilla, the puff-bread title Virginia Dooley had achieved in the last Fiesta parade, was summoned to "Take that bowl to the kitchen!" That ended the tape session so that we could continue to enjoy the fine, golden, autumn day in the Sangre de Cristo mountains.

After my two guests departed to the East, I settled back into running the gallery in earnest. On Thanksgiving Day, I looked out my window toward the lovely mountains. Snow had fallen, so I decided to try a ski run down them. I was due for dinner at the ranch owned by the head of the Arts Council, but there was time for a few hours on the slopes. My skis had not arrived yet from New York, so I opted for a rental pair at the slopes. Not bothering to check the equipment, I started up on the chair lift. An amiable college student and I decided to descend the slope together. Wouldn't he like to stop partway down for a morning drink at the inn? It was too early in the day, he thought, but maybe on the second run. I did not drive, ski or do much of anything else well in the morning without first having a drink.

Turning around to see if my new friend was following, my skis crossed. I toppled in perfect weather and easy ski conditions. I heard and felt something in my right leg—it was broken in three places; spiral breaks, which occur in slow accidents, are the hardest to heal. While being strapped onto a toboggan by the ski patrol to be brought to an ambulance, I asked my new friend to return my ski equipment and call Margaret Jamison. Would he ask her to come to the hospital later with a bottle of "white wine" (my code word for champagne) and tell my hostess for Thanksgiving dinner that I would not be there. Finally, I asked that he call ahead to the hospital and speak with Fritz Scholder's wife, Ramona. As head nurse, she could arrange the best room possible for me. He was then dismissed, and I began the painful descent. To my outrage, I was not permitted a cigarette or a drink. I was in shock.

The enchanting days of riding Nellie, the Tennessee Walker that Margaret had loaned to me were over. Almost every day, I had gone out to Winnabelle Beasley's ranch in the early morning or late afternoon to ride through arroyos and over foothills. Nellie was white, and I rode her wearing white gloves, short white windbreaker and white trousers. Always, I wore the orange bandanna of Giorgetto's Italian cavalry division around my neck.

Winnie called me one day with an invitation for dinner with her "g-r-r-rand and elegant friends." I was warned not to use

Winnie plucks her washtub.

four-letter words, however. I accepted the invitation but wondered why she especially asked me not to use swear words, since I did not usually do so anyway. I arrived, unsure of how I could correct her mistaken notion, but I knew that inspiration rarely failed me. I greeted her "grand and elegant friends," all of whom I had known for some time. I was speaking with the newly appointed head of the Arts Council, and I told her about Winnie's odd comment. "But, Eric, you don't use them and even if you did, so what?" Then, inspiration burst forth. I asked the pillar of society whether she would use a four-letter expletive if I cued her at the table. She agreed—as did every other guest that I surreptitiously cued at the predinner cocktail party. Winnie was done up in bright red velvet hot pants and golden pantyhose. Her wide, Imogene Coca eyes seemed to betray a private madness; they opened wider than I imagined possible as she surveyed the dinner table. She rose to her feet, reaching for a platter of food. Her eyelids glittered and her long lashes fluttered. "Er-r-r-ic! Would you like some more?" "No, thank you, Winnie dear," I replied pleasantly. My arm struck a conductor's pose, which was the cue for all at the table to do their thing. "Shit! Fuck! Damn! Cock!" Expletives flew from each guest's mouth while Winnie looked around, confused and stunned. I was the only one there who did *not* use a four-letter word! I drank to that.

Christmas found me still wheelchair-bound, with a long recovery ahead of me. Margaret finally permitted me to do a group show of young artists from the area, perfect for customers wanting to acquire Christmas presents that were both inexpensive and artistic. It helped to acquaint the public with the many tal-

Governor Bruce King attends my Jamison Gallery Christmas show.

ented young artists working in the area. Press and public crammed the gallery with Governor Bruce King and his wife there for photo opportunities. I held court from the wheelchair, attired in my muskrat vest, holding the ubiquitous drink in one hand. Little did I know that that exhibition would encourage other galleries to flourish. I created a monster that now seems out of control in Santa Fe.

Edward Steinbrecker, astrologer and wizard, gave an astrological New Year's party at the large house he had rented in Arroyo Hondo. It was a "New Age" costume party. To cover my crutches, I wore a long, hooded, burnt-gold velour robe. It had an orange and pale blue Greek key design around the border, which I echoed on a painted mask. The owner of the house, who I think had been involved with the formation of the Boys Scouts, the organization Mother never allowed me to join as a young boy, had a large chapel connected to the house. A stairway into the chapel led from the main floor of the house. While the party was going full-tilt, I entered the chapel and surveyed the revelers from above. The organ intoned slow, somber chords. People in papier-mâché headdresses and exotic costumes bobbed about below. Slowly, balancing myself against the balustrade so I would not tumble down the stairs, I declaimed loudly, "I've been saved . . .I've been saved!" waving my crutches in the air. When all eyes were upon me, I hurled the crutches into the chapel. I do not know how I thought I would move from there without them. Happily, Jacques the hairdresser, rushed up the stairs with the crutches and helped me back to a seat in the house. That kind of behavior may explain why Ed Steinbrecker told Faye Dunaway upon introducing us that "Eric is the most likable disliked person in Santa Fe." It puzzled her and dismayed me.

Being an invalid in a snowbound place and in a house with stairs made it clear that I should consider returning to Ysabel, now that she was back at "955." The house I had rented after leaving Margaret's big place did not suit someone who had mobility problems. "Come here, darling, where there are not steps and there is a maid to help you," Ysabel implored. I moved my things into the studio of the artist Mike Selig, who had moved away. It was an inexpensive, cozy accommodation in the foothills just off the Old Santa Fe Trail.

The anthropologist Bertha Dutton was the director of the Navajo Museum nearby. She had asked me if I would like to give talks to the visitors on Indian ceremonial art. She knew of my avid interest and intense reading on the subject. I could deliver the talks from my wheelchair. It had given me purpose and meaning, assisting my recuperation, too.

Eventually, I closed up my little house and returned to New York to accept Ysabel's invitation. To celebrate my arrival, the maid waxed the entrance hall to the Fifth Avenue apartment as part of the sprucing-up. I entered on crutches, which immediately slid out from under me, the marble was so highly waxed.

Happily, no injury resulted but I had to laugh at leaving Santa Fe for the "safety" of the New York apartment.

Life with Ysabel regained its daily sense of madness and excitement. Uncle Monkey, Ysabel and I went to Wednesday matinees on Broadway. Each of us took turns buying tickets for the play, while the other would provide lunch, in rotation. One day I sent the others ahead to the theater while I paid for lunch. I caught up to them on my crutches along Sixth Avenue. As a joke, I made believe that I did not know them. I asked Ysabel if she could spare a buck for something to eat. She stopped, opened her bag and took out a dollar bill. Suddenly, she crammed it into my mouth. I lurched backward from the force of her thrust. A stranger caught me while the crowd gasped at the deranged woman pushing over the nice guy on crutches. The vodka martinis were showing.

After the matinee, we hailed a taxi back to Ysabel's for much-needed refreshment. I got into the front seat with the driver. There was just enough room in the back for Ysabel, Uncle Monkey and my crutches. "955 Fifth Avenue," I directed the handsome young driver. We spoke a while. He liked to play chess, as did Ysabel and I, which prompted an invitation to come up. While discussing taxi holdups, he revealed where he hid his wad of dough. Busily concentrating on the heavy traffic, he was shocked to feel me reach into his shirt to take his roll of bills! "I held him up," I told Ysabel as I passed her his money. She was delighted; Uncle Monkey a bit appalled; I laughed. The poor guy was not sure what to do, hoping it was a joke and that he would get his money back. He parked his taxi and joined us upstairs. The driver and I played chess and drank. Ysabel took to kibitzing, which annoyed me tremendously. Finally, I took the chess board and hurled it across the room. Infuriated at my disrespect for her chess set and the rudeness to her, she ordered me out of the house. I led the driver to the street and we planned to go to Uncle Monkey's. Ysabel threw my clothes out of the eleventh-floor window, finally stopping at Uncle Monkey's intervention. Passersby saw clothes flying out of an elegant Fifth Avenue residence, as though we were in a Neapolitan back street. The taxi driver, who had never had sex with a man, liked me and indicated that he would try it with me. It would have to wait for another day, however, as he had to catch up on making fares for that day's quota.

I needed ongoing physical therapy if I hoped to walk again without a limp. My first thought when the accident happened was not, "My God, I'll never walk again." It was "My God, I'll never *waltz* again." I prided myself on my Viennese Waltz, which I performed to great acclaim. I wanted to walk and to dance like I used to, and I worked long and hard to achieve it. With three screws holding my leg together, I needed to learn how to move without any indication that the leg had ever been damaged.

My longtime friend Nina Micheleit, whom I had first met in Provincetown, had a house and business in Falmouth. I visited her and worked out daily in the indoor pool of a local motel. My first steps free of crutches were with Nina at Race Point in Provincetown and then at Long Nook in Truro. As the weather was still cold, there were no tourists. I was delighted to start my recovery on Cape Cod, so rich in memories for me.

My English friend Allegra sent me an announcement of her impending wedding to Douglas Campbell, a Canadian stockbroker. "Not *that* Douglas Campbell," I asked her, as there were a couple guys with the same name knocking about New York City. This one had a strange reputation. "I'm afraid so, but don't worry . . . I'll change him," Allegra assured me. While they were on their honeymoon in Idaho, I was invited to use their Holmby Hills home in California. Because I needed therapy, the swimming pool, Jacuzzi and sunny southern California weather would be just the thing. Daily workouts in a warm environment encouraged more rapid healing. Ysabel planned to go to Beverly Hills to visit some friends who took a house there. I did not particularly like them, as they put on airs of superiority that did not sit well with

me. Typically, and hypocritically, I took extreme pride in telling
them that I had a well-appointed house in Holmby Hills *above*
Beverly Hills.

George Michaud, an artist I knew from Santa Fe, had a
charming house in Manhattan Beach, south of Los Angeles. He
maneuvered me around in his van and introduced me to many
swinging places where I could meet young men eager to come for
a swim in a Holmby Hills mansion. Languid decadence best
describes those days under the jacaranda trees. Allegra and Doug
returned and we had some perverse days that greatly eroded the
charming surface of my English hostess. Doug found ways to torment her so that each evening ended in tears. I was next on his hit
list.

Douglas sought the company of Robert and Rosemary
Stack. Doug wanted to be close to the actor, his fame and status
in the L.A. community. One evening, Allegra, Douglas and I went
over to the Stack's Brentwood mansion to pick them up for dinner at a chic, new French restaurant. I admired the olympic-size
pool and the tennis court adjacent to the house. "You can play
there anytime you want," Robert told me warmly, "but not when
Janet Leigh is playing. She uses the court all the time." Robert
engaged me in conversation, and I got the impression that he
would enjoy getting to know me much better.

During dinner, I spied Janet Leigh across the room dining
with a couple of people. She gave me a good looking over. When
she finished dinner, she strolled over to our table, greeted Robert
and Rosemary and then turned to me for an introduction. I mentioned that we had talked earlier about playing on the Stack tennis court and that I understood that she played there all the time.
The actress took a deep breath, which extended her ample bosom
even farther. A simple gold chain fell into her cleavage as the
polyester two-piece outfit she wore stretched. "All the time? Oh,
no," she meaningfully insisted. "I spread myself all over town!"

One day Douglas announced that he had chartered a yacht

to take us and a few other people for a two-day cruise along the California coast. It promised to be a pleasant jaunt, finishing with a lobster and champagne dinner in Santa Monica harbor. Jack and Phyllis Nugent were called ship-to-shore to join us at the pier to be picked up for the dinner that Douglas decided I was to host.

Glowing with a vibrant suntan, I donned a Balinese sarong borrowed from Allegra. I wore a Tunisian silver necklace over my bare chest and tossed my golden, salt-bleached locks in a shake of readiness. Jack was very much a New England, JFK kind of guy, in his Topsiders and simple cotton sportshirt. He looked askance at me during our introductory comments. His wife Phyllis had an easygoing manner and a broad smile. When Jack finally asked me if I was going to get dressed for dinner, I fingered my solitary necklace. "Oh, yes," I replied. "I am going to put another necklace on!" Phyllis laughed and we formed a lasting friendship.

Bearded in the Pacific.

I left Holmby Hills and the internal war without truce for the peaceful retreat of New Mexico. The Campbells thought about my invitation to visit. They decided to come to Santa Fe. We chartered a small plane and swooped over the Canyon de Chelly and other picturesque sights in the Four Corners. I explained that my little house was very simple, but they insisted it would be okay with them. I wanted to make a gesture to repay them for their hospitality, yet felt my abode was inadequate. It was. Douglas told Allegra loudly that he would not spend the night there; La Fonda Hotel was more to his liking, and he made arrangements to move there. Allegra was mortified that he had humiliated me, and he would continue to do so. Knowing that I liked Phillip van Rensselaer, he told me that Phillip had died. I did not know that this was a lie, a perverse invention on his part. We were driving across the high desert, possibly to Taos. Douglas was never content until he had someone in tears. It was my turn to weep. I was glad when Douglas and Allegra went back to Holmby Hills, although I felt sorry for Allegra. The marriage was doomed and Allegra was the worse for it. She had developed rheumatoid arthritis, probably resulting from the continual strain. Douglas also managed to leave her financially strapped after an ugly divorce.

I returned to Santa Monica in time for the Nugent's New Year's Eve party. It was a delightful way to bid farewell to 1972. I stayed with Phyllis and Jack and helped to decorate their beach house, which had once belonged to Harold Lloyd. Nestled between what had been Marion Davies's beach house, where her benefactor William Randolph Hearst died, and the place that Mae West still owned but only came to on Thursdays, the house was ideal for parties. Patricia Nation was one of the New Year's Eve guests, whom I was to party with on an ongoing basis on subsequent visits.

I kept a distance from Douglas but managed some commiseration with Allegra in those last days before the divorce. At that same time, Maureen Feehan resurfaced. I had not seen her since London at the time of my "crash." She was soon to go to live in Oregon, where she would be married and become the mother of three children. It would take years before I would catch up with her again. But life consists of concentric ellipses that become vibrantly evident with constant networking.

When I packed up my belongings in New Mexico, I had the company of a young Navajo named Lee. He was an artist in need of recommendations to get into art school. I gladly complied, and he got admitted. His family, in appreciation for my efforts, gave me a strand of turquoise together with the ground, white shell discs called *hishi* that belonged to the family. I was to keep it "until." I accepted the honor and understood that the "until" was a subtle Indian way of giving it to me without officially doing so. Family beads are to be kept in the family, so I had them "until."

Margaret Jamison had reorganized her gallery yet again, now that I was no longer available for directorship. I still did some promotion for the gallery as part of my hastily conceived "Art Unlimited" that freelanced jobs in the art market. One assignment was to place carefully written publicity about Jamison Gallery artists into the press. This was obviously a gesture on Margaret's part to throw me some business. For a few months it went well, but I knew my efforts had to be placed in a larger market. It was time to make another geographic move to New York, where I could reconstruct my life more meaningfully—or so I thought.

Lee helped me load the U-Haul for our ride to New York, where things would be placed in my rented apartment within my family's home in Montrose. I bid farewell to Santa Fe at a fancy costume party given jointly by Margaret and her grand, super-rich sister, Betsy Bennett. After many festive drinks, I left the elegant Monte del Sol hacienda dressed as Rudolph Valentino, and got into the van to drive through the night with Lee.

When Lee left for school, I concentrated on forming theater design collections for institutions, using Ysabel's Fifth Avenue floor-through as home base. The Cooper-Hewitt National Museum of Design was preparing to open at the Carnegie Mansion on Fifth Avenue at 91st Street. I had given my orange cat, Tyrone, to the museum's administrator a few years earlier when I was departing for Spoleto. He knew about my theater design background and suggested that I help the museum update their collection. A small grant was forthcoming, so I began contacting many of the designers to acquire their work. The success was considerable and it did not go unnoticed by Lisa Taylor, who was to

open the museum as its director. Married to handsome, rich
Bertrand Taylor III, Lisa had ambition, intelligence and taste.
Gradually, I confided in her, she had such a nurturing nature. I
think our special bond came as we were walking down a flight of
stairs near her office. Quoting lyrics from a Bessie Smiths song,
"Nobody knows you when you're down and out," I revealed how
on-the-rocks I knew myself to be. If Ysabel did not offer me a
wonderful place to live, I would be destitute. The quandary for
me was that traveling in my world of distinction and elegance,
one could never reveal such an inappropriate state of affairs. I
had to continue to dress well and seem successful, or I would be
treated like a pariah. Lisa told me that I was one of the most hon-
est people she had ever met.

Various odd jobs augmented my modest income from the
museum project. Alan Klaum, a friend with a travel agency, asked
me to cohost a bus trip to Washington, D.C., to attend the American Ballet Theatre's performance there and visit the newly
arrived pandas from China as well as the French Impressionist
collection from the Hermitage on view at the National Gallery.
Each bus had a bar in the back tended by Alan or myself. With
relish, I served drinks and encouraged refills. Those drinks
greatly increased the money we earned. My bus was rollicking en
route to Washington, D.C. The passengers in the other bus noted
our glow at the rest stop and some of them left Alan's bus to join
mine. I remember a man who left *our* bus to go with Alan
because he could not read with all the partying going on. My bar
ran dry by arrival, Alan's supply was barely touched.

The last day presented a programming problem. Alan's bus
opted to skip the pandas, as the crowds for the Hermitage collection might delay getting in to see it. They decided to play it safe
and go only to the National Gallery. We, on the other hand, bused
over to the zoo and greeted the pandas. With time for a "pick-me-
up," my group made for the National Gallery. Upon arrival, the
lines were very lengthy. I hastened my busload to the front of the

line and imperiously informed the guard that we had VIP clearance to enter without waiting in line. The guard expressed confusion and no knowledge of the arrangement, but I insisted. Further, I stated, the rest of our party was already inside and it was imperative for us to leave together. He granted my wish and we went in to see the splendid exhibition. What I did not know was that Alan and his busload of visitors were still in line. A couple had noticed my group pass them by and enter without waiting. They left the line and followed us in. So we managed to see the pandas and the exhibition, all because of alcohol-driven aplomb. The return to New York City was another financial success for me, as the bar was again depleted. My thirst was attended to and my pocket had a small bulge.

Nancy King Zeckendorf, on the board of American Ballet Theatre, was with us on that trip. Years later, in the Opera Club at the Santa Fe Opera, she expressed how "off the wall" I had been. She was the one had who fed me a warming drink after my plunge into the decorative pool, in the spirit of Zelda and F. Scott Fitzgerald, at Iris Love's dinner-dance some years earlier. Nancy made sure she changed from my bus to Alan's as politely as she could. Her career, as dancer from Brooklyn and then wife of Bill Zeckendorf, whose family financial dealings were always the subject of dubious speculation, was made up of careful choices, a prerequisite to her social standing.

Eleanor Steber was going to perform at the Continental Baths in the Ansonia, where she lived. Anthony Bliss and many other top opera people made their New York homes there as well. The rising pop singer Bette Midler had performed at the notorious gay bath some weeks earlier to great success. "Black tie or black towel" was the dress code. Ysabel and an out-of-town friend were to meet me there after I attended Grace Bumbry's performance in *Salome* at the Met. It is a short opera, so I could easily get to the baths on time for Steber's 10:00 or 11:00 p.m. recital. Instead of going backstage to greet Grace, I hastened to the baths. With time to kill, I wandered around the cubicles to see who was there. An attractive young man caught my attention and he invited me in. Even though the door was closed, we could hear Steber when she began. I asked him why he did not go outside to hear the diva. The guy refused, saying he was not aware that this was going to happen in the baths and he wanted to avoid publicity if he got caught there. He told me that his name was Jimmy Goldwater and that his father would not appreciate any comments about his son frequenting a gay bath. Before the finale of the recital, I showered and dressed in my black tie, and entered the pool area where everyone was seated. Greeting Ysabel, she noted that my hair was wet. I later revealed the accessory details of attending a recital at the baths.

My birthday was approaching, which meant mandatory days of celebration, although bacchanal would better describe it. In Santa Fe, Calla Hay described in her newspaper column that my birthday resembled a novena! Jerry, no longer Larry Jones's lover, came to New York to celebrate our birthdays: his was the same day, but a few years later. We began with lunch at Uncle Monkey's. The costume designer Patricia Zipprodt helped us to celebrate. She wore a shirt she had designed for a Richard Burton Shakespearean role. Jerry was fascinated with Pat, as I was, but his fascination became an obsession. We drank and went for dinner with Uncle Monkey and then drank more back at his apartment. Pat, Jerry and I decided to stay the night and continue into the next day. On the third day of the drunk-a-thon, we bid each other fond farewells. Despite the extravagance and drama, there was desperation under the enforced merriment.

Ysabel's apartment was an ideal playground for an expansive alcoholic. My great friend from graduate-school days in Pittsburgh, Audrey Holland, was in New York with her new beau Bill, who taught communications at Hunter College. They came up for a drink at Ysabel's. I had my French friend Jean-Charles coming for a drink, too. As he arrived before they did, we played

around a bit in the living room. Just as I was appreciatively performing fellatio on his very responsive penis, he straightened his
position on the couch. I looked up and noticed his eyes on the
marble entrance hall across the long room. I turned and saw
Audrey and Bill watching us. I got up from my knees and greeted
them. After kissing Audrey hello, I said in a stage whisper, "Does
my breath smell of cock?" What else could I do?

Turkish beauty Zeynep Turkkan took me to a cocktail party
in honor of Duke Ellington at River House. Guests included
members of the Ellington family, and dancer-turned-choreogra-
pher Alvin Ailey, whom I had been eager to meet for a long time.
We had an immediate rapport. If "black is beautiful," then Alvin
was riveting. I yearned to get him alone. Ysabel had departed for
Europe and rented the apartment. I took a one-bedroom suite on
a top floor of the Hotel Wales. It had become ramshackle with
neglect but had the distinction of being designed by Stanford
White at the turn of the century. I lived there in exchange for
doing restoration work in the lobby. Its coffered ceiling cried out
for repainting. The horrid green had to be replaced by cream and
gold; the walls had to be stripped of hideous papers and painted.

Ailey was intrigued by my talk of forming an Alvin Ailey Collection of designs based on original works created for his ballets
over the years. I invited him to come up and see me on an
arranged date. I was going to a white-tie-and-tails waltz party that
night but he could come up before that, which he did. He helped
me get dressed, inserting buttons, studs and so forth in the complicated procedure. We were growing to really like each other. I
made a preliminary play for him but he jokingly said, "Whatever
would we do together in bed?"

What did come out of our session together was a plan to create the collection of designs for him. That gave me continued
access to his company and a glimpse into the Ailey dancers' daily
regime. Judith Jamison was his leading female dancer. She was
going to dance a role based on Bessie Smith, and she wanted to

view footage of the singer from the archives of the Museum of
Modern Art. A private viewing was arranged and I got myself
included.

Alvin inscribed a photo he gave me. He thought I was
"Quite, quite divinely crazy!" In conjunction with his new season,
my exhibition of the Alvin Ailey Design Collection opened at the
City Center. At the party afterward, I met again the extraordinary
Lena Horne. I reminded her that I
still had her raincheck for a dance
since the St. Regis Roof wedding
of Hal Prince to Shirley Chaplin.
Grace and charm personified, she
nodded and claimed to remember
her promise.

Uncle Monkey counted on
my company more and more.
Nina invited us to visit her in
Falmouth. It was not far from Provincetown, where her sister Grace
owned a beachfront house. The
ground floor of it was for rent,
which Uncle Monkey decided to
do so that he could have a change
from the Upper West Side. The
proximity to so much gay activity
was an added attraction for him.

". . .Quite, quite divinely crazy."

I completed the monumental Hotel Wales lobby facelift
and gave up the corner apartment with the view of the reservoir
in Central Park, packing for a couple of months on Cape Cod
with the old gentleman. We got along terrifically well when the
vodka consumption was kept at just the right flow. Too much
made him unstable and irrational; too little made for unremitting
grumpiness. Naturally, I was fine all the time, or so I had everyone believe.

Alley-catting and drinking defined those months on the Cape. I itched to get back to Santa Fe for the early part of July. The Bells loaned me their guesthouse on the Pecos Trail. I took Barrie Bell, their lovely daughter with tunnel vision (the result of a motorcycle accident) to the opening of the Santa Fe Opera, saw friends and caroused before continuing west to California via Phoenix. I hopped from friend to friend, hoping not to stay too long to become tedious to anyone. Drinks flowed as did my charm, which I thought helped to pay my social debts. After visiting the Adlers, whom I knew from their patronage of the Jamison Galleries in Santa Fe, I made my way to Chattaugua Boulevard in Santa Monica.

Near the Nugents but nearer still to the Friendship Tavern, the Tumble Inn was cheap and convenient to everything I wanted. Between a gay bar and a gay restaurant and a very brief walk to the gay beach, my no-tell motel provided an ideal nest. The older woman who managed it had been in the movies at one time; her faded headshot hung in the office. When I asked her why she charged only double rates for the rooms, she replied, "No one stays here alone for very long!" I know I did not.

George Michaud and I had driven up the coast to San Francisco the year before and partaken of gay, abandoned times there. This time, I went by myself by Continental Bus. I heard about a guest hotel in Chinatown that catered to gays. I checked in there to meet a few interesting guys. One of the most interesting guys, though, I met in a restaurant at lunchtime. It was a family-style restaurant, where you took a seat at a large table with other diners. He sat next to me and we talked. Each liking to hike, we agreed to meet the next day. We did go hiking in the mountains and had a torrid cocktail hour, too, but I was not allowed to spend the night. He had an arrangement with his girlfriend that precluded night visitors. So he checked me into a Chinese-run hotel in Chinatown, right across the busy avenue from my previous dwelling. Being ditched after an intimate afternoon was a disappointment. It was enough to drink over, which I did then and on many other occasions.

The alcohol trail led me back to Santa Monica and to Santa Fe. I had arranged to be the tour leader to "The Land of Enchantment" for Alan's travel agency in New York. Some of my friends signed up. While in Spoleto with my design gallery, I had met a spirited, humorous woman from West Virginia, Eloise Long. She was on the Metropolitan Opera's National Council. Whenever she came to New York, I went with her to the opera and social functions. She was a wonderful fairy godmother. Being a "walker" is useful, sometimes a lifesaver. Eloise brought along her daughter Margo and her husband Christopher from Boulder, Colorado. A few other ladies signed up from New York, too.

My plan for the junket was to have a few wonderful homes belonging to friends opened for visitors so that they could appreciate how Santa Feans lived. Also, they would see them at the opera, making the scene more familiar to the visitors. One of the most impressive homes belonged to Nancy Thomson Taylor, who was becoming a valued friend of mine. Nancy could still walk a bit, with the help of crutches. A polio sufferer dating to World War II, the attractive brunette had had two husbands, and two children from the first marriage. We bonded over the years over many glasses of scotch and champagne. Bertha Dutton arranged a special welcome at the Navajo Museum, and the Bells did something at the ranch for all of us. The junket was a success, owing to my arrangment of picnics in Indian ruins, visits to reservations for tribal dances and my many local friends.

After the tour, Nancy took me to dine at the New Mexico home of Washington, D.C. bigwigs Susan and Christian Herter. North of the Pojoaque Pueblo, their view of the desert formations was spectacular. The editor of the *New Mexican* newspaper was there with his Hungarian wife, whose daughter Edmée became a friend. Edmée and her two young children returned to New York on the same flight I was on, giving me an opportunity to know the

sensitive young woman better and to help her cope with two restless kids in flight. Her very conservative husband I had met years
earlier when I was squiring Nannette Cavanagh. But their marriage did not seem to be able to sustain itself, so Edmée was next
seen at my exhibition at the Cooper-Hewitt a few years later with
another man, who would change
into yet another man, the son of one
of my best friends, Valli Firth. He
married Edmée.

During this period of vaga-
bonding to New Mexico and California, a Provincetown friend,
Ginny McKenna, was free to join
me on one of these jaunts. We
stayed at the Bell's guesthouse and
later hitchhiked to California and
back, with a stopover at the Grand
Canyon to celebrate her birthday
under moonlight. That caper was
full of amusing anecdotes, after the
fact. While we were hitching on a
highway in the Arizona desert, a
police car stopped. We were asked
for ID and informed that hitching

*Ginny hitches with me across
the wild West.*

there was not against the law but they wanted to know who was
out there in case something happened to us. It was for our protection, not the drivers'. One ride was made in the cattle pen of a
truck driven by an Indian squaw whom we thought might be
delivering us into white slavery. Another car, packed with
drunken Indians, squashed us in with them, empty vodka bottles
rolling about underfoot. They were jolly after having finished
picking potatoes somewhere.

Our entrance to the dignified El Tovar Lodge on the rim of
the Grand Canyon was unusual. A hippie van drove us into the

porte-cochere. The uniformed doorman was startled by the wildly painted vehicle and the rock music emanating from within. We descended with only one small suitcase and proceeded into the lobby as if we were royalty. The scariest episode was on our way back to Phoenix. A self proclaimed ex-con asked me to drive his car. Rambling, he claimed to have a trunk full of guns. He was going to get even with the world that had sent him unjustly to prison. Sizing Ginny up, he asked me if I would trade the woman for his car! Quietly soothing him, we anxiously watched for the mileage to Phoenix to drop to zero. Each mile seemed an eternity fraught with fear, but both of us tried to seem calm. Upon arrival at the bus station, we made a dash to the nearest toilet to pee. It was the ladies room, but what the heck! Safe at last. We discovered how chancy, if not dangerous, a hitching trip across the desert can be. Cocktailing heavily, we merrily wended our way, doubtlessly under divine protection. Upon return to Santa Fe, "Ma Bell" chastised me for the risky hitching caper and wished us a safe return by plane to New York.

Greta Keller returned to New York to sing at the cabaret in the Stanhope. Notwithstanding many preshow drinks, I marred her performance by arguing with some arrogant daughters of Bilitis I was with about God knows what. Greta had to stop the show to request that we desist from loud talking. Happily, the women had to share the blame; but we were all friends of Greta, which made it more disgraceful.

Elaine's Restaurant was all the rage. Freddy Wittop invited me to join him at Elaine's with his life-mate, Gil. I was indignant when Elaine herself told us that she did not have a table, that we would have to wait at the bar like tourists. I haughtily informed her that Freddy Wittop, a genius of the theater, should not be treated that way and strongly implied that I should not, either. I urged Freddy to leave, and we went down the street to Pat Hemingway's.

Needing to relieve myself, I asked a waiter where the men's

room was and went to the door I thought he indicated. I found myself in the alley so I peed there. It did not seem odd to me that I was in a state in which I could not even locate a men's room. Life was a big, expansive party. Minor things were of no significance. Driven by alcohol, I was smug in believing that I could do what I wanted, where and when I wanted.

A One-Man Show . . .

One subject, many artists, different times.

Eric in his "Hall of Fame" bathroom.

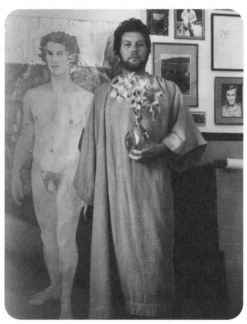

Artists whose renderings are not included are R.C. Gorman, Porter Jean Dunaway, and Cynthia Bissell.

Chapter 12

GAILY LIT BOULEVARDS

"They were so big, they were so black," Ysabel murmured. It was not yet dawn, but we each stirred from sleep at the same time. As only couples who have spent years together do, I instantly knew Ysabel's frame of reference. Our minds were focusing on the same incident from the previous night. "Did I do the right thing? . . . Kissing them?" I mumbled, still half-asleep in her oval bed. Ysabel sat bolt upright in bed: "It was mandatory! It was obligatory! You were the only man there!"

As culmination of an ongoing competition between the illustrious opera star Grace Bumbry and Ysabel, a tit contest had been held in the quiet of Grace's bathroom. The rivalry began jocularly when Grace arrived at a birthday party Ysabel threw for me. She was wearing the multicolored off-the-shoulder gilded gown that she had worn at the closing of the old Met. Grace did not know what she was in for when she entered that marble hallway. I had decided to wear a white Mexican wedding dress, since Ysabel was wearing a long white lace dress. As it was see-through, I put on my well-worn gilded bikini and placed a pre-Columbian gold piece in the front as a crotch decoration. It was my birthday and I was the guest of honor, so I decided I did not have to wear black tie as the other men were instructed to do. Startled to see me in the white dress, Grace then met the hostess-in-white. Ysabel crooned, "Oh, Grace, I read about your standing ovation at the Met last night. How thrilling! But, you know I sing better than

251

you do!" I expected Grace to fume and stomp out. Rather, she sized up the impertinent hostess and playfully patronized her. I introduced the Navajo artist R.C. Gorman to the diva. He was thrilled at the prospect of meeting the celebrated singer and nervously touched her shoulder, asking, "Is that your real color?" I almost fainted. Grace looked down at his finger and up at his brown face and replied, "Yes, is that yours?" She was more of a trouper than I expected. Shortly, Grace and Ysabel were hiking up their evening gowns, comparing their legs.

On and on it went, continuing weeks later at Grace's party. While distinguished figures from the music world were mingling, enjoying a dinner party Grace gave in her apartment, the two women were comparing boobs. When I knocked on the door, having heard their voices within, Ysabel directed Grace to let me in and have me decide. Grace undid her bodice, revealing two very ample breasts. Glancing at both sets of mammaries, I leaned over and kissed Grace's nipples the winners.

Grace Bumbry after a supreme performance.

Before leaving for that party, Ysabel had been taking far too long in her elaborate preparations. I left her at "955" so that both of us were not tardy for Grace. Ysabel told me to go on ahead, she would be there soon. "Where's the *prima donna assoluta*?" Grace asked me upon entering. I assured her she would be along shortly. John Coveney, the head of Angel Records, asked me who was expected. Several music world bigwigs started trying to figure out the *prima donna assoluta*'s identity. Maria Callas was out of town, they noted. "You will see," I parried their inquiries. It took much longer for Ysabel to arrive than expected. When she finally appeared, she told us the amusing story of getting there. When she had gotten off the elevator, she had gone to an apartment where a party was in progress. Downing two martinis while talking with acquaintances who happened to be there, she inquired, "Where's Grace, and where's Eric?" No one knew who she meant. It was the wrong apartment!

Ysabel told Grace that upon entering she had noticed how well her hostess danced. "Well, finally a compliment," Grace said in French. "And, to use a French phrase, there is something else that I do better than you, and that is fucking!" Ragnar Ulfung, a tenor of noted amorous proclivity, wandered by and heard the comment. He leaned over and suggested that he be allowed to be the judge of that! Diva and ersatz diva were a stunning combination in tandem.

To give some validation to my aimless existence and to keep the wolf from the door, I went on another trip as a guide for Alan's travel agency. The New York City Opera Guild organized a tour of Vienna and Salzburg for Christmas and New Year's. Ysabel was going back to Europe, having rented out her apartment for a year. She decided it would be delightful to accompany us before going south to Italy. Never one to pack carefully, she ended up just piling a few of her fur coats into my arms. We left for the airport in a state of disarray only to find our flight was delayed for hours! A cocktail bar was set up for the tour's use, and in our case, abuse. Despite the fact that I was the leader of the tour, I proceeded to get smashed before we even took off. It set the tone for the trip, which had several mishaps before finishing, all of them the result of alcohol abuse.

One woman in the group was particularly impressive. Alice Fordyce was elegant, imperious and gracious. Everyone knew she was the sister of the philanthropist Mary Lasker, who entertained royalty and statesmen at her annual Christmas parties on Beekman Place. I gravitated toward Alice, and she toward me. We walked arm-in-arm from sight to sight and really bonded at the dinner-dance in Schloss Louden, for which we all dressed to the nines. Alice wore a black ruffled Dior gown with boa. We waltzed in ecstasy over the uneven eighteenth-century parquet. Each of us discovered the other's passion for waltzing. Alice invited me to join her back in New York for the next Waltz Series, of which she was a member. She was a widow, perhaps in her late sixties, with a married son. I made her blush easily and gave her the expectation that she would have a dancing partner.

Life at the Hotel Imperial in Vienna was splendid, interrupted only by the visit of the Shah of Iran. Mobs of angry protesters filled the street outside, creating tension and havoc. Ysabel and I managed the same within, spurred on by excesses of vodka and champagne.

Alice had a woman friend traveling with her, staying in her own room. That woman invited me to St. Martin in the West Indies when we returned. Perhaps she thought I was "available," as I seemed to have cozied up to Alice. When it was clear that she and I had different notions of how I wished to spend my time on the island, she poured my whiskey down the kitchen sink and ordered me out of the house. I spent the night drinking, then sacked out with a friend of a decorator I knew there. In the morning, I fled to New York on the first plane available.

Alice commented that that sort of thing would not have happened if she had been there. She invited me to the eightieth birthday party for the legendary Josephine Baker at the Sherry Netherland Hotel. After the historic lady sang a few numbers, it was time for the guests to dance. I requested a waltz. To my delight and amazement, Baker stood at the edge of the dance floor watching Alice and me. She even clapped at the end and told us how well we danced the waltz. Another of my entertainment-icon thrills!

I was preparing to play the role of Christ in a new play conceived by a sexy Anglican lay priest from Australia. It was to be performed in the nave of the Cathedral of St. John the Divine. The director-playwright assured me that he would help me to develop my acting skills. It was an unusual reinterpretation of Christ: the guy ranted and raved a lot. My artist friend Nathalie played Mary Magdalene à la Emily Dickinson; an opera singer and a society publicist, also friends of mine, were cast in supporting roles. It did not make complete sense to me and I felt awkward in the role. However, it was amazing how many people came up to me

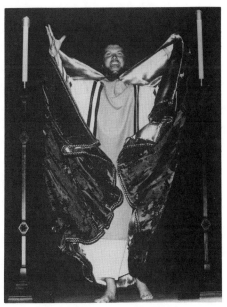

Playing a deranged Christ.

afterward to congratulate me on my performance. Uncle Monkey was there with Alice. The three of us went to dinner on Broadway near the Cathedral; I had no interest in going to the cast party. The director had bedded me more than coached me, then cheated me on my pay for the pretentious drivel.

Alice enjoyed going to the ballet as well as to fancy balls. Once, we did both in one night. She had expensive tickets to see the Royal Ballet and have supper afterward with Princess Mar-

garet and her husband, Lord Snowdon (a.k.a. Anthony Arm-
strong-Jones) at the Lincoln Center. The charity ball was held at
the Plaza Hotel and began with dinner before the dancing. Thus,
we saw the ballet but had to forego the supper following so as to
go to dance at the ball. Having subscribed to four costly meals, we
did not have a bite to eat! The princess was rumored to have been
in vile humor that evening. Could it have been because while
"God Save the Queen" was played, her husband was flirting with
me? The bouquet of yellow roses in her hands quivered. I
thought she was about to swat her husband with them. The
throngs of attentive onlookers may have deterred a royal tantrum.

The Whitney was having its invitational openings, which I
always attended. The public relations woman, Roberta
Montelbano, usually gave me a batch of free drink tickets. Once,
I sold several of them, pocketing needed cash. Then, on leaving
the museum, I sat in a museum wheelchair, asking my friend to
push me around the corner to "955." The guard did not stop us;
the doorman at "955" looked alarmed when he saw me in a wheelchair. "Don't worry, Tommy, it is only temporary." A woman with
a large dog passed me as I was about to enter Ysabel's building.
Her dog sniffed at my legs, but the woman dissuaded her pet
from lingering, parting with some sympathetic word. Upstairs,
Ysabel was reading and looked across her immense living room at
my wheeled-in entrance. "What happened, darling?" I sprang out
of the chair, laughing. She thought it funny, too. In the morning,
I called the museum to tell Roberta about my escapade. She was
glad that I did, so she that could alert the guard to expect the
chair's return, as though there had been permission to begin with.
Outside "955" the same lady with the dog happened by again. She
seemed startled to see me on my feet. "Yet another miracle," I
told her, continuing on my way to the museum around the corner,
pushing the chair along. I picked up some "thank you!" flowers
for Roberta.

One memorable evening, I escorted Alice to a charity ball.

There, I was introduced to a charming woman named Lila Tyng at our table. Little did I know that the amiable lady would become intertwined in my life for the next twenty years! Lila and I danced agreeably together and shared small talk, as one does at a ball. A few days later, Alice greeted me in her United Nations Plaza apartment with a piece of blue notepaper in hand. She told me that Lila Tyng had just written to her, requesting that Alice bring me to a dinner dance at the St. Regis Roof. Lila was involved in the event. Alice asked if that would interest me. I answered in the affirmative, of course. Alice could not have known then that it was the opportunity for Lila and me to begin our long, deep friendship. It would inevitably spell the end of my being Alice's dance partner.

Alice invited me to her summer place in Sakonnet, where one viewed Newport over their trashcans. I prided myself in getting uptight Alice to drink magnums of champagne, rather than tiny splits that did not have the same flavor or verve. We even enjoyed them in the morning, as Ysabel would have. One of my favorite tasks at Sakonnet was to create dinner-table decor. I wanted to show my appreciation for the many kindnesses that Alice had bestowed upon me. I waded into a lily pond and plucked a water lily. To keep the blossom from closing, I dripped white candle wax on its petals. I floated the lily on top of water in a large brandy snifter. The spotlight above the table pinpointed the white lily. When the guests sat down, they could see below the lily. A conch shell was placed in the bottom of the snifter. On one of its uppermost protrusions dangled a large tear-shaped pearl with a ruby set above it. It was one of Alice's costume jewelry earrings that took on an air of underwater treasure.

Lila began inviting me frequently to Lu Shan, in New Jersey. The house had been built for her by her first husband, Henry Luce, publisher of *Time, Life, Fortune* (which Lila had named) and other magazines. By selling the first weekly news magazine, he made out very well at the end of the Depression. They searched for a location convenient to New York City for a country house in which to bring up their two boys. The French-style chateau was the result of Lila's francophile tendencies, together with those of her ever-present mother, "Muddie." Lila claimed to have built the walls to accommodate the French furniture she and her mother had collected early in her marriage, while living in New York City and later Ohio. In the winter of 1939, Lila and the boys were ensconced in the wonderful estate. The son of a Presbyterian missionary to China, Henry Luce did the unthinkable: he fell hopelessly in love with another woman and was never to spend a night in the place. A very determined Clare Boothe fascinated him to distraction. He asked the totally unaware Lila for a divorce so that he could marry Clare. It was called the American "divorce of the century." Over the years, I pieced together the many intricacies of the tapestry of the life of Lila Hotz Luce Tyng, slowly at first, because I ambled between Sakonnet and the ever-enticing visits to California via Arizona and New Mexico.

Northern New Mexico beckoned to me annually. "The Land of Enchantment" nourished my parched soul. It was also an open invitation for celebration, as that is what my friends did best. A friend decided we should drive a drop-off car to California as a cheap means of going west. We made arrangements with a New York office, and agreed to get the car to Los Angeles within a ten-day period. The Tumble Inn in Santa Monica was available for pleasure, as always. How transitory those pleasures were, and I found myself doing the rounds in New York again by autumn.

Holly Woodlawn, star of Warhol's *Trash,* which I had seen stoned on those pot brownies, was introduced to me at a New York gallery opening. I found the transvestite endearing, promising to catch her show at the Grande Finale. In a none-too-rare moment of bizarre creativity, I had a wrist corsage delivered backstage, an anthurium whose pistil penetrated an orchid. With that less than subtle pornographic floral delight I sent a large plastic bag full of colored blown-up balloons. Inside, in clear view

"Love you madly"
—*Holly Woodlawn*

was an autographed black-and-white glossy of me looking vigorously butch and healthy! Holly was delighted; she carried on like the winner of a lottery afterward. She took to sending me gushy love notes with big lipstick kiss marks sealing the envelopes. We played at attraction, but despite a couple of sheeted adventures, it never went anywhere. The last attempt was after a Museum of Modern Art experimental film screening. Holly came up to my East Side apartment for a brief romp. When it was time to leave, I stood naked at the door and mentioned that he/she could easily pick up a taxi outside. Holly, outraged that I did not get dressed to secure a ride home for her, slapped me hard across the face. "That's no way to treat a lady," she snarled and stomped down the stairs. I think we were both drama queens in search of a vehicle.

The Met auditions came and went every year with fairy godmother Eloise always appearing and having me walk her around to dinners, social functions and opera performances. Annually, Eloise and her counterparts from various cities in America gathered at the Waldorf. Two other elderly women from Minneapolis and Wichita joined Eloise and me at Peacock Alley in the Waldorf for a nightcap. It was a ritual. One night, a young man with a woman who seemed to be his wife looked over at me with the older women in their gowns, furs and jewels. He commented to me how lucky I was to have three attractive dates. "They are not my dates," I blurted in a moment of abandon. "They work for me. On Monday, this lady works the lobby; on Tuesday . . . " I indicated another of the ladies. "You mean, they are . . . " he inquired in stunned disbelief. "Yes," I said, "and if the woman you are with would like some work . . . " My dowagers suddenly became "youthful" with the enchanting notion of being "ladies of the night." We had a wonderful laugh over my outrageous notion.

Another time, the same three ladies were impressed when Zsa-Zsa Gabor approached, on the arm of Huntington Hartford. I knew Hunt from various parties at Allegra's when she was still in New York, working at the United Nations. Zsa-Zsa I had recently come across at a friend's home in the Santa Monica Canyon. A Hungarian noticing a handsome young man with three dowagers in the Waldorf would have set off a bell or two. I was delighted that I could generate further esteem in my friends' eyes with the acknowledgment from the two celebrities.

Eloise met Ysabel at "955" and I think had some reservations about her influence on me. This was tinged with a degree of jealousy, although Ysabel was a bit outlandish for the more sedate West Virginian. I do not think Eloise ever met Lila, as I was not yet enmeshed with life at Lu Shan at that point.

One of the last times I saw Eloise before her stroke was when we were invited to Alice Tully Hall to attend the premiere of a new opera. Someone I knew was producing it, and he decided Eloise would be a good benefactor to cultivate for the future. Instead of having us sit together, he gave me ticket elsewhere in the theater. It was clearly an affront to me and a means of having Eloise to himself. I took my ticket and gave it away to a stranger in the lobby, wishing both of them a good evening. In black tie, I walked the short distance to the Met, where Baryshnikov was performing with the American Ballet Theatre. The house manager told me that the house was full but that he would give me a box seat that had other people in it. He reminded me that his wife was a young opera singer and that she could use some publicity. As I wrote an occasional piece for *Opera News*, thanks to my friend the editor, Bob Jacobson, the bribe was obvious.

There, sitting in the box in a tasteless cloche, was Elizabeth Taylor. She had suffered threats when she turned to Judaism and a bodyguard was a constant in her life at that time. The bodyguard did not frisk me, but made a great display of doing so when I went to the dinner-dance at the State Theater afterward. How ridiculous, I thought; if I had wanted to harm Liz, I could have done it close-range while in the box. With great pleasure I told Eloise about the ballet and Elizabeth Taylor and the dinner-dance when I telephoned the Waldorf the next morning. Reports about the new opera were not thrilling. I suppose I should have thanked that conniving impresario for my change in program. I adored walking out of one would-be glamorous event, only to walk into something far more interesting.

Ysabel and Lila met on a couple of occasions. Although Ysabel abhorred the idea of being considered a lady, she had a deep sense of breeding and cultivation. With Lila, she displayed warmth and appreciation for both the exquisite taste that Lila displayed at Lu Shan and the individualism Lila expressed in her everyday life. Ysabel's days in New York were coming to a close and she expressed great relief that I had Lila in my life. She felt, as both Lila and I came to appreciate, how important we would be to each other. Ysabel knew that Lila and I had a symbiotic resonance that offered us a happy life together. Ysabel thought that finally I might find stability, with Lila's kindly influence.

The terrifying fact of suddenly waking up one day to find that the family's fortune had been dissipated was a shock to Ysabel. Ninety million dollars existed no more. How could that happen out of the blue? Well, it had not. It had been going on for some time but none of the women in the family took time to notice the signs and final proof until it was all over. Ysabel's mother had been named "Woman of the Americas" on two occasions; she began each morning talking with the archbishop and the president of the country by phone over coffee from her bed. Ysabel's father had been general of the Colombian Army before his death. They were considered the oligarchy in the country. Undercurrents of political power worked against them. Their lands were taken away for airports and road construction, with pennies given in recompense. A cousin was covertly tapping funds for his own bank account in Miami. Gross mismanagement and neglect finally left the family of three sisters and their mother stripped of the fortune they took for granted.

Regrouping was the order of the day. Country houses were sold off. The sister I had met in Paris came home to Bogotá to live with her other sisters and mother. The big city house was disposed of. The ladies lived together in an apartment in Bogotá. It was the first time ever that they had been reduced to such circumstances. With great pain in her heart, Ysabel dismantled her apartment. She gave many mementos to her friends and her son and his successive wives in New York. She attempted to live modestly in a rooftop *pensione* in Rome, but in the end she, too, went to Bogotá. It was hard for her to do. She hated the weather there. "Good only for frogs." Living under her mother's roof put a serious damper on her existence. Poor health and emotional stress brought her back to New York, where her doctor-son tried to help her subsist.

For the couple of years that Ysabel was gone, New York was not the same for me. The loss of "955" was dramatic for me, too. I shared a walk-up with a young man I met at a museum reception. We had a flirtation and decided to share the humble apartment. My nervous system rebelled, doubtless upset by my alcohol intake. I got lesions on my feet and my hands. "My stigmata" is how I jokingly referred to the palm wounds that might suddenly open, spilling blood down the front of my shirt or tie. Sometimes,

my feet began bleeding. I
felt my socks getting soggy
as I walked. One day, Alice
gave me a pair of her
deceased husband's soft
velour slippers, which were
too large but comfortable on
my lesioned feet. My doctor
had repeatedly told me to
cut back on my drinking. He
told me I was an alcoholic,
and I readily agreed. I did
not see the reason to diminish my drinking though, as it
seemed to be a source of

*Martha Mitchell sounds off
at MOMA gala*

relief from the problems of my life. I thought I coped better
when I drank; I tolerated the condition of the world better with a
few drinks; I believed I needed alcohol to get through the day or
night. I invited alcohol to take its toll on me.

My doctor had social ambitions as great as mine. Many of
his clients were rich and famous. One June evening, he invited
many of his patients to dinner in a noted restaurant. It was the
same restaurant where I had thrown myself into the decorative
pool at Iris Love's dinner-dance years earlier. I remember chatting up a very agreeable Mrs. Warburg before getting to my feet
to deliver a ridiculous "Happy Birthday" toast to the host. It was
not his birthday, but what the hell!

The group were invited to a dance at the Museum of Modern Art. The blond, loud Martha Mitchell entered with me. She
made sure the press noticed us as we danced by, asking them not
to photograph us. The "Garbo" stunt worked again. Flashbulbs
exploded all around us. Eric and Martha Mitchell made the press.
It was not long before the poor woman spilled the beans about
Richard Nixon. She died under suspicious circumstances shortly

afterward. I liked her outgoing, unassuming gregariousness. It was clear that Martha Mitchell was a very needy woman and that she drank lots trying either to find something or get away from something. Whatever it was, she was manic. Nice, but manic. Then she died. Many people held her husband and "tricky Dick" responsible for her death as a means to quiet her.

On the lighter side, Alice took me to Cape Cod for a performance by Kitty Carlisle Hart in *You Never Know*. I was intrigued by the actress's presence. Being last to leave her dressing room after the performance, I remember the lingering, warm look she gave me. Unknown to me at that time, her leading man also bestowed many a warm look on me in years to come. Small world, indeed.

Lila began fashioning weekend parties around people both of us knew and liked. Ruth Page, a chum of hers from Chicago days way, way back in their youth, was often in New York during that period. Two books came out about the ballerina, who had danced briefly in Pavlova's company; studied and danced extensively for Adolph Bolm; and who had later started the Chicago Ballet. The Library for the Performing Arts housed her collection of memorabilia, with a party to celebrate. In the midst of all of this, Ruth and I developed a friendship. "Sky diving, Viennese waltzing and fucking have to be the three greatest thrills

Kitty Carlisle Hart in quiet conversation.

in life," I dared to blurt to her one day in the boxwood maze at Lu Shan. "I don't know about the first two," Ruth responded with her pixie smile, "but I'd agree with the last one."

Jane Engelhard, the uranium heiress who lived on nearby Bernardsville Mountain, invited us to join a select group for dinner at her estate. It was a pleasant evening that promised interesting company over dinner, with a dance in the poolhouse afterward. The notorious Doris Duke appeared, with a gigolo escort complete with Vaselined hair and a shiny black satin dinner suit. In contrast, Doris herself was a complete surprise to me. She looked glamorous in a white chiffon evening gown held with spaghetti straps. A graduated diamond necklace fell into her ample bosom. I had not expected her to be so well built or attractive. The necklace was incredibly well designed and fabulously understated. My Parke-Bernet training had taught me to appreciate the enormous value of that piece of jewelry. I was impressed. What astonished me most was the quiet conversation we had about the restoration of Newport that she was helping to sponsor, and Buddhism, of all things! She seemed admirably spiritual, which belied the nasty things I had heard about her lurid past. When the orchestra played a Viennese waltz, I asked her to dance. "I'm afraid I'm a little rusty," she informed me apologetically as we made our way onto the dance floor. The New York society columnist Eugenia Sheppard ran a piece in her column a few days later, indicating that "Eric Gustafson took the rust off Doris Duke but left her her diamonds." That prompted many a phone call to me from friends. I explained what the columnists comment was all about and everyone had a good chuckle.

Lisa and Bert Taylor had grandstand seats to see the tall ships in New York harbor for the national bicentennial. I accepted their invitation and appeared dressed as an admiral. Street vendors everywhere offered interesting things to eat; the subways were free, to allow sightseers to get around easily and to encourage people not to drive in the city. We ended up at the

Taylor's apartment in the late afternoon for a farewell drink. I was setting off to Phoenix to deliver another car as part of my annual pilgrimage to the Southwest.

I had plans to meet a friend in St. Louis for a champagne boat cruise before continuing to Santa Fe for the opening of the opera, and finally Phoenix. Driving through the night, I had vivid images of those tall ships. When I wanted a change of pace to keep me alert and awake, I reran Mae West movies in my mind's eye. I laughed at her witty, suggestive remarks; what a campy woman she was! Cleverly, her off-color remarks usually made it past the censors of that time. I resolved to write her a thank-you note for the pleasure she had given me as soon as I arrived at Phyllis's home in Santa Monica. Remembering that her house was very close to the Nugent/Harold Lloyd house, I promised myself to drop the note in her mailbox.

After delivering the car and seeing my dear friends Tony and Joan Adler, I flew to Los Angeles. My letter to Mae West was delivered as planned, and I made my usual rounds in the Santa Monica area: The Friendship Tavern, The Golden Bull and The Pink Elephant for early morning drinks. One day, I was thrilled to receive an autographed 8 × 10-inch black-and-white glossy of Mae West, delivered to me care of the Nugents. Mae came to the beach house only on Thursdays, and she did not spend the night. Her musclemen cleaned the sand on the beach side of her house, picking up cigarette butts as though they were barbells. Then, they would depart. "For Eric, Sin-cerely, Mae West" the photo was inscribed. It was quite a while before I noticed the hyphen between "Sin" and "-cerely," which made it even funnier and so in keeping.

Mae West's beach house had once been furnished in all-white. After years of use and disuse, everything was off-white, grayish and faded from the original pristine white. The house is elongated, with the end facing the ocean shaped like the bow of a ship, 1930s-style, probably because that was when it was built.

"Sin-cerely, Mae West."

Entering the narrow hallway, one was dumbfounded by a mural running the length of the staircase that hugged the wall: naked men painted in flesh tones, diminishing in size up the staircase, with a classical folly in the background near the entrance to the bedroom floor above. All the men were very well endowed and had erections painted in gold. At the bottom of the staircase, a small framed pencil sketch of a naked woman stretching backward over a boulder was inscribed, "Mae West, 1935." While viewing the sex goddess's bedroom, I surreptitiously opened a cachepot on her mirrored dressing table. In it were two objects: a cheap crucifix without a chain, and a bobby pin with a plastic butterfly on it. There was a white round bed and a chaise longue with a white mantilla carefully draped on it. That was the only new, purely white object in the house. At one time, it must have been a pleasure palace. Now, it needed sprucing up, which was hardly about to happen, as the place was for sale.

During my wanderings from New York to California, I conjured up the idea for *The Kaleidoscopic World of Opera*, a book in which I would interview a cross-section of people who made the art of opera happen: divas, directors, public relations and administrative people, musicians and supernumeraries. Finding my way back to Santa Fe for the revival of Virgil Thomson's *The Mother of Us All*, I interviewed the noted singers Helen Vanni, Ellen Shade, Evelyn Lear and her husband Tom Stewart, and the designer-artist Bob Indiana.

Robert Earl Indiana had made a big splash as pop artist and creator of the L-O-V-E graphic. He was interested in selling his original designs for *Mother* and I agreed to help him. Lisa Taylor told me that although she was interested in having them for the Cooper-Hewitt Museum, there was no money available. I next turned to Robert Lynn Batts Tobin, the theater design collector who had close ties with the Santa Fe Opera. Over lunch in the garden of the Compound Restaurant, I encouraged him to acquire the complete collection for his vast holdings, which have since become a museum in Texas. Indiana promised me a commission should this materialize, which it did, and I left for more interviews in San Francisco at the opera. I was never paid the commission of $60,000.

There was just time before departure from Santa Fe to attend a very wet *vernissage* R.C. Gorman was having. He requested me to wear the legendary layered blue chiffon trousers that Stavropoulos had created for me to wear to the opening of the Cooper-Hewitt. It was the only creation the "king of chiffon" ever made for a man. Gorman had read about them in the newspaper and wanted me to share the unique fashion statement at his show. He had a table of friends gathered in the back room of the Palace Restaurant following the *vernissage*. After a bluette from Texas departed, having secured R.C.'s autograph, I coyly asked him if he would give me an autograph, too. "Sure, on your ass." I stood up and loosened the top of the chiffon, revealing my right cheek. R.C. took his felt-tip pen and drew something there and signed it. When the next bluette appeared asking for an autograph, he suggested she ask me to show her the one he had given me. I told her where it was and requested $2 for a viewing. To my utter amazement, the little lady from Texas opened her beaded purse and placed $2 on the table. I lowered the trousers. Soon other curiosity seekers were lining up, $2 in hand, having been alerted by the Texan lady about the unusual artistry of R.C. Gorman. It was not until much later, in the shower of a Hispanic admirer, that I realized that I had washed off my livelihood without ever having viewed it!

Calla Hay's column about Santa Fe goings-on, *"Pasa por aquí,"* mentioned that I had gone to a costume party that week at La Fonda dressed as Quetzalcoatl, with a huge sunflower as my scepter. What was not mentioned was that I did not return home that evening but paid a surprise visit to the English conductor Raymond Leppard. While he did not object to my materializing in the darkness of night, he was dismayed in the light of day at the smears all over his sheets from my body paint. Then, there was the total disarray of his bathroom, with my discarded plumed serpent accessories that included a six-foot sunflower watering in his toilet! As delirious as the evening had been, morning presented a clear indication of how inappropriate my behavior had been.

Rick Brockman, who had worked for me at the Capricorn Gallery while doing his graduate work at the Fine Arts Institute and the Metropolitan Museum, now worked at the Phoenix Art

Museum. He planned to visit me at the Scottsdale home of the Adlers. We would take a swim in the upper pool, as the lower one had too much shade at that time of day. In the changing cabana there, Rick suddenly indicated why he had sometimes arrived early at Capricorn, when I was still in bed. Now married, he still wanted to experiment, so we did. I was very surprised and wondered why it had taken me so long to get his message.

That brief and pleasant interlude brought me back to the warm sands of Santa Monica, where I decided to spend my brief visit at the Tumble Inn. The first day, I was arrested with a divinity student from Yale for swimming nude in the ocean. The West Los Angeles police were out for vengeance, having been humiliated by a large group of gays on that beach earlier that week in a demonstration. It was a hideous experience I dealt with by plea bargaining down to the misdemeanor of littering. It left a bitter memory and an indication to be more cautious in my behavior.

My notes for *The Kaleidoscopic World of Opera* were growing. Over an early morning brandy or two or three with the wig department head of the San Francisco Opera, I was learning about Richard Stead's notion of being a "Confidence Man." He told me that Beverly Sills was not slated to be at the opera that day, which was too bad as I was running out of interview time in that city. As we left the bar and approached the opera house, I spotted a redhead ahead of us that looked like Beverly. It was. She greeted me with a hug and asked how everything was in Santa Fe. When I told her about my book, she said "Kaleidoscopic? Why I don't want to be in anything pornographic!" We laughed and promised to catch up in New York.

I lived out a peripatetic, desperate clutching-at-straws existence: wandering from one city to another, making a feeble effort to work on a book, staying afloat with celebratory drinks and reunited friends. "Gaily Lit Boulevards" germinated within me during that nadir in my existence. The bleak piece was written in one sitting, without changing a word, while brooding in Montrose during a particularly low moment. There were lots of those moments when I was at wit's end. Thoughts of suicide were frequent. I decided to kill myself by escalating my drinking, living more flamboyantly, ending with a glamorous, alcohol-induced flourish. I glorified those tormented writers and artistic souls who had died of drink. I belonged in their company. The only hitch was that I did not die. I spent more than another decade in an increasing blur, with more intense desperation than ever, after exhilarating moments of devil-may-care "bedaucheries."

GAILY LIT BOULEVARDS
I suppose
The culmination
Was that morning
When I looked into a mirror
And saw a bloated aging queen
With only the slightest resemblance
To my mind's image of myself.
The total of the various experiences
Afforded by a-quart-a-day rampages
Flooded my consciousness.
There was a mixture of delicious mad abandon
Tinged with embarrassing, aggressive bad taste:
A magic horror show!

It seemed at that moment-
The only moment possible-
The decision had to be made.
It was time
To hang up those roller skates.

I was thoroughly tired of careening
Down gaily lit boulevards
Only to find myself
At some dead end

Or in a darkened alley-
Usually with someone
I did not really want to be with!

Gaily lit boulevards can be fun
With all those vibrations;
Alluring inducements promising the unattainable;
Scintillating illusions,
Shimmering aspirations;
Nightmarish loss of control or proportion-
A topsy-turvy world
With little meaning
Outside of the quest for fresh pleasure
And an insatiable thirst.

Broken roller skates make a horrible sound.
Direction is lost and perhaps unimportant.
The lights blur,
Swim before the careening figure.
Few notice or seem to care.
The pulse continues;
Echoes fade
With new voices
Soon to add to the sum memory of
Inconsequentia.

There is no winner in this marathon block party.
Endurance
With grace
Is the badge inconspicuously worn
By the least of the losers.

Chapter 13

FALLING FROM THE REGAL EAGLE'S NEST

Father was improperly declared insane at Mother's instigation. He died a broken, befuddled man in an upstate New York institution. After his retirement, he had faced life with Mother on a full-time basis for the first time in their long marriage. Diagnosed with Parkinson's disease, he needed constant care, which she found overwhelming. She was used to operating freely, on her own terms. Father was a burden. It was about then that I began to refer to Mother as "The Field Marshal."

I gave a benefit at the Capricorn Gallery for the Parkinson's Disease Foundation on December 16, 1969, in conjunction with a major exhibition of theater designs. It generated much favorable publicity, which put me in good stead with the Foundation. I invited Beverly Sills and Jane Pickens, of the historic singing Pickens Sisters, to be hostesses. Celebrities from the performing arts turned out, Leontyne Price and Ethel Merman among them. Tallulah Bankhead spent an hour on the phone with me explaining why she could not come. She was not supposed to talk as she had emphysema, and how I adored the generous, madcap gesture.

273

Beverly Sills, hostess for my theater design benefit opening night.

The Parkinson's people offered to treat Father with L-Dopa. The drug was not yet available to the public, so it was a special honor to have the invitation to possible recovery. Mother would not hear of it, which led me to believe that a cure was not what she had in mind for Father—too inconvenient for her agenda.

Flo suggested that a professional man be hired to tend Father at home. She would help to pay for it, and perhaps others in the family would help out. No, Mother would not have a stranger in the house. He would have to be tended to elsewhere. To have it covered by insurance, she convinced her doctor that it was imperative to have her husband declared insane. It would be too much for her heart to take more of his ranting and strange, erratic behavior. She was very effective in her case. Dad was put in a local hospital for observation. There, he was tied into his chair so that he could not move around. Never having been restrained in this manner, he attempted to walk out of the hospital with the chair strapped to his back. They declared, "He's insane!" When we heard about it, Mother insisted that her heart could take no more stress. She would collapse and die if we made a fuss, and she would be sure to cut us out of the will before expiring. Her control and intimidation were absolute. I bristled with deep resentment, guilt and frustration at not being able to help Father.

My visits to Montrose became less frequent. When I did visit, I shut myself away most of the time. I took pleasure in shocking Mother or openly emulating my father's drinking. One New Year's Eve, I invited Ruth Warrick and a young man who amused me to come to Montrose. We had been invited to a party not too far from the house. Ruth wore a daring, plunging-neckline gown that caused gasps. Over it was a floor-length mink cape. It was beyond Mother's comprehension and sense of propriety. On our way out, we made a special trip downstairs to wish her a good evening. Ruth strode in smothered in fur, then briefly exposed herself in the clinging gown underneath. That gave Mother enough to talk about to her cronies for some time.

After an initial visit, I never again went to the institution to see Father. I thought that would legitimize the situation. To me he was dead. No amount of coaxing from Mother could induce me to approve of her action. On one of my trips to Europe he died officially, so I was not there for the funeral. I had long since buried him in a vault of resentment deep within me. I had learned to stifle feelings long before.

The Cooper-Hewitt Museum was open and going full swing. At one of the receptions, I met a short, bright-eyed young man at the bar, who had just been hired as curator of decorative arts. It was a very prestigious position, as this was the National Museum of Design. I noticed David McFadden had a limp, which inspired my sympathy. We chatted with animation, each of us laughing at everything the other said. It seemed obvious that I should go to his nearby apartment for a nightcap, especially as his name was David. In the sparsely furnished apartment he had only recently moved into we enjoyed more drinks while I waltzed

Visiting Royalty birthday party: Marie Antoinette minuettes with Gustav III.

around the parquet floors. He had some blue silk fabric lying on the floor, which I fashioned into a gown, doing an impromptu "Ethel Merman sings opera for your pleasure." My heart was captured by David IV; a whirlwind romance developed. Between his immense knowledge and my network of social connections, I could see our union as a dynamic one. We certainly seemed sexually compatible, and his leg, although withered from polio, was not an impediment.

Being so charming and well versed in antique silver, David adored coming to visit Lila at Lu Shan. He told her many fascinating details about her silver collection as well as the many other treasures that filled the chateau. We planned a costume party to celebrate my birthday. Everyone had to come as historic heads-of-state in full regalia to pay homage to young "King Gustav III's" birthday celebration. It seemed in keeping with my passion for the court theaters of Europe: Gustav III of Sweden during the eighteenth century had played a prominent role in that colorful history, for which I had a great affinity. I had just had another portrait of me done; this time as Gustav III. Having rented the costume for the portrait sitting, I kept it long enough for the party. Diane Spencer came as Gustav's great friend, Marie Antoinette, with a silk sailing ship on her head; Alice Fordyce came as the Fairy Queen; Valli Firth dressed as Eleanor of Acquitaine; and there was a Prince of Darkness and a Bacchus. David made his own costume, appearing as Pope Gregory. Lila was Li-Ping, Empress of China and all Orientalia. The servants and musicians were decked out in Chinese regalia befitting the court of the empress.

Invitations had been sent from Venice using cards that showed the royal gondolas of the eighteenth century in a flotilla on the Grand Canal. Lila, her son Peter and his delightful but soon-to-be jettisoned wife, Ann, spent a couple of weeks there with me. I showed them the wonders of Sicily, Rome, Florence and Venice. I left them, continuing on to Munich and a tour of the castles of "Mad" Ludwig of Bavaria. My hostess on that trip was a descendant of Maria-Theresa of Austria (mother of Marie Antoinette). We passed briefly through Austria to reach Neuschwanstein and Linderhof castles. Theresa exclaimed joyfully how much nicer the air was there! My research on the court theaters of Europe gained greatly on the visit. I was preparing lectures on the subject and organizing a small book as a companion piece to illustrate some of the salient points and places that I spoke of. It seemed peculiar that no one before had amassed a compendium of information about the various court theaters in Europe. There was literature available on those in France, England or Sweden, but nothing summing up all the European court theaters. My work was cut out for me.

Lila and I began to make annual trips together to Europe. Apart from sightseeing, which we both enjoyed, she relished time away from telephones and social engagements to work on a book about her family. I heard the daily clatter of her typewriter while I read or wrote. Time permitted forays into the local terrain in search of historic sights as well as those of somewhat more dubious educational value.

Lila's eightieth birthday was approaching, with a large celebration planned by her son Henry to be held at the Plaza Hotel. The ballroom was hired for dinner and dancing; the adjoining

Lila preferred balloons to pearls.

room for cocktails. Our waltzing had become our trademark. She was so light and responsive to my every lead. Lila claimed I was the best partner she had ever had. We both displayed energy and enthusiasm for the dance and maneuvered fast spins, stops and reversals with accuracy and grace. Lila was enraged that her son revealed her age in the "fourscore" invitation, but she disguised her feelings, as was her nature. She gave an amusing after-dinner speech: "After the middle ages comes the Renaissance . . ." The orchestra struck up a waltz and I began to twirl Lila around the empty ballroom floor. Spontaneously, as we passed each table, each person at the table stood, applauding us. Spinning and spinning, we whirled about the expanse of the grand room with the applause growing louder and louder. Finally, everyone was on their feet showing their approbation. It was a thrilling moment, although Lila later claimed to be unaware of it as it was happening. I was stunned and delighted to have been able to show off the remarkable lady to her friends and relatives so superbly.

My research into the Swedish court theaters was about to reach fruition. I received an invitation to stay as guest of honor in the royal residence of Gripsholm Castle, north of Stockholm. Its curator I had met through David IV when Åke Livstadt was visiting in New York. I had had a brief encounter with the present king when he was still the royal prince, and I knew Björn Bexelius from our "sea battle" days and his wife, opera singer Kerstin

Meyer, the court singer who proposed the invitation. My creden-
tials were in order.

Uncle Monkey suffered a fall and was abusing the bottle,
which resulted in his hospitalization at Roosevelt Hospital. I went
to see him the day that I was to leave for Stockholm. Later, as I
was finishing my packing, the telephone rang. He had collapsed
in the hospital shower and died. Before getting on the plane, I
made all the necessary arrangements, including a *New York
Times* obituary. I felt loss and utter dismay. Lila and I decided to
hold a memorial at her Park Avenue apartment when I returned.
David promised to write. Ysabel was away, in deteriorating
health. I relied on stiff drinks to get me to Stockholm.

To my surprise, Björn was at the airport, as he was in the
neighborhood doing business related to his position as head of
the theater in Uppsala. Although I had been instructed to get off
the airport bus at the first stop, I was too under the weather to pay
attention and ended up at the Stockholm center station. Åke had
sent his friend Lars to meet me, but I did not appear. I had some
difficulty getting a taxi driver to understand where I wanted to go,
only to find no one there upon arrival. After a wait in an accommodating neighbor's apartment, Lars arrived. He let me in to
Åke's apartment and took me to bed.

It was exciting to spend a couple of days in the guest room
of honor at Gripsholm Castle. Much remained as it had been in
the eighteenth century during Gustav III's reign. The walls were
hung with the original leather decorated with painted designs;
many of the windowpanes were original; the floorboards
remained intact, as did the bed and small table. The horsehair
mattress had a catalogue number on it and may have been the
original, but I think the sheets were modern. Certainly, electricity
had been added. Alas, I did not have a valet sleeping in the alcove
reserved for that purpose. Sleeping, it turned out, was what I did
the least of at the castle. Research, food and drink seemed the
unending pastimes, with saunas, skinny-dipping and other

pleasures to consume the time. I read everything available about
the castle and toured the historic rooms carefully. Passionately, I
absorbed details and notions about the colorful history of the
place, both for use in my book-in-the-making and for the after-
dinner speech I was expected to deliver that evening.

The toastmaster arrived from Uppsala with individual copies of the various toasts for each of us. Agneta Hernmarck, the
king's representative, instructed me on protocol during the dinner. I could drink the wine or beer at any time, but the aquavit
was taken only after a toast was given, and there were many to
enhance and prolong the evening's festivities. I dutifully drank
when prompted, feeling emboldened with each toast.

The young king Carl XXIII Gustav and his German bride,
Queen Silvia, were at Drottningholm Palace, so Agneta stood in
for the royal couple. She and I had several delightful drinks in the
setting sun in the courtyard of the castle before everyone arrived.

*Agneta and Björn in front
of Drottningholm palace.*

I had some trepidation about
standing up after dinner to
give my speech of thanks to
the august assembly of
learned people. She lent
moral support and kept me in
good humor and steady until
it was time to acknowledge
the honor bestowed upon me
that drink-filled evening.

Invention being the
mother of necessity, I rose
woozily to my feet. Knowing
that bluff should always begin
in established fact for fancy to
work best, I startled everyone
with a comment about the
New York Times. Counting

on the improbability of anyone having been able to read that day's newspaper, I told how thrilling it was to be there at Gripsholm Castle, especially after reading the sensational piece in the *New York Times* that morning. I began telling about a sunken ancient Swedish ship, located off the Florida coast. There, a watertight chest was discovered that held documents relating to this very castle. I told the known history of monks having been on that spot, losing the property in a dice game to the royalty who later built the castle. I threw in a few Indians from the New World having come over for the king's inspection at that time, and then returned to America. The tale got more and more fascinating as the historians, curators and toastmaster hung on every word. They did not know what to think and they seemed confounded by my talk.

Agneta knew that I was making up much of it, and as she sat by my side I could sense her pent-up humor. I got to the part where a princess went up into the tower, indicated with my arm pointing upward, during a siege of Huns. Her returning lover had to be warned. She made a fire and removed her undergarments to increase the flames and send smoke signals. "That, ladies and gentlemen, was the first woman to burn her bra!" Agneta tittered; the group was appalled at my twisting history in such vulgar fashion. We all had another toast while I circulated my personal booklet of toasts, requesting everyone to draw or write something on the other side of the printed pages as a memento of this unusual evening. It is a wonderful conglomeration of doodlings, including a caveat about not trusting some of the people present, a drawing of the rune stone in front of the castle but with Verdi lyrics inscribed on it, and one sketch inviting me to a nocturnal visit in someone's room in the palace.

Leaving the rune stones behind, and bidding farewell to my room, whose first occupant had been Mme. Cederstrom in 1782, first lady-in-waiting to the Court of Gustav III, I departed Gripsholm Castle. Agneta promised to show me Confidencen,

Drottningholm and the Haga Palace of Gustav III in Stockholm. A small, delightful luncheon was given for me at the latter place by the curatorial staff.

That year of hopping about Europe inspecting court theaters and renewing friendships in Denmark, Holland, France and Italy gave me the opportunity to visit Freddy Wittop on the Spanish island of Ibiza. He and Gil had retired there. It was there that I hoped to receive some long overdue news from David IV. Nothing.

As usual, I had had the joy of dining with Sir Harold Acton at his Villa La Pietra outside Florence, where I made the acquaintance of the writer Joan Hazlip and Helen, Queen of Romania, whom I managed to distress after lunch. Sir Harold invited the guests to join him for a postprandial stroll through the formal gardens. Her Majesty demurred, preferring to rest in the enormous marble entrance hall. Thinking it a polite and thoughtful gesture, I offered to keep her company. "You must be about twenty-one years old," the Queen informed me. Forgetting that one does not disagree (or choose the subject of conversation with royalty or the Pope), I gently corrected her. Thanking her for the compliment, I indicated that I was considerably older. "I noticed your youthful gait when you entered, but I guess I am a blind, old woman," she retorted, punctuating her words with a stomping of her cane on the marble floor. Mollifying words followed. When the group returned, Joan Hazlip invited me to her villa with the notion that Lila and I might rent it for a couple of months to continue our writing projects. That did not work out, as we discovered other choices, the Canary Islands and Costa Rica.

My thoughts were often with David. Strengthening my network in each port of call, I kept wondering why I heard nothing from my love. My travels continued, my notebooks were crammed with information for the court theaters project, my camera retained for posterity shots of foreign places of interest with appropriately notable people. But what of David? After a couple of heady months of visits around Europe, I was homeward-bound.

Life as a homosexual is unusually precarious. The ready availability of hungry men ever eager to usurp one another's lovers and the lack of that structure which is automatically included and sanctified with the heterosexual marriage vows, make the situation rife with problems. Or, turning to my own case, was it that I was an overwhelmingly controlling, demanding flame who extinguished individuality in those immediately around me, consuming them with my needs and wants? Whatever it is and was, I returned to an empty nest. Yet again, that ill-fitting slipper—David had found someone younger, less overwhelming and challenging. The price for a strong, willful personality. I'll drink to that!

Paul Stiga, my theater designer friend, and Rita Simon, my artist friend and collaborator, encouraged me to mount an exhibition at Pace College, near City Hall in lower Manhattan. "New York Collects New York" opened to nice fanfare in the press. Photos of Ruth Warrick, Betsy von Furstenburg and Tammy Grimes, the opera star Maralin Niska and a sprinkling of theater designers and social figures circulated in the papers on the opening of the exhibition.

A few months later, Lisa Taylor, director at the Cooper-Hewitt, arranged with me to have a major exhibition of theater designs. As mentioned earlier, I had helped expand their collection of theater designs before the museum officially opened. Now, I curated "20th Century Theater Designs" for the Cooper-Hewitt, which was an instant success. All of the remarkable designs, many of historic significance, were for sale. The museum made good money and my floundering career was boosted, at least momentarily. Although married to a powerful, rich man, Lisa had started out at the Smithsonian, selling postcards in the gift shop. Lisa was careful not to reveal much about her past but I knew she related to my ongoing floundering in a hard world. We

To Eric – Blessing
Helen Hayes

Helen Hayes signed this to me at
her 80th birthday party.

developed a mutual admiration and regard for each other that was very special while it lasted. As director of the National Museum of Design, Lisa told me that she met a tremendous number of people, many of them very interesting. Having gotten to know Lila through me, she felt that Lila was the most unique and delightful person she had met in a very long time. High praise, indeed.

Lisa gave me a sumptuous formal dinner after the museum opening. This was one of my moments of fulfillment in having "arrived." Bert and she had a huge Fifth Avenue apartment that was gorgeously furnished. Many of the walls were hung in heavy Fortuny silk, which would have made Elsie McNeil Gozzi delirious with joy, as she owned the Fortuny factory on the Giudecca in Venice. (Once, while dining at Elsie's wonderful villa, also on the Giudecca, we were joined by a journalist from the *London Times*. He asked what Fortuny silk was like, not having done his homework. Before Elsie could reply, I said, "Fortuny is to silk, what champagne is to wine." She beamed appreciatively.)

On my left at dinner was Jackie Onassis's sister, Lee Radziwill, whom I found enchanting in her conversation and charm. Lila was on my right, with Valli Firth diagonally across looking dazzling in a Stavropoulos cherry-red chiffon. (The

cherry-red chiffon did not have a long life. One evening, at a dinner-dance at Valli's apartment on 70th Street, I engaged her in a
bit of exhibition dancing. I grabbed her hand, having wound her
up in my arm and instructed her to spin out as I gave her a tug to
unwind. Forcefully, she spun out into the room with me clutching
the torn red chiffon from her skirt that had gotten caught in my
hand. Being a lady of great elegance and breeding, Valli excused
herself with cheery words, hastily donning another gown. I
meekly handed her the ripped skirt with lame apologies. I was
grateful we were in the privacy of her home with good friends and
not on the St. Regis Roof or Grand Ballroom of the Plaza! Somehow, that never happened to Fred Astaire's partners in the movies.) Also at the dinner, my Argentinian designer friend, José
Varona, told me about the extensive collection of costumes that
Dame Joan Sutherland owned and used in her international tour-
ing.

Wanting to expand my reputation as a curator of theater
design exhibitions, I met with the head of the Library for the Performing Arts at Lincoln Center. I proposed putting together a
survey of twenty-five years of Sutherland's career, using original
designs, programs, posters and memorabilia as well as the costumes themselves. The exhibition would examine the designers'
intent and show how the costumes actually looked; then, how the
diva looked in them through photos and posters. If Joan Sutherland and her conductor-husband Richard Bonynge agreed to
cooperate with loans and lend their approval, I would have the
go-ahead. I wrote Sutherland and Bonynge to propose the idea.
As I would be attending a performance of *Don Giovanni* on
March 27 at the Metropolitan Opera House in which Dame Joan
would be singing, could I speak with them backstage afterward?

For years, I had never bothered with putting my name on
the list to see performers at the opera house; I just walked back
into their dressing rooms. This time, I thought I would behave
correctly. I had my name on the list and instead of bursting ahead

of everyone, I purposely waited at the end of the line. That way, I thought I would have more of the star's attention with no one left to interrupt us. I was surprised to hear my name called while I stood in line. When the pager found me, I was told to follow him. He announced to a very disappointed mob of well-wishers that Dame Joan was not seeing anyone but me! If that is not enough to make one's heart stop, what is? Imagine, the great diva would receive only me that evening! In all my grandiosity, I never would have imagined being singled out for that distinct honor.

We had a warm conversation, agreeing that the Bonynges would do everything to assist me in my project to get "Designs for a Prima Donna: Dame Joan Sutherland" mounted at Lincoln Center. I made arrangements for Bonynge to meet with me and the head of the library at a later date to discuss details. Dame Joan then bid him goodnight as he was going "off with the boys," she explained. She and I talked some more and agreed that I should come to their Brooklyn home to look at the costumes. Thrilled and elated, I went into the night whistling a happy tune!

It took a year and a half to curate and pull together that large exhibition, one of the largest mounted at the library. I chose my birthday, October 7, 1980, for the opening. It made it easier for me to remember for future reference. Otherwise, things easily got jumbled up in my mind. I decided to compile a list of all the operas Dame Joan had performed in, with locations and dates. Another list was of the designers. Then, I chose materials: photos, posters and memorabilia, together with the actual costumes. An exhibition floor plan was devised and placards printed, describing the exhibits. There was enormous resistance from staff in preparation for the exhibition. I was treading on other people's terrain, and the task of putting up a terrific display with little time allotted was challenging. I had a couple of helpers who were willing to put in long hours, but we were locked out of work areas when the regular staff went home. There were attempts to slow down and impede progress for the opening, but we persevered.

The press and public were highly enthusiastic at what they saw. One of the workers who had helped to install the exhibition told me on the sly, careful not to be heard or noticed, that he thought it was the best exhibition ever mounted in the space. Despite all odds, with next to no budget and little cooperation, "Designs for a Prima Donna" opened to critical acclaim. The Bonynges told me that they had heard nothing but praise, even from cantankerous opera queens who tended to be vicious in their comments. In preparing the printed program, I had requested an introduction from Lord Harewood, England's "Mr. Opera." He had been in London for Sutherland's debut as Lucia at Covent Garden in 1959 as well as her earlier appearance as The Bird in *Siegfried*. After a period of time, not receiving his response I panicked. I contacted Franco Zeffirelli with a similar request for an introduction to "Designs for a Prima Donna: Dame Joan Sutherland." Harewood's reply crossed with my letter to Zeffirelli. I ended up with two introductions, even better than my original plan.

R.C. with the Italian Navy in The Colesseum, Rome.

There was plenty of time before the exhibition opening, so peregrinations were in order. Having enjoyed attending Ruth Page's eightieth birthday party in New York, with sculptor Isamu Noguchi, the actress Geraldine Page, one of Page's favorite partners of years gone by, Freddy Franklin and the critic John Gruen, I departed for another European sojourn. As a result of recently having taken the Navajo artist R.C. Gorman on a whirlwind tour of Italy with his fourteen-year-old nephew who had never been off the reservation, Ruth Warrick asked me if I would make a similar trip with her. Ruth had heard about R.C.'s requests for me to introduce him to titled Italians, meet the Pope and a film star while in Rome, and "do" Florence and Venice. R.C. had raved so much about the people and places I took him to that Ruth had her inspiration. "Phoebe Tyler," soon to be Professor Wallingford's bride on *All My Children,* would be going on a honeymoon. Ruth had created the role at the inception of the program years before, and had achieved a large, enthusiastic following. As Phoebe was going on a honeymoon, Ruth had the opportunity for a vacation. The program made occasional references to Phoebe's whereabouts that coincided with our itinerary.

Traveling with a vintage actress has distinct drawbacks. I had pleaded with Ruth to arrive in Rome with a minimum of luggage. She appeared with twenty-three pieces of assorted cartables. Each day, we planned a program of sightseeing delights. No matter what hour had been chosen, Ruth was at least another hour delayed. I soothed my frustrations with a vodka, then two or three more. The brilliant morning sun became hidden by daily midmorning rain clouds before we managed to depart. By that time, I was under my 90-proof cloud, too. In various Italian cities, we were accosted by strangers. After countering their inquiries about whether Ruth had left *All My Children*, she would smile and slip her arm through mine and announce, "No, I am on my honeymoon!" I was observed by her fans with scrutiny and odd glances.

Sutherland/Bonynge interview in Rome.

Sir Harold Acton produced his usual fine luncheon in the villa La Pietra on Via Bolognese just outside Florence. Ruth and he were enchanted by each other. We strolled through his spacious formal gardens sprinkled with eighteenth-century statuary an ancestor had brought to the spot. We admired the outdoor theater where many a celebrity had performed. An attractive man staying at La Pietra accompanied us back to our hotel on the Arno. He posed with Ruth on her terrace for our cameras and then joined me in the small garden adjacent to my room in another part of the hotel. In conversation, I mentioned that I had interviewed Dame Joan Sutherland in Rome and indicated the tape on my dressing table. Commenting that it was worth its weight in gold, I explained how it would be broadcast over radio station WQXR upon my return to the States. Alas, it never came home with me as it disappeared at some point during my stay in Florence. It was lifted from my hotel room sometime after my remark about its value. I resolved to make another one in San Diego in September during a planned meeting with the diva, who had agreed to sign some posters and photographs there. Beverly Sills and Joan Sutherland were to make their only appearance together in *Die Fledermaus* at the San Diego Opera. I did not intend to miss that event.

Just after our arrival in Italy, Sutherland invited Ruth and me to hear her in *Lucrezia Borgia* at the Rome Opera. Backstage, she commented to Ruth apologetically that her acting consisted merely of throwing her cape one way or another. Dame Joan was aware of Ruth's career as an actress on film, stage and television. She claimed, in seeming modesty, not to be up to Ruth's dramatic achievements. I made arrangements with Bonynge to do a taping interview session in the coming days. Dame Joan claimed not to be able to take lunch first, yet her husband made arrangements with me for the four of us to dine at Ranieri's near the location for the taping. I learned that if you wanted the diva to do something, do not ask her; make arrangements with her easygoing husband.

It was fascinating to observe how a world-famous diva manages to escape an overwhelming mob of fans. A personable man in her immediate coterie backstage at the opera had a batch of small autographed color photos of Dame Joan. He stood at one end of a hallway distributing them to her fans. They flocked around him,

Waltzing in Venice with Ruth.

eager to possess of one of the mementos. While they struggled with each other to get the photos, Joan, Ricky, Ruth and I walked to the waiting limousine almost unnoticed at the other end of the hallway. A graceful exit with promotion built in, I noticed with some admiration. Our luncheon and taping went off pleasantly and smoothly with an evening of *Lucrezia Borgia* thrown in. Farewell until New York, we waved and parted.

Bernard Berensen's great Florentine villa, I Tatti, hosted a lovely dinner for Ruth and me. Lila had introduced me to the American couple who ran I Tatti for New York University. I had come to look forward to visits there as well as to La Pietra each time I passed through Florence. It was a supreme combination of privileges few people could boast about, and I was smitten with awareness of this signal honor.

Elsie Gozzi entertained us in Venice. She always treated me with deference. I was fond of her recollections of Mussolini, life in Italy and her run-ins with Peggy Guggenheim. Elsie had saved the Fortuny industry during World War II by wooing "Il Duce" into letting her keep her shipping intact, despite the war. Knowing his weakness for postage stamps and great-looking women, she sent him a large envelope carefully covered with diverse stamps. In it was a request for an audience with his august self. When she arrived through a succession of doorways down a long marble hall, he was stunned at her verve. She nonchalantly dragged a mink stole and wore a dress that accentuated the beautiful breasts for which she was famous. Our visit with her was the last time I saw Elsie. Her health was declining and she was unavailable again for visitors on subsequent visits. Only Elsie sported an olympic-size swimming pool in Venice, where space is at an ultimate premium. With her passing, Venice lost a lively bit of its history.

To complete our "honeymoon," Ruth and I spent a couple of days at the Villa d'Este on Lake Como. Stockard Channing dined at an adjoining table with a very handsome man, whom I quite fancied. When she was called off to the telephone, I glanced over at him. Catching his eye, I blurted, "Perche mi guarda così? Che vuole fare con mio corpo virginale? Eh?" The response to my blantant aggressiveness was like a lead balloon in a downdraft: I thought it hilarious to refer to my virginal body; he abruptly left the table. Ruth and I went out to the dance floor on the terrace overlooking the romantic lake. Knowing her penchant for exposing as much as possible of her "body of an eighteen-year-old," I cautioned her about provoking Italian men. During one dance with a man who asked her onto the floor, I caught the inevitable moment when the actress could resist no longer. While briefly turning apart from her partner, her hands managed to separate the floor-length skirt. For a moment's revelation, a gasp of surprise issued from the audience gandering at the full-length leg exposure. Then, all went back to polite dancing as though nothing had happened

The Furies were driving me onward, across the face of Europe, while Ruth returned to the television world of *All My Children*. While in Italy, I dined with Maria Luisa Belgiojoso in Milan, and visited the ducal palace in nearby Parma. Until World War II, when Allied bombs destroyed it, it had one of the best-preserved court theaters in the world. It was from that theater that Louis XIV's mother borrowed actors and technicians to bring theatrical arts into France. Giacomo Torelli, designer par excellence, was among them. Now, only the shell of the theater remains, with drawings of the original to stir the imagination.

Alfred Biolek, the star of German television's *Freddie's Bahnhof*, expected me for a few days in Cologne. Since he had been my guest in Tunisia, where I had appeared in his movie, he had been to New York. I had taken him backstage at Ruth's soap opera, where he was impressed by the high quality of production. He had invited us to see *Evita* on Broadway, and was amazed at how people swarmed around Ruth. As I was on my way to see Agneta in Stockholm, I had the long mink stole Ysabel had given to me to cover my bed pillows. Agneta was prone to depression, so I thought the furry object might cheer her up. Freddie was amused at my dressing up for the party he gave for me in his Cologne flat. I borrowed his Roman centurion helmet, donned the ubiquitous gold bikini, over which I wore a filmy gold and turquoise silk robe, and draped the stole down the back of one shoulder. It was a strange sight, for which only many cocktails could have provided the inspiration!

My hands often betrayed my stigmata and my feet still bled despite dermatology. My nervous system seemed to be in rebellion, but the Furies would not let up. My odyssey brought me through Paris, Amsterdam and Copenhagen en route to Stockholm, all familiar stomping grounds. A mandatory London visit to see my girls: Allegra, LoRaine and even Phyllis, who was now in residence in Chelsea with her wayward Santa Monica beach kids. She felt English schooling would enhance their social skills. Katya Douglas, from my Irish brothel times on the Embankment, drove me with a new chum, Rupert Cavendish, to Leeds Castle, where I had an invitation to visit for the day. Another day was spent in Brighton visiting the theater writer and critic Charles Spenser.

Other names and incidents blurred during the passage to a land I had long avoided from increasing prejudice: Ireland. I was finally going to visit Ireland for the very first time. In college, it was impressed upon my receptive imagination that the Irish had consistently suppressed, even burned books of which they did not approve. With only a couple of exceptions like Lady Gregory or Yeats, writers had fled or were expelled from Ireland. People such as Oscar Wilde, James Joyce and George Bernard Shaw were perfect examples of the artist seeking benevolent climes. It is true that the Irish monks had saved Western civilization's literature during what are called the Dark Ages, but the nineteenth- and twentieth-century history of abuse to artists in Ireland seemed shameful. Trying to achieve a semblance of objectivity, I decided to explore the shamrock isle. Adding to the new experience was the thrill of being invited to stay at Knappogue Castle with its American owners, Edwin and Lavonne Andrews. The delightful Houston couple had extended the invitation while dining with Lila and me at the Colony Club. I followed up, arranging to meet them after scrutinizing Dublin, Limerick and Waterford.

I was amazed at the spray-painted messages on the sides of buildings in Dublin that boldly stated with pride the assassination of the distinguished statesman Lord Mountbatten, with the additional question of who would be next? The IRA may not be synonymous with the Irish people, but why were such disturbing, ugly messages permitted? They were not only permitted but also flaunted in public with no intention of being removed. Such naked impropriety appalled me. To increase my disgust with the Dublin scene, I watched with dismay as the wrecker's ball systematically destroyed rows of lovely Georgian town houses. The recklessness against some of the only beauty left in Dublin seemed inappropriate and barbarian. So much for dispersing my prejudice.

Arriving by railway at the appointed time, I spotted my hosts on the platform. A very handsome, blond driver took my luggage while Lavonne and Edwin chatted with me in their car. We stopped for lunch at Dirty Nellie's, near Bunratty Castle. A delicious gin martini seemed to evaporate too quickly in my glass. Lavonne seemed to have the same reluctance to abandon the bar for lunch. She insisted we have another, to which I enthusiastically acquiesced. People like that really warmed my heart.

The next day, Sean Hanrahan was in charge of showing me around the neighborhood. He not only drove the car, but also managed the estate in general. He told me of his interest in acting with his amateur group, and he showed off the achievements of local artisans. Of particular interest to me were the molded wall hangings done after ancient designs, dried bog covered with worked metal. One, of an angel looking over the Three Wise Men, caught my fancy. Sean gave it to me as a memento.

Sean, too, caught my fancy, but I suppressed any notions in that direction after he talked of his wife and young children. We were inspecting a historic building that had a tunnel leading to the surrounding fields. A storm came up quickly with rain pelting down. We ducked into the tunnel as Sean said something about "capturing the moment." It was a propitious moment for a flirtatious advance. Even though I felt the expectant tension in the air, I resisted responding to the handsome man at my side. Just as well that I remained neutral, as some visitors seeking shelter suddenly popped into the tunnel. When the shower subsided, Sean asked me to look at a site he was considering in the woods, to which a historic chapel might be moved. We walked there. It was obvious that Sean kept checking to see whether anyone was around. We were alone and he made an advance. The pent-up yearnings in his closeted existence found expression.

Another blessing was about to be bestowed upon me. Back at the castle, my hostess explained to me that from time to time an honorary Earl of Knappogue was chosen. Lots of tourists came to the investiture and much mead was drunk. They decided to confer the title upon me! There certainly were perks attached to knowing the right people. How agreeable it was to have a title given to me; how appropriately in keeping with my fascination with the courts of Europe. Naturally, I would need a lady with me on the dais. Lavonne suggested joining me. "You could be my Earl-ess," I joked, playing on the fact that she was rich in Texas oil, oil being pronounced as "earl" by Mae West and others with Brooklyn accents. Not missing a beat, Lavonne retorted, "In more ways than one!" Wearing an ermine-trimmed mantle and holding a large ceremonial sword, I bid all the guests welcome in the Gaelic I had memorized beforehand. On the day of my departure, my host gave me a navy-blue silk tie on which is embroidered the image of the castle in silver, another memento I cherish to this day.

Returning stateside in August permitted my annual visit to

My "Designs for a Primadonna: Dame
Joan Sutherland" at Lincoln Center.

the white sand beaches of East Hampton. Walter Herlitschek's
home was a resting place for many a transient friend over the
years. It was convenient to New York when matters pertaining to
"Designs for a Prima Donna" occupied me. Lila invited me to use
the guest room at her Park Avenue apartment whenever I
planned to be in town.

Ysabel was in and out of the hospital. Her son was affiliated
with a hospital in White Plains. When she was not in a hospital
bed, she stayed at his home north of White Plains. I visited often
and was expected to supply her with her "lifesaver" vodka, despite
her son's warnings.

Rehearsals for *Die Fledermaus* began in San Diego in September. I flew out to redo the stolen interview, which annoyed
Dame Joan, who was soothed by Ricky. With many photos and
posters signed, programs printed, costumes steamed and in place,
we were ready. After many long hours and tedious hardship
imposed by the jealous in-house staff, "Designs for a Prima
Donna" began its two-month run. My tape was aired for broadcast and the publicity was terrific. Nannette Cavanagh agreed to

Sutherland/Sills in a unique performance of Die Fledermaus *in San Diego.*

host a luncheon for Sutherland and Zeffirelli to add further zest to the project. Zeffirelli was filming in the New York area and agreed to come. So did ABC, CBS and NBC! All three television stations found it an event worthy to share with their viewers.

The telephone in my quarters at Lu Shan rang one morning, just days before the gala luncheon. Sutherland's voice sweetly informed me that Beverly Sills had told her how exhausting it was to jet back and forth between California and New York. The performances demanded a requisite amount of rest. Dynamo Beverly had to be in New York at the same time as the luncheon, but she had managed to convince Joan not to come. It seemed evident to me that publicity for the other diva is not what Beverly wanted when she was in town. If that was the case, why didn't shrewd Joan realize it? She was obdurate. No, she was not coming to New York, even if the three major television stations were willing to cover the event honoring her. Luciano Pavarotti had a birthday at the same time. I heard from his agent that he would like her to participate in that event. She told me that they probably wanted her to jump out of the birthday cake. Perhaps that was reason enough to turn down putting my exhibition on televison. It did not happen. What did happen at the end of this exhibition was far more serious.

I had gone to London to deliver three lectures on the court theaters of Europe: at the Institute of Contemporary Arts, the

Slade School at the University of London and Croydon College.
On the day of departure from New York, I received a letter from
the Duke of Devonshire. It was in reply to my request to visit
Chatsworth, his palace where the Inigo Jones sketches for the
English masques were safeguarded in the duke's library. It was a
long distance north of London, near Manchester. The duke
invited me to visit Burlington House, now the Royal Academy,
that week, where he would open the exhibition featuring works
by Inigo Jones. I was welcome to go to Chatsworth, but the
designs would be on view in the center of London. That seemed
much easier.

Ironically, the designs had once lived in Burlington House
during the seventeenth century, before the ancestral Duke of
Devonshire married Lord Burlington's daughter and became
heir to the art treasures. I was going to be a houseguest of Rupert
Cavendish in London. He and his socially ambitious mother
could join me to meet with another Cavendish, the Duke of
Devonshire. Upon entering Burlington House with his crested
stationery in my hand, I asked the whereabouts of the Duke. He
was in the second room on the right, I was informed. With
mother and son Cavendish following, I approached the aristocratic gentleman. He spotted his crested paper and very cordially
greeted me. When I introduced the two Cavendishes, he seemed
disoriented and nervous. "You must be from the American
branch of Cavendishes?" he falteringly inquired. You could have
slapped Hazel Cavendish in the face with a clammy dead fish and
not gotten such a shocked reaction. She was utterly crestfallen
and humiliated. I found it funny, but I realized I had put the duke
at a disadvantage. He probably thought he knew any English Cavendish there was to know. Rupert's Swedish lover was delighted
when he heard of Hazel-the-Grand being accused of being an
American!

With only days to go before my exhibition was to be dismantled, I returned to New York. The Grolier Club featured a show-

ing of drawings from the Botanical Gardens in the Bronx, put together by my Montrose neighbor, Bob Long. I invited him back to the Park Avenue apartment after the Grolier Club reception. My plan was to feed him a plate of spaghetti with a bottle of fine red wine to wash it down. I hung up my formal clothes and put on a seductive striped silk robe from Morocco. I was soon to regret that decision. To get the water to boil quickly, I used the pressure cooker. Unfamiliar with a pressure cooker, I opened the top without releasing the pressure. Boiling water gushed forth, scalding me! The water came through the light silk with devastating effectiveness. Too bad I had not stayed in dinner clothes for protection, but who knew how stupid I was? The expensive bottle of red wine was in my left hand. I watched it drop in slow motion to the floor. My only thought was "Don't break!" while my right hand, happily, held the pot lid in front of my face so that I did not suffer facial wounds. However, my right side was badly burned. So much for my dinner and seduction. The doctor at the emergency room decided to flay the skin, to avoid scarring. A large area of me was anointed and bandaged. In pain, I dismantled the exhibition two days later and loaded the gowns for their trip back to the house near the Brooklyn Botanical Gardens.

The Bonynges were out of the country at the time. I wrote them that I had left the costumes at their house. Because of my injuries, I may not have left them as orderly as I would have ordinarily. I looked forward to doing the book about the exhibition to which they had so graciously assisted with loans of costumes and drawings. They had written to me earlier that they liked my idea of capturing the essence of the exhibition for perpetuity in the form of a book. Another letter from Bonynge confirmed that all was well regarding the costumes. He thanked me for kindly delivering them despite my injury, and wished me speedy recovery. There was a long period when I heard nothing further.

Between preparing for publication of *The Court Theaters of Europe* and lecturing on the subject, I received a phone call from good friend Paul Stiga. "Are you sitting down?" he inquired. I was, but I stood up, sensing something amiss; I prefer to stand in a crisis. Paul told me that Sutherland and Bonynge had published my idea for the book on the exhibition. The photo-art work had been done in Japan. It was boxed as a very expensive book; over $200 and was available at the Met gift shop. Appallingly, my name did not appear anywhere in the book. The only acknowledgment was to their secretary. I had been contacted by several people in different parts of the globe, inquiring about the new book about Sutherland. I had thought they were referring to one of the two other books that were in the making. What a blow to have my concept plagiarized. I had worked so hard creating the exhibition and generating the publicity for it. It was natural that I should do the book, and I would have gotten to it sooner if it had not been for the burns, and perhaps my insatiable thirst to wander, drink and carouse! Lawyers advised me that a title cannot be copyrighted; that, although they had behaved high-handedly and I had proof that I had originated the exhibition and concept, it would be costly and grievous to all concerned to pursue it in court. I was advised to drop any proceedings against Dame Joan Sutherland and Maestro Richard Bonynge.

It is amazing what surfaces when something like that happens. I would tell someone about their bad behavior and stories from others exposing what Joan Sutherland had done to them would be revealed. I wrote a letter to their domiciles, in Australia, Switzerland and Brooklyn. I complimented their taste in using my idea and title for the book they published. I requested a copy for the Apollo Muses library, which was in the process of formation. No response—ever. Later, in Australia, I held a press conference in Sydney. Albeit sympathetic, the press was instructed that Dame Joan was a national treasure who was not to be assailed in print. The story was squelched. The same happened on television when I spoke with an interviewer on a program equivalent to the *Today Show*. Any unfavorable mention of their beloved monolith was deleted.

Dysfunction in my everyday life increased; travel became more frenetic and the grim reaper was relentlessly active. Mother had finally become hospitalized and lost a considerable amount of weight. I went a couple of times between trips, tricks and pressing engagements to visit her. I was startled by how different she looked under medical supervision. She looked pathetic, incapable of having been a field marshal. The house in Montrose had long since been sold. Her life consisted of assorted objects needed for subsistence in a small apartment north of Peekskill. My sister Helen was dutifully her protégée-companion whenever possible. Flo stopped in from time to time as did her daughter, Lori. While staying with Gladys, dowager Lady Burney in Mayfair, London, I received a cable from Flo, sadly informing me of Mother's death. Again, I was not there for the funeral; I was conveniently out of the country, just as I had been for Father's funeral. They were laid to rest together in a plot on the north shore of Long Island. The idea that they are at rest together seems ironic to me; I can not imagine my mother letting my father rest—especially in such close quarters!

Ysabel wanted to return to New York City. Life with her son and his family in Westchester had reached a limit. Because she was so financially distressed, her son agreed to rent a one-bedroom apartment for her in the East 80s of Manhattan. He would write it off as a doctor's expense. Her oval bed was moved in, together with those pieces of furniture and paintings from the Fifth Avenue apartment that her son and others had stored for her. Constantly ill, usually in pain, Ysabel at least had a New York view and a flow of visitors not possible in Westchester. At one point, in the Westchester hospital, Ysabel "died" on the table: she claimed to have seen her body from above and observed a doctor working on the body. "He's not fucking me right," was her observation. Then she was revived. Advanced alcoholism, cancer of the uterus and other complications left her a shell of her previous self. She had a zipper on her chest so that doctors could enter quickly. Ysabel did her crossword puzzles, sipped strong black Colombian coffee, then switched to vodka or champagne. Her life was no longer vibrant or thrilling. She was immobilized, worn out with pain. She begged her son to give her something to end the suffering. "He is too much of a coward to kill me," she disdainfully remarked.

Often, I spent the night on her couch so that I could hear if she needed something. One morning, before her son was expected, she asked me to bring something from the kitchen. She needed to relieve herself but she was too heavy for me to lift into the bathroom. Her son had not thought of providing a bedpan, or a nursing attendant. For three days, she needed to be put back into the hospital. There was no bed available, her doctor-son said about the hospital where he was a staff member. In a few more days, perhaps . . . Glancing around the kitchen, I grabbed a large, flat frying pan. That should be easy to get under her. When Ysabel noticed what I had brought to relieve herself in, she was furious. "The silver bowl, darling, not the frying pan." The silver bowl had a crenelated edge I was certain would hurt her delicate skin. But, apparently, that was better than injuring her pride. Astonished but amused, I complied.

I returned to Lila's apartment tired from the vigil. The phone rang. It was Alberto, Ysabel's son. "Ysabel just died," he informed me with remorse and helplessness in his voice. I returned immediately and instructed him on the things that had to be done. I gave him Ysabel's bank card and told him the ID code with instructions to empty the account quickly. I helped him to facilitate her cremation, according to her wishes. I located a couple of close friends to help me organize various items that needed safeguarding. Alberto gathered the jewelry, giving me the pre-Colombian gold piece Ysabel had always referred to as mine. We all sipped champagne in her memory. A mutual longtime friend, John Githens, called to inquire about our beloved Ysabel. When I told him of her demise, he rushed to the apartment. After some commemorative champagne, he helped me back to Lila's apartment with some things Ysabel wanted me to have. We brought another bottle of champagne from her stash and opened it. That opened the floodgate of my tears. Frustration and loss, mixed with dry champagne and wet, bitter tears.

Later that day, I went out to Lu Shan. I fixed a strong scotch at the bar and took Chou-Chou out to the apple orchard for a contemplative walk. Until now, Chou-Chou had been Lila's German shepherd pet. The dog loved company, walking close beside me. I burst into tears thinking about Ysabel, sobbing uncontrollably under the apple blossoms. Chou-Chou pushed against my legs sympathetically. My glass empty, I walked back for a refill. In the Gothic Hall, Lila spotted me, stopping in her tracks. "What has happened?" She hugged me in sympathy when I explained the circumstances. Chou-Chou continued by my side. From then on, she was my dog. No matter where I was in the house, she would lie outside the French windows of that room. She took to sleeping by my bed and following me around. What a wonderful creature she was, such a comfort in the great loss of my beloved Ysabel.

For almost two decades, Eric and Ysabel had shared experiences that were thrilling and expansive. We shook up the world around us but always managed to be available for the many possibilities our bizarre lifestyle made possible. It was a rare and exotic land we inhabited in joy together. That was now finished. Ysabel had been glad I had Lila's environment in which to continue my life. I was glad the grand, poetry spouting pre-Colombian chicken had finally found rest.

It is comforting to realize that although losses happen, gains happen, too. A treasure in my hoard of friendships arrived in the person of a young playwright from Nebraska, Bruce Whitacre. Few people in my lifetime have been so attuned to my inner being as completely as Bruce. Our whirlwind romance soon turned to deep friendship, but we had breathless days exploring Cape Cod as well as my particular spheres in New York and New Jersey. They were worlds foreign to Bruce's immediate life. He was overwhelmed and amazed when I dashed off to Palm Springs/Rancho Mirage with Lila for a month's writing retreat. Then I returned to present a salon concert at Lu Shan, the beginning of Apollo Muses. A junket to Santa Fe and Taos, leading a group of friends through my beloved "Land of Enchantment" followed, giving Bruce another breather from my relentless energetic attentions. Then off to Europe for what was left of the summer. It was no wonder Bruce opted for another alliance, one with seemingly fewer peripatetic, manic elements built in. Turning a lover into a friend was, in this case, the best thing we could have done. In some ways, it was as good as any glass slipper could provide.

When Lila and I decided to accept Beneficial Insurance president Finn Casperson's invitation to use his newly acquired desert home in California as a writing retreat, we did not realize how beneficial it would be for us. Little did I know when we went to The Springs on Bob Hope Drive that I would return five years later, across the road on Eisenhower Memorial Hospital grounds in the Betty Ford Center. Between a life of utter indulgence and a life of reconstituting a shattered existence, there was only a road and an attitude adjustment.

Lila's younger son Peter had a new woman in his life. Betsy, a slightly chubby Carol Burnett type with a receding chin, arrived with him for a pleasant visit. In the plush antiseptic community set in picture-postcard desert beauty, it was assumed that nothing untoward would ever happen. The water sprinklers started on cue, the Mexican gardeners clicked their hedgeclippers and golfers hit their balls around the manicured greens. No other sound or activity disturbed the utter perfection of the day. Intruders could not gain admission through the highly secured gates.

Is it that the dramatic attracts me, or is it the other way around? One evening, I heard rustling in the empty house on one side of us. To my surprise, a bleached-blond and a burly dark-haired guy were putting things into the kitchen. I could easily see them, that is, by standing on the large wooden coffee table in our living room. I called Lila to join me. We observed them with some interest, as that house had been empty the entire time we were in residence. The next morning, our neighbors on the other side called me over. Casperson's previous CEO for Beneficial lived in that house, enjoying desert retirement. He told me that my neighbors had arrived. When I said that I became aware of them last evening, he urgently asked me if I had spoken to them. He was relieved when I answered in the negative. He opened the newspaper in his hand and pointed to the bleached-blond's picture. It was my neighbor! "Actress to be tried for murder of sixth husband." Sleuths at heart, Lila and I spent time perched on the wooden coffee table in the evening observing the kitchen of the adjacent house. We searched for telltale signs of guilt in the soon-to-be married couple next door. Our view was the only one possible into their secluded house. We hoped to dig up some kind of evidence pertinent to the trial. Both of us were naive kids from a Nancy Drew novel. Peter and Betsy were there at the time of the wedding reception next door. They thought we should go over with a wedding gift of new knives. The bride's previous husband had been slain by more than sixty knife wounds, so some sharp knives might be in order!

The Court Theaters of Europe was finally published, just in time for my slide lecture at the Bruno Walter Auditorium at the Library for the Performing Arts at Lincoln Center. Nathalie Marshall had edited it and created the design, but things got slowed down at the University of Miami. It was hastily printed in New York only hours before people gathered to hear my talk and get their autographed copy. Ruth Warrick graciously agreed to introduce me, so I thought it a good idea to have the chief of the Performing Arts Research Center, Thor Wood, introduce her. He was nervous, rambling on about her long career in Hollywood, her "forty-odd" films. Thor made Ruth sound like Methuselah, which was *not* what that actress wanted as an image. To restore her sense of youthfulness, Ruth began her introduction by talking about how long we had known each other. Paraphrased, she indicated that it seemed like we could have gone to school together. Lila, not hearing too well even in the front row and being just a bit jealous of Ruth's glamor and pizazz, loudly said, "*What* did she say? Go to school together . . .?" After a titter from the audience, all of whom knew me and many Ruth, she continued with reference to Thor's unfortunate wording in the awkward introduction: "I knew that some of the films that I did were odd, but not all forty-something . . ." It was a *simpatico* evening, with a reception following. Flo was there as well as many longtime friends who were happy to get my published work on the court theaters. My lectures, now that I had a companion piece to go with the talk, expanded across the country to Denver, Boulder, Viscaya in Miami, the Colony Club and then to New Orleans as part of the tercentennial celebration of Louis XIV's formation of Louisiana.

New Orleans was a city that I could never could spend time in without something terrible or outlandish happening to me. The first time involved my "scandal" at Antoine's Restaurant in the French Quarter. I had been invited to enjoy dinner there by a doyenne of New Orleans society. As she had to hostess another event, she had a younger Doris Day–type society woman accompany me. Well known by the owners, my delightful new friend and I got a table of distinction and proceeded to order champagne. I was wearing a dark blue Italian silk suit. Each time I moved in the cane bentwood chair, I felt something snag my jacket. There was a nail that threatened to tear my costly suit, so another chair was brought by our black waiter, together with apologies. Now, whenever I turned to the bubbly blond, I was glued to the seat. Bubble gum! As warm asparagus and cold champagne were in front of me, I declined going to the men's room to remove the trousers so they could be iced clean in the kitchen. Gracefully, I slipped the trousers off under the long white tablecloth and handed them to the shocked waiter. I proceeded to eat the delectables in front of me. No one noticed what I had done or could see my underwear because of the ample tablecloth and napkin on my lap.

My friend asked what color underwear I had on. I replied "orange, bikini," discreetly showing her a peek of orange from under my napkin. We sipped more bubbly, giggling at the sea of dark faces peering through the kitchen service-door window. My trousers were being ungummed with ice in the kitchen while we leisurely continued. Imagine how uncomfortable it would have been to miss all this while huddled in the men's room without my trousers on! Much better this way. It was considerably more difficult to get the clean trousers on, but I managed to do so without making a spectacle. The head waiter told me that I had made Antoine's book of firsts, offering us complimentary after-dinner drinks. The owner's son had left the restaurant for the evening before all this business had begun. (We agreed to meet him the next day, at a fancy luncheon given by my friend. She comandeered all the ovens to make individual soufflés for her guests. As she was an important client, it was permitted.) I was taken to view the trophy room at Antoine's after dinner. By now, we were the last to leave and we did a waltz around the trophy room. We bid each other a mirthful farewell at my hotel lobby. She had parked her car in the garage there and started off for home.

My phone rang later. My friend excitedly told me of her adventure after leaving my hotel. Taking a shortcut through a seedy neighborhood, two black youths jumped into her back seat as she waited for a red light to change. Quick-thinking, she kicked her purse back under the driver's seat, and turned her diamond ring around, showing only the band. She flicked on the inside light and opened the glove compartment, indicating the lack of

contents. She explained to the young thugs that she had only been
out dropping off a friend. There was nothing to steal. Luckily, a
police car cruised by and saw a blond in the front seat of the car,
the inside light on and two black youths in the back seat. Something was amiss there. Without asking for her identification or
written statement, the two black men were hustled off to jail with
no further questions asked. That was Louisiana: white supremacy
was enforced. Upon arriving at Antoine's the next day, the entire
luncheon party wanted to know exact details from our evening
the night before, all about the chairs, the table location. It was
hilarious in retelling but got out of hand as we left the restaurant.
The owner and his wife, together with his son, were at the door to
greet the various distinguished guests at our table. Somehow, the
staff had related a greatly exaggerated tale of events from the
night before. It was said that I had danced seminude in the trophy
room, and worse, that we had planted the bubble gum in the second chair. My dinner partner was so shocked that she took off her
shoe and sarcastically said, "Yes, look, my heel swivels to release
hidden bubble gum that we sneaked in to put on the chair!" The
owner's son stated that had he been there when all this happened
last night, he would have had the police throw me in jail (just like
the two black guys) and throw away the key! The owner, who had
been having a chat with me, interrupted his excitable son. I had
spoken intelligently and with praise about his wine list and the
food preparation. The owner took my side and refuted the possibility of what they heard had happened. He stated that he
thought me a well-behaved and intelligent person. Thus, a rocky
scene was diffused and we dispersed with a lively story with many
convolutions.

A year later, when my blond dinner partner was in New
York with her husband, he claimed that it was not possible for
someone to remove their trousers at a restaurant without people
noticing. We went to some new place in Brooklyn for dinner.
There were about ten of us. At the end of dinner, I rose and pro-

posed a toast to my host. Further, I lifted in my other hand my trousers, which I had surreptitiously removed sometime before without anyone noticing. He was outraged, and he tried to get my trousers away to hang on the light post in the street. How people hate to be proved wrong!

The second time in New Orleans was equally disastrous, or fraught with the disagreeable. Part of the tercentennial festivities revolved around continual partying. I was to deliver two talks there but slept little in order to keep up with the rounds of drinks and other goings-on. I was the houseguest of two gay men who had a historic house in the French Quarter. Stopping to check out a nearby gay bar, I met a sexy young man who invited me back to his place. It soon became clear that he was a hustler, even though he had denied it earlier. Further, his girlfriend appeared, and I thought it best to get out. He followed and suggested that we get a bottle and go to my place. The implication was that it was not a hustling arrangement but a friendly one. I took him up to my quarters and realized that he was more than I could handle. Yes, he wanted some money and he was not going to leave quietly.

After several trips to my bathroom, where I assumed he was taking drugs, I became anxious. I had a dressing room adjacent to the bathroom where I kept jewelry and cash. I found him handling an envelope I was to deliver to a friend in Houston in a few days that contained a Victorian beaded necklace. He wanted to take it, but I saw Lila's writing on the envelope and was outraged. We fought over the strand and it broke, scattering beads over the floor. My hosts heard the *contretemps* and inquired if I was okay. I should have thought to get them while he was in the john but I was so drunk, tired and embarrassed that I had not. When he heard their voices and saw two guys appear at the bedroom door, he lunged for my expensive camera. Again, I grabbed at it, catching the straps. He pushed me over but I did not release my grip on the straps.

He made a dash, empty-handed, into the hallway to a win-

Flo shortly before her death.

dow leading to the roof. The three of us stood gaping at him as he lunged through space onto another rooftop. The space was enormous, the drop terrifying had he not made it. The interloper had stolen my tranquilizers, but did not get any money or jewelry as far as I could tell in my drunken state. I decided it best to call Houston and plan to arrive the next day, slightly earlier than arranged. I was glad to leave New Orleans.

That first night in Houston, my brother-in-law called me with the awful news that Flo had just died. I spent the night crying, doubtless making moans of grief that kept my hosts uneasy all night. I booked a flight the next evening to grieve in my New York apartment and prepare for the funeral. Excessive drinking to assuage the pain of my sister's death began on the flight back to New York. I remember ordering a scotch and feeling very despondent. Florence was my closest link to my family; she had always been supportive. We had a very warm relationship. Now, her disease had taken her life. When she had called me before I left for New Orleans, she explained that the prognosis was not favorable. She did not want to shock family members with her death but wanted us to be prepared. I did not accept that it could possibly be as serious as she claimed. Surely she would not die, not in her early fifties. How could that be? While ordering another scotch, I requested a Bible, if there was one on board the plane. When it was brought, I hoped to find something to comfort me. Tears kept rolling down my face. Those around me tried to no avail to comfort me. More scotches were brought, this time "on the house." Time to collect my luggage at the terminal. I knew I could not maneuver well enough on my own. I asked for a wheelchair and assistance. The airline complied, assisting me into a taxi to take me to the small East Side apartment Lila and I shared. Her large Park Avenue apartment was

Lila and "Charlie," Canary Islands Mardi Gras.

sold in a moment of being practical. She decided it was more important to support White Russians, as though there were any left, as a means of fighting Communism, than to maintain a large apartment that was not used much anymore.

It had become routine for us to plan a couple of months in Europe at least once a year. Lila wrote away at her book and we saw friends and sights. One year, we did the French Pyrenees, the next Lac d'Annecy, or the Pilgrim's Route to Santiago de Compostela. I got to know the Canary Islands that way, as well.

Champagne in Paris with Sylvia.

Although the meaningful people in my life were dying, our trips and excursions with the International Society of Bibliophiles kept Lila and me stimulated, an international spectrum of places and people. Weekend parties at Lu Shan and circulation at watering spots such as East Hampton, Cape Cod, Santa Monica and Santa Fe/Taos kept my network strong and the flow of celebratory liquor flowing endlessly.

Young people struggling to create careers in the arts have always been up against enormous odds. Singers and musicians are constantly looking for a showcase for their talents. I started to present musicales in Lila's Louis XV salon, which delighted her and her invited guests. The barns at Lu Shan had long been abandoned. There was wonderful space both in the barns and on the terrace and grounds around them. I had been told by two different people in the arts that the environment was perfect for concerts and other events such as art exhibitions. When I asked Lila what she thought, she looked at me and without hesitation reminded me that "Nature abhors a vacuum—have at it, sweetie!" Thus, Apollo Muses was born, now celebrating its fifteenth year of presenting a diverse program of music, theater, art, dance and stimulating talks on the arts.

Remembering how delightful it had been to have refreshments with the artists at the Spoleto Festival and to be able to go to events of contrasting disciplines in the same day, I fashioned "Sundays." Keeping the ambience informal in a lovely setting with nature abounding amid music, art and other disciplines made the arts accessible and nonthreatening to anyone who chose to attend. Michael Redmond, then the senior music critic at the Newark *Star Ledger*, told me that some people thought Apollo Muses was an elitist organization, serving only a chosen few. I quickly corrected that notion with the statement that Apollo Muses was not for the chosen few but for the *few who chose*. He liked that, and as a result we formed a durable friendship.

Lila and Anne Jackson in the barns for Apollo Muses poetry & music.

"Sundays" at Apollo Muses: Eric & Tova (center) with her sculpture.
NJ Ballet ballerina Rosemary Sabovick-Bleich,
Music Director Frank Daykin, Maestro George Marriner Maull,
and two NJ Shakespeare actors.

To make a strong statement the first year we presented programs on the farm at Lu Shan, I created a season of ten Sundays.
It nearly killed me! At least, I thought, there were ample hiding
places for the vodka bottles, whose contents kept me going. No
one hired to perform counseled me against imbibing so continu-
ously. They wanted to keep their jobs and knew I would not tolerate interference. In grandiose, Godlike fashion, I swaggered
about determined to make the project "fly." I created the publicity, took phone reservations, handled logistics of parking, food
preparation (everyone got a free lunch to ensure they were there
before performance time) and transitions between programs. I
greeted the audience at the start of each program with pithy,
humorous comments.

Between selections, I sometimes got up to deliver a few
words. Fred, my wire-haired dachshund who sat in the back with
me, would clink his dog tags following me to the front. Once, I
decided I could be the moderator in a special arrangement of
Mozart's *The Magic Flute*. Faltering occasionally, I managed to

get through the piece with no major mishaps. But who knows? The soprano at the performance had shown the audacity to try to wrest a clutched vodka bottle out of my hands before I went on stage. No one else had ever tried to do that. I was angry, but I forgave her as I admired her talents and she was one of my favorite performers. Sometime later, at a reception in New York for another group, she told me how well I looked. I explained that I had been to Betty Ford Center and given up drinking. She sighed relief and expressed how glad she was. When I mentioned to her that drinking never got in the way of my performance and that I never missed a cue, she looked at me squarely and meaningfully stated, "Not that you are aware of!"

How right she was. There were many things I did under the influence that I was not aware of, whether because of blackout or simply lack of focus and confusion. No longer able to feel well or to sleep, I wanted a rest to help me get back into my old self. There seemed to be a corrosive feeling in my innards that saddened me, and revolted me, too. I was full of fear, anxiety and ongoing desperation. Dying would have been easier. On two occasions, I had out-of-body experiences that greatly frightened me. Unable to sleep, I kept the television going every night in my bedroom. A bottle of vodka was under the bed for security. A filled glass was on my bed table. I passed out or had blackouts but did not enjoy real sleep. It was eerie to find myself floating above my body on those two occasions. I remember loitering in the far corner of the ceiling, frightened to go out of the room. With effort, I returned to the safety of the body I saw lying there. I was exhausted but unable to die or to help myself accomplish it. I called the Betty Ford Center to arrange admittance. It was time to hang up those broken roller skates, finally.

Chapter 14

An Altered Life

It was a bright morning when I landed at the Palm Springs airport. The trip in the small plane from Los Angeles was bumpy, making the frantic last swigs of Stolichnaya from my silver flask difficult, causing splashes down my front. They were my last splashes before committing myself into the Betty Ford Center for alcohol abuse treatment. A hefty drink of vodka at the airport would help calm my nerves. In the terminal I spotted a man in the red, white and blue uniform of the center waiting for me. I ducked into the men's room before he noticed me. One last swallow of vodka was what my body urgently craved.

The orderly tried to make the ride across the desert to Rancho Mirage more comforting by quietly explaining what a wonderful experience I was about to have. He told me that he, like many of the other volunteers and staff, was also a recovering substance abuser. Despite his quiet encouragement, tension mounted as I pushed open the thick glass doors of the Betty Ford Center, entering the great unknown. A young blond gave me admission papers to examine and fill out. I decided I was hungry. Could I get a sandwich while doing the requisite paperwork for my twenty-eight-day stay at the famed treatment center? When the sandwich arrived, I noticed a water tumbler on a shelf behind the young woman. When she asked what I wanted it for, I blithely replied that I wanted to have my last drink of vodka before going into the center. I produced the silver flask. She firmly stated that

I was already in and asked me to turn over the flask! Tom-toms
beat the message across the campus that there was a live one in
admissions.

To my disappointment, she did not respond admiringly to
the line in the admissions form requesting who had referred me
to the BFC. I carefully entered the names of Elizabeth Taylor
and William Hurt, which obviously made me a VIP. No response.
Months before, Bill had come to Lu Shan with a girlfriend Lila
and I found common. They drank all day and, finally, Bill passed
out under the chandelier in the hallway. I "never" drank that way,
and I was repulsed by it. Grandly snapping off blazing lights, I
told the girl to help him to the car, as the guestrooms were full. I
did not like the girl's vulgar pushiness. A couple of months later,
I saw Bill on television, receiving his Academy Award for *Kiss of
the Spider Woman*. He looked together and sane. When I asked
about the difference, he told me about his treatment at Hazelden
in Minnesota, recommending that I think about help as well.
Elizabeth Taylor's admonishment to "get your ass over to Betty
Ford" (though directed to R.C. Gorman, I took to heart) rein-
forced Bill's words. Doctors and friends had repeatedly advised
me to do something about getting my life and health in order, but
I would not listen to them. What did they know about the artistic
spirit and my destiny to die of drink so dramatically and tragically!
I *did* pay attention to the high priestess of the cinema and the
newly acclaimed actor, who seemed to have made decisions
about alcohol that I had not considered.

Over decades of alcohol abuse, my once shapely body was
swollen from excessive drinking. I was more than sixty pounds
overweight. My face was barely recognizable. People who had not
seen me for a long time would pass me on the street and not realize who it was. When they did, they were shocked. Sometimes, I
got a reprimand for allowing myself to lose my good looks. I did
not care, or so I said. My best friend was alcohol, which protected
me from the harshness of the world. It gave me courage and

energy to keep Apollo Muses going for the welfare of the cultural life of the community, if not the world-at-large. I was a martyr to the arts!

Opera had spiced my daily life. Donning one of the several long robes I had had created by an artist friend, I lip-synched arias, grandly gesticulating, vodka in hand. My clothes were greatly splattered in those days of sloppy eating and drinking. Not only did I play the heroine, but I also took on all the roles that interested me. What soul-wrenching performances I gave in the blue silk-walled living room. My best performance was *Norma,* with the divine assistance of Maria Callas.

When the telephone rang, I quickly swallowed vodka for courage to answer it. Since my broken-leg period, stairways frightened me. If I came upon one suddenly, I would momentarily freeze. I never descended my stairway at Lu Shan without taking a drink first. And never did I attempt to drive the car without at least three comforting drinks to calm my nerves. It did not seem possible that I could exist without the bolstering vodka in the morning and scotch at night, with lots of wine and such in between. When I had the buzz just right, I was larger than life. That required constant attentiveness.

I had pockets created in suits I designed and had made at Scaglietti's in Costa Rica. The pockets held flasks that were not discernible, thanks to superb tailoring. The ashtray in the car held two miniature liquor bottles. If all went well, I could get from watering hole to watering hole without falling into a craving for another fix. I did not go to parties where liquor was not served, or I brought my secret supply, gratefully imbibed in visits to the lavatory. The Scaglietti suits had to be replaced regularly, as my waist expanded and the volleyball in my abdomen got larger. The suits were skillfully draped to hide my grotesque form. I avoided really looking at my face in the mirror. Never did I to try to brush my teeth first thing in the morning, as nausea was a sure result. A couple of hours after I had a good flow of vodka in my system, I could tolerate my morning brushing.

The servants hated my rampages. Of course, exhausting as it was for me, I felt an obligation to inform the gardener about the finer points in gardening, the cook about special seasonings for the dish being prepared. The serving girl was instructed to keep my water glass filled with iced straight vodka, and could she not understand that the placement of the knife was directly below the water glass, not the wine glass? On and on my compulsive perfectionism intruded itself in every event. Meanwhile, Lila and I pursued a thrilling life with colorful people, interesting places and always a waltz to spin us into the fantasy world where only beauty and excellence existed.

Lila did not believe that it would do any good to try to get me to reform, she revealed later. She was right. Just as my doctor was ineffective in getting me to subscribe to a healthier way of living, I would not have listened to Lila or many other people. It was exhausting to have to run the world, but who could do it better than I? What mattered was keeping my festival going and Lu Shan running smoothly. However, I had to get myself in better shape. I would try the Betty Ford Center treatment, as what I really needed was a rest. It was not a question of giving up the bottle. Heaven forbid! So, I allowed myself to take the time and effort to enroll in the program in the lovely California desert. Phyllis, with a friend, Stephen Garrett, who was the director of the Getty Museum, had dinner with me the night before I was to leave Santa Monica for BFC. As a final gesture of free-spirited Eric on a toot, I mooned the crowd at the "in" Venice restaurant before being taken back to my room for a good night's sleep. Photos of the display were sent to me at BFC as a reminder of what alcoholic behavior was like.

At last, I made it to the Betty Ford Center to get help and enjoy a respite from my disease. Forms completed, I was directed to North Hall, where my counselor, Suzanne Smith, would continue the indoctrination. Tough but competent was how she was described by the admissions woman. A slight shudder of anticipation ran through my tortured body.

A plump young man from Idaho escorted me to North Hall. He told me that he had heard I was involved with music. Would I like to be the conductor or leader of their kazoo marching band, he inquired. The previous leader had just left the Center and everyone at North Hall would be pleased if I accepted. I was flattered though shy about accepting. I did not know what a kazoo was, but I wanted to fit in and please my new friends. I liked the idea of being singled out for leadership so soon upon entering "the campus."

Immediately inside North Hall, I met my counselor. She was tall, thin and almost pretty, with a slight skin problem. When Suzanne heard my name and established that my family was Swedish, she lapsed into the typical snide remark Norwegians are prone to make. Her family being Norwegian, she had learned early on to say, "Fifty Swedes ran through the weeds, chased by one Norwegian." Nervous, tense, angry and confused, I did not endure being baited. "I have a good mind to give you a swift kick in the ass," I heard myself saying, as she leaned over the file cabinet. Silence in the office was heavy as the other counselors and administrative staff waited for her response. Slowly, Suzanne straightened up and looked at me with restrained anger and a reddened face. "It's nice to see that you can still blush," I bantered with arrogance. Thus began the rocky road of my recovery and self-discovery. No way was I going to help her find a chink in the armor I had so carefully constructed for protection from the world. Finally, Suzanne spent a very long session with me in private. She admitted defeat in reaching me, and felt that as there were so many people waiting to get into BFC, it was probably better if I withdrew from the program. Stunned and panicked, I pleaded for another chance, promising to be more cooperative.

Predawn walks around the lake helped me to focus on my

relationships with family and friends. Observing the heavens and the craggy mountains as the sun dawned, I was thrilled by the beauty as well as the possibility that I might be helped into a better sense of being. The other "inmates" were very encouraging, extending friendship and help getting into the pace of life at BFC. My nervousness at the new environment soon gave way to acceptance and the camaraderie of my new friends. Even if it was intended as a joke, I took my leadership of the kazoo marching band seriously. I enjoyed leading my pals to meetings and conferences across the campus, playing and singing simple songs, the only ones any of us could remember. Breaking a small branch from a tree, I covered it in tinfoil obtained from the cafeteria chef. That became my baton, easy to see and follow.

After my predawn walks, we gathered in front of North Hall to say the Serenity Prayer, arms linked around each other's waist or on the shoulders. Then, off to breakfast with the rest of the "inmates." Each house-group sat by itself, instructed to keep to itself at all times, even when exercising in walks around the lake. We were discouraged from any talk with members from the other three houses. That was to keep our focus on ourselves and our recovery. It was fun to arrange small liaisons with someone in another house, just because it was strictly forbidden!

A redhead from Margaux Hemingway's hall caught my eye. We did not know each other's names but playfully sent messages back and forth. We devised cunning ways to communicate clandestinely. I would empty a small box of corn flakes and refill it with Cheerios, no significance in mind other than its being odd, and slip a funny greeting inside. Then, I would drop it on the table in front of her while passing with my tray. Often, she would have an older woman in a wheelchair pass me with something in a bag or napkin together with an equally amusing message. The "agent" in the wheelchair we thought was a brilliant foil, as who would suspect her of being a go-between? Once, I collected somewhat wilted flowers a departing patient had left behind. I put them in an elegant florist's box and delivered them to the front desk in the administration building with my friend's name on it—I had only recently learned her name. She was thrilled to receive the flowers, wilted and all, and the attention.

Things culminated the pre-Christmas morning that my roommate and I decided to have our North Hall recite a Christmas carol at breakfast for the entire campus to enjoy. We wrote it the night before, based on "She Walks In Beauty" and the Johnny Carson introduction, "He-e-e-e-re's Johnny." While the group "innocently" recited the Christmas carol, I slipped behind the chair where my new pal, "Carol," was sitting. In my hand, behind my back, was a wreath made from bent wire coat hangers, twisted with old ribbons and leftover flowers and greens from discarded bouquets. Motley colored streamers cascaded down the back of the wreath. At the end of the ode, as they canted "Ho-o-o-oly Shit! He-e-e-ere's Carol!" I plopped the wreath on her head and disappeared into the North Hall crowd. For the next few days, Carol strode the campus, proudly bewreathed. She refused to remove my gift until she was threatened with expulsion. It was a grand success and we have remained friends ever since.

I had the handsomest roommate at North Hall, to the envy of the other men and women. The gentleman from Virginia was poised and sexually vibrant, traits he counted on for getting through life. Supposedly straight, it became clear that an intimate interlude was possible. I realized that his suggestiveness was really a ploy for me to be another of his acolytes on campus, so I ignored the advances. Also, I was told not to have any sexual relationships for the first year of sobriety—staggering news that I was not sure I wanted to subscribe to, even if I could. But, "for today," it was okay.

Notions of God redefined themselves during those salubrious days in the desert. Beginning with my early-morning focus on nature while walking around the lake, I began to count on an informal kind of prayer. I learned to listen for the first time. I thought I had always listened, but that was not true. I began to relate to my fellow mates in recovery with a more open heart and a mind that reevaluated everything.

The most startling news came one day when I was told that I did not *have* to drink. I thought I did so to keep going. After a massive dose of tranquilizers upon entry, I was weaned off dependence on alcohol. Replacing it were interesting talks, films and friendly interplay with others having the same problem. Concentration on overcoming my addiction became paramount in my day's activities.

Each day was filled with programs of recovery. There were films interspersed with talks about aspects of substance abuse. We had group as well as individual therapeutic sessions; we had individual sessions with a nutritionist, a spiritual counselor and a doctor so that all aspects of our recovery could be considered. Prescribed reading and daily summations of my activities and thoughts were written up for the counselor's consideration, returned with comments the next morning. Exercise in both the swimming pool and the gym were mandatory in the program, too. There was little time for dallying and no time for isolation. Peer pressure and support were a constant. Within days, my weight started to drop; my bloat diminished and the volleyball in my belly got smaller until it was not there anymore. I liked my fellow inmates and we indulged in delightful, often childish pastimes that took on special significance there in the desert retreat.

Christmas was coming, a dreaded time for many people—especially alcoholics. The pressures inherent in the season accentuate dysfunction. The stress encourages acceleration in drinking; problems become compounded. I purposely chose to be at the Betty Ford Center during the holiday period, which had come to signify desperate unhappiness. Each house had been requested to prepare a twenty-minute skit for the annual Christmas party, held in North Hall. The subject had to deal with substance abuse. No one seemed to have any inspiration in my group. Finally, I

proposed a playlet called "The All New Nativity Play." I knew
how salubrious laughter is for people in recovery. By holding an
outrageous comedy, I sought to cheer everyone up as well as send
a message to the inmates. Although the notion of a Nativity play
was agreeable to North Hall-ers, no one seemed at all interested
in directing it. So, not being a controlling person, I wrote and
directed it. I also starred in it, playing the Virgin Mary—as Mae
West would have interpreted her! I created humor by casting in
an outrageous way: Joseph was played by a wimpy, slight, short
guy; the baby Jesus was a large, muscular guy in diapers. I had the
Star of Bethlehem played by our house Jewish American Princess, draped in fairy lights, standing on a bookcase. The Three
Wise Men became "the three wise guys from the East" as interpreted by two of the older women and our white, deep-south
young man cast as the black Wise Man. One of the shepherds was
played by a twenty-one-year-old boy who had been brought in on
his birthday by the arresting sheriff, his father. He was a Bible
freak who spent much time writing poetry. I asked him to write a

poem about what Christmas
meant to him and read it in
the playlet. Another shepherd read portions of Luke
and Matthew having to do
with the Nativity.

Ever-reliable Oscar Murillo.

Now that we had a ter-
rific script and cast, what
about costumes? I called
Oscar Murillo in New Jer-
sey. He had helped me with
Apollo Muses and knew my
wardrobe from years of
being around me and Lu Shan. I requested that he send me the
formal Louis XVI wig that I wore combed out for other such trav-
esties. Also, the Santa Claus outfit, a few robes from north Africa

together with headdresses. "Please hide some fireworks in the costumes for use on New Year's Eve, as well."

As rehearsals progressed, there were murmurs that some of the audience would consider the playlet sacrilegious. I wanted to protect the humor of the play without offending anyone. Hence, I devised a preperformance speech to be delivered by Santa Claus, to the effect that what was about to be seen was in bad taste, childish and possibly offensive. Anyone not wanting to be subjected to the nonsense was free to leave before it began. With that warning, which no one heeded, the performance began.

Holding candles, some singing and some playing their kazoos, we entered to "O Little Town of Bethlehem." Shepherds led the procession. The Virgin had a blue mantle (a bedspread) over her pink gown (a borrowed flannel nightie) with her head turned toward the baby Jesus walking between her and Joseph. No one could see her face as the wig and mantle obscured it from the audience side.

Small stuffed animals were around the large cardboard box the baby Jesus was stretched out on, legs and arms protruding over the sides. Mary had her back to the audience, tending the child. It was not until Joseph looked stage left and declared, "Hark, Mary, I hear noises in the distance. Why . . . it is three men . . . approaching from the East on camels . . ." that Mary got to her feet and spun around to the audience. She gazed toward the approaching men, straightening her outfit and adjusting the wig. Screams and guffaws filled the room as my inmates realized who the Virgin Mary was. When I said, seductively, "O-o-h, are you the three wise guys I've been hearin' all about?" accompanied by hip wiggles and Mae West expressions, the house collapsed into convulsions. Margaux Hemingway stood on her chair and shouted, "Eric, I love you!" *Succès fou!* Nervous about how the football-player types would respond, I was thrilled when they hugged me and congratulated me on the best interpretation *ever* of Mae West.

That led me to further extravagances. I told the exercise instructor at the pool that I preferred classical music to the contemporary noise she played. She brought a disc of *Swan Lake*. She was in the ladies' room changing into her bathing suit when I put the ballet music on. I proceeded to teach the football-player types the roles of the cygnets. Holding each other's hands crisscrossed, *en pointe* in the pool, they pliéd and followed my directions in improvised ballet movements. As the music crescendoed, the Swan Queen made a terrific *grand jeté* into the pool just in time for the instructor to catch the incredible scene! She claimed never to be able to attend a performance of *Swan Lake* again without thinking of our performance in the pool that day. Only in an institutional environment would those guys have given themselves permission to play ballerinas, giving me such warm support in my fantasies. That may be one of the reasons that I liked the institutional experience.

Daily meditations and prayers while circling the lake in the predawn hours grew in fervor. Somewhere along the twenty-eight-day period of adjustment and recovery I succumbed to a willingness to free myself from the enslavement of alcohol. An increasing sense of well-being, resulting from good eating habits and good company, the ability to sleep well and budding spirituality got me to consider real change in my life. It was overwhelming to contemplate the extensive work needed to bring me back into the land of healthy, balanced living. The concept of "just for today" bore fruit. I knew I would have to pace myself, working slowly and patiently. I accepted the notion that I had been insane, out of control. I started working on my Fourth Step list of resentments. The hurts I had suffered, real or imagined, had to be examined.

My list grew so that it seemed that the only living thing to escape my resentment list was my dog Fred. The days flew as I tried to absorb the steps to recovery. I would soon have to face another human being and talk about my list and my life. How embarrassing! But, I was instructed that the deliverance of the Fifth Step was mandatory to my graduation from Betty Ford as well as obligatory for my development in recovery. When the day arrived, I was introduced to a young, handsome member of the clergy. I slowly, nervously began my confession. He quietly encouraged me with an occasional "Oh, my . . ." giving credence to my astonishing admissions. At the end of it all, perhaps an hour later, I was advised to walk around the lake and consider what I had talked about. There was not a soul to be seen from the campus as I walked around the lake. It was an ordeal I was glad to have made it through. I was relieved that it was over. Now, I had to make sense of it all. I looked up at the mountains and the clouds skipping across the sky. God, I thought, Give me some sort of a sign . . . some notion of where I am to go from here . . . Something . . .

A roar of approbation filled the air as eighty-nine colored balloons floated into the heavens above the campus, startling me. I was in awe. *Wow* . . .Thank you, dear God! I thought in response to the miracle. What I did not know was that the other eighty-nine inmates had been gathered together and requested to write their outstanding resentment on a slip of paper. Tying them to balloons, they released them on cue, giving a shout of joy in getting rid of them, pulled skyward by the balloons. It worked for me; it worked for them. There is no such thing as coincidence.

Daily prayers on my knees resulted from this experience. Since that day eleven years ago, I choose to begin each day with words of gratitude and thanksgiving to God, together with a request for divine guidance. It provides a sense of focus and an appropriate agenda for the day. What a relief to have a manageable program of events in my daily life, free of the onerous task of being responsible for running the world. How much easier my life became when I gave up feeling the need to control everything and everyone.

Though God found a conscious place in both my mind and

heart, I was not deprived of my impishness or need to participate in flamboyant behavior. As I was about to be graduated from the Center, I thought a memorable act of self-indulgence was in order. I was sitting in the whirlpool bath to assuage my swollen ankle, a carry-over from the ski accident in New Mexico. My colleagues were still in the exercise room finishing stretching. My bedroom was nearby, so I slipped over to it to get my white terrycloth bathrobe. Removing my wet suit, I returned to the exercise room to sign out. As the class was finishing, I put my name on the list and turned to leave. Margaux Hemingway and other pals were following directly behind me. A few steps onto the sidewalk, I loosened my robe and slowly took it off, dragging it behind me. Startled exclamations from Margaux and others were heard as I sauntered, bare-assed into my room. I was enormously pleased with myself for creating that sensation, a final gesture of self-will run rampant. Rome was not built in one day, as they say. I still had much to learn, but at least I was on my way to a new life.

Margaux left the Center a couple of days before me and we promised to stay in touch. The Center disapproved when she held a press conference directly upon discharge. Administration and inmates unanimously agreed that it was not a healthy policy of recovery to cash in on publicity when anonymity should have been applied. When Betty Ford started the Center, she had used her connections, making her own case public as a means of getting others to seek help or to give support to the cause of recovery. Elizabeth Taylor also tried to use her own experiences to help others. I certainly would not have gone to a rehabilitation center without her directives. William Hurt made public his battle with the bottle. Through the valiant efforts of Betty Ford, Elizabeth Taylor and Bill Hurt, public awareness has grown. In my case, attraction to what they got led me toward recovery. Hence, I feel free to mention them. Margaux's case was different. Whether it was an agent who advised her or her own need for attention, it was generally conceded that we would not go her route.

How fearful it was to go back into the "real" world after the protected, nurturing environment of the Betty Ford Center. I made my way to Santa Monica to visit briefly with Phyllis before going to Santa Fe. I wanted time to let recovery take hold by going to "The Land of Enchantment," which was so close to my heart.

Jane Gray and her husband, Byron Treaster, were going to spend some time in New York. We agreed that they could use my New York apartment and I would house-sit their wonderful modern house situated high above the arroyos in Tesuque, just north of Santa Fe. A.A. meetings were plentiful and uplifting to this "green" alcoholic in recovery. I enjoyed the combination of living in the high desert in a terrific house with commanding views of God's miraculous landscape and the spirituality of the meetings. Feeling energized, I decided to plan a concert for my New Mexican friends.

A pianist from California was willing to perform on Jane's baby grand for about twenty invited guests. My impresario urgings were stimulated. I got some rust off my professional self and put sober living with its accomplishments to a gentle test. Flying high on a pink cloud, some of my old habits were hard to overcome. I counted on control and ego responses deeply ingrained in my daily behavior. Ann Luce flew in with her new boyfriend to visit and enjoy the concert. Other local friends attended and got to see the sober Eric at work. My enthusiasm took to proselytizing ad nauseam. One of my best artist friends really needed guidance. I was certain that I could be living proof that alcoholism could be overcome. She resisted, denying any need for help. That was a dismal failure for me, and it continues to be. We have given up trying to maintain our old friendship, as a deep sea of vodka separates us.

R.C. Gorman was interested to see what I would be like

sober, as we had years of riotous cavorting together, with many a bottle emptied en route. I brought him a mug from Betty Ford Center, which was a status symbol he could easily relate to. He stopped for a while, but controlled drinking was the route he chose. Each has his/her chosen path, and the Twelve-Step program suggests that we are where we are supposed to be.

Fred, my wire-haired dachshund, did not know what to make of me when I returned to Lu Shan. He heard my voice in the courtyard and responded with a yelp and wagging tail. He started toward me. Then, stopped and crawled toward me as though there was something suspicious about me. There was, indeed. I did not smell like the Eric he had known all his life. I had been alcohol-free almost two months. To my dog, it was my voice, my outward appearance but not my smell. An impostor?

There are so many "firsts" when one enters sobriety after a quarter of a century of alcohol abuse. Getting into white tie and tails to go waltzing seemed familiar enough. It was the waltzing. Something seemed wrong, missing or different. It was not as much fun twirling; the event seemed lackluster. It took a while to realize that booze had given me such a buzz that without it, the world was calmer, more sedate and definitely less manic. Indeed, it was calmer for all those around me as well as for myself. No longer needing to help everyone do their tasks and demanding perfection, I was relieved at how much easier everyday life seemed. The servants were content to go about their tasks undisturbed by my ranting. I began to go to Twelve-Step meetings and general recovery meetings. Rather than seek to relish those things that made me different from everyone else, I learned to appreciate what I had in common with the rest of humanity. I truly began to feel a part of the human race, enjoying that sensation.

Apollo Muses became a seasonal event each July. "Sundays" were sold out and the programs of diverse disciplines made a delightful way for participants to enjoy a day in the country at the

Friends of Apollo Muses

Clockwise, from above: Celeste Holm and Ruth Warrick join me for an Apollo Muses concert/dinner and Apollo Muses Lyre presentation; Another season with Franco Corelli, Lucia Evangelista, Ruth Warrick, Jerome Hines, with host Eric aboard BargeMusic; Chatting with opera star Frederica "Flicka" von Stade; Afloat with the Hon. Douglas and Suzzie Dillon, who attended Apollo Muses 15th annual concert/dinner; Dinner on Malcolm Forbes's yacht with Dorothy Dillon Eweson and Christopher (Kip) Forbes; World revered "Madonna of the Clay" Toshiko Takaezu exhibits work at Jack Lenore Larsen's in East Hampton.

and Related Events

Above: Esteemed actor Wesley Addy at Eric's home with his wife, Celeste Holm. Top right:As Mother Ginger, my "Carol Channing-on-acid" yearly opening night performance in NJ Ballet's Nutcracker. *Lower right: Cheek to cheek with Celeste. Below: The Forbes helicopter at the ready.*

Lu Shan Farm. Making use of my many contacts in various disciplines over the decades, I was able to intermingle young, aspiring professional musicians with seasoned talents who were willing to share their expertise and experiences. Accomplished actresses such as Celeste Holm and Ruth Warrick generously participated, as did Anne Jackson, who enjoyed reading poetry to us. The authority on rare books from Sotheby's came to discuss illuminated manuscripts, as an outgrowth of our talking on a dusty bus in Turkey. Museum directors and curators came to share their knowledge, as did noted artists. The world-revered ceramist Toshiko Takaezu shared her talents, throwing clay on the wheel; costume and scenic designers explained their artistry. Ballet star Eleanor D'Antuono talked of her career at a program of dance featuring Carolyn Clark's New Jersey Ballet. Frederica von Stade joined many other luminaries in the arts on the Advisory Board of Apollo Muses.

Every Sunday had the multifaceted blend that constitutes the totality of the arts. When the weather cooperated, which it usually did, we enjoyed lunch on the terrace overlooking the lush central New Jersey valley. The silo and barns made a bucolic backdrop for direct contact with nature and the arts. A break between programs permitted an interlude of relaxed communication with the artists, nature and each other. It was an ongoing success, but we barely broke even; admission fees were kept to a minimum to permit access to those less financially endowed than my neighbors. When the weather was tempestuous, audience and artists gathered even closer together. Once, Ruth Warrick was telling of her film experiences when a thunderstorm broke overhead. It was hard to continue, but in their efforts to stay dry and safe, everyone seemed to bond. The project and the location were stimulating and enchanting.

Storm clouds gathered over more than the barns. Lila and I continued to go on European trips, which got increasingly more difficult with the onset of her advanced age. I was careful to think everything out ahead of time to avoid problems in her travel. I usually rented a car and drove it myself. The itinerary permitted stopovers that assured her restful comfort, in places that interested her. Picnics were a delight for both of us. Often, in the morning while Lila was having tea and reading, I would go to local markets to secure delights for our picnic basket. Both of us were of one mind on many things, which made travel a joy mutually shared.

History from a royal point of view fascinated us. Chateau hotels enchanted us; we were game for anything that promised adventure. A small inn was chosen over a chateau if the chef was especially competent, or the location permitted accessibility to sights we wished to see. We looked inquisitively at the local sights, bringing a fund of information with us, too: we always read and prepared before going.

France was of special interest to us. Man'ha Garreau Dombasle was a longtime friend of Lila's. She had married a French ambassador whose stations had been worldwide. Man'ha was one year older than Lila, and in her nineties still dressed elegantly in high heels, sporting a bit of cleavage in her fetching ensemble. A poet and mystic, Man'ha was proficient in providing a superb meal in the most genteel surrounding. Trappings of her long career in the diplomatic world were evident in every room of her apartment. I first met her when she occupied a large apartment on the Avenue Victor Hugo; thereafter she lived for some years across from the Bois de Boulogne, and finally in Deauville.

Her granddaughter, after years of struggle and determination, achieved success as an actress in the French cinema and on stage and television. Arielle Dombasle has a radiant personality, with inimitable quirks of humor I have always found irrepressible and amazing. Recently married for the second time, the actress wedded France's handsome, controversial writer Bernard-Henri Lévy. The quaint town of St. Paul-de-Vence in Provence was closed to traffic to accommodate their wedding reception. Arielle posed on the cover of *Paris-Match* in her unusual wedding outfit. The press adore her for doing, wearing and saying the unexpected.

Lila always looked forward to long visits with Man'ha in her duplex in Deauville. Arielle had a suite of rooms there that were rarely used, so Lila had a perfect place to roost. While she and Man'ha talked and sipped tea for days on end, I went on trips elsewhere. Knowing Lila was in safe hands, I could investigate Paris or other sights that had interest for me. Our life together over the two decades had become very meaningful and intensely loving. We cared deeply about each other, while spinning out our lives in an agreeable, stylish manner. For many years, many of our friends considered us a very special "couple." We had many of the same interests and relished them.

The infamous Clare Boothe Luce, who had seduced Henry Luce away from young Lila and their two children, said on occasions before she died that there were two things that she regretted in her life. Startled but avid listeners would hear her say that she had never gotten to see Lu Shan. Lila had promised her mother that an invitation would never be forthcoming to that husband-stealer. The second loss to Clare was that she never had an Eric in her life! Lila was greatly relieved, too. She did not feel like losing the two most important men in her life to Clare Boothe Luce. One was devastating enough!

Many people claimed that I kept Lila young and interested in life. Our symbiotic life had aspects of a fairy tale, complete with bad witches or wicked step-sisters (of either sex), and intrigue that seems to come with money. Lila always said that money was corrupting. She was worried what would happen to me when she died, and made provisions in her will. Lila considered others getting bequests, too: Halina Kudzin, the Polish cook who gave such loving care to Lila; always available Oscar, whose loyalty on her behalf was above reproach.

When Henry Luce abandoned Lila to run off with Clare

Boothe, Lila's sons were left in her care in the beginning. The eldest son, Henry III, grew up to be a surly, self-important megamillionare. Although I think he loved his mother, I got the impression that he was too busy to be involved in the machinations at Lu Shan. For a couple of decades, I had been there to amuse his mother and keep her out of harm's way as best I could. I was not on the payroll. On the contrary, at one point the question had come up of my receiving a salary. I had refused the notion of being "hired help" during my tenure as resident impresario. I loved Lila and was grateful for all she did for me. Money *was* corrupting and I preferred to live life free of grubbing vulgarity.

Her younger son, Peter, on the other hand, expressed to a previous wife his malcontentment towards his mother. He felt it was her fault that his father ran off with Clare. Peter believed that Lila spent her whole life more concerned with balls and social events than being a good wife and mother. He was full of resentment, even at being a Luce of *Time* magazine fame. Peter went to Colorado to live anonymously in Boulder, where he dabbled in land development deals. He did not achieve notable success in these ventures, but he did participate in aviation, which absorbed much of his time and interest. His second wife, Ann, learned to fly to keep him company. Then she enjoyed it so much that she got her own plane, which she used in her expanding enterprise, Alarion Press. Peter did not appreciate the challenge of her success in creating the business of supplying schools with video kits that taught art to children of all ages. Peter, wanting to be less challenged, beguiled by a younger woman who did not seem a threat to him, dumped Ann. Lila and I were sorry Ann was treated that way, and we became aware that Betsy would snare Peter into his third marriage, despite her protestations that "the last thing she wanted was another entanglement."

After their marriage, subtle changes became evident. Peter had gone over Lila's will and diminished the amount I was to get.

Lila had given me a run-down gardener's cottage with a piece of nonprime land. She wanted to make sure I had something if anything happened to her. After all, had I not taken care of her without financial reward for two decades? Peter was furious. My eventual inheritance had to be cut down. He put in a clause that did not concern me at the time; I thought it typical of his fussy thinking. It stated that each person was to get the stipulated amount on the provision that they were with Lila when she died. The housekeeper was not mentioned in the will, but Halina, the cook was, she pointed out. Maria had opened the safe and read it. Then she came crying to me to do something about the oversight. She had xeroxed a copy and given it to me. Maria appeared sweet and sincere. How could I imagine the machinations she had concocted with Peter and his new wife?

Halina's estranged husband had just died in Poland, then still under Soviet domination. At Maria's insistence, she returned to Gdansk to settle matters, despite her children's warnings not to get stuck there by returning. With the mighty righteousness of Halina gone, I was the biggest obstacle to a takeover at Lu Shan. Lila suffered a fall in her bedroom and contracted pneumonia as well as broken ribs. In her nineties, there was a great chance that she would not recover. The net was closer to being cast with the arrival of Peter and Betsy. Lila finally came out of her coma. I had been to her hospital room a few times, and found her hallucinating. She thought she was with her husband, Henry. Lila imagined there was a fire. She seemed concerned about *Time* and raved incoherently. Once home, she was weak but on the mend.

One day, Oscar called me to tell me that the locks at Lu Shan had been changed and that anyone who admitted me would be fired immediately. Shocked, I called Lila. It was obvious that someone was listening on the phone. I asked her to meet me outside the house. She was bewildered when I told her about the strange development. She would straighten it out; she could not imagine my being locked out of Lu Shan. Lila suggested I take a guest room and live there, near her. I did not relish having a continuous internal struggle.

Lila did not have the strength to challenge her "two treasures," her sons. She could not give up the illusion that they were anything but wonderful and loving. I believed that if she did, the truth might have killed her. She did not want to give me up, either. She kept calling me, asking me to return. I could not until things were reversed, which was not going to happen. If Lila was not strong enough to defend us, I had no hope of living a sane life around the Luces. It seemed that it was time to be de-Luced. I had always thought that it would happen after Lila's death. I was wrong.

What would the community be told about my disappearance? There were so many questions posed by the new turn of events. Oscar, a good influence on Lila's well-being, and in my camp, was dismissed with one-day's notice! I got him a place to live and called various friends who were only too delighted to hire him on a freelance basis. He ended up making more money and enjoying a diversity of work, but he regretted losing contact with Lila.

Halina, who tried to return to Lila's household, was denied a visa. Each time she went to Warsaw to the American Consulate, a handwritten letter from the USA was pulled out and inspected. Then, she was told that her request was denied because she had worked illegally in the United States. Someone had written to report her. "Don't worry, Halina," Maria had said, encouraging her to leave the country for Poland, "we'll get you back here." Fat chance.

"Things were beginning to disappear," people were told when they inquired why I was no longer around. I would not be surprised if things had begun to disappear; I resent anyone thinking it was me who lifted them.

All telephone calls to Lila were monitored, the mail inspected and no one was admitted without clearance. "This is war, and I'm Hitler!" Peter told someone who tried to reason with him. Betsy may have encouraged him into those actions he never would have attempted on his own. With Maria's inside help, Lila was truly helpless.

Henry III also had a new wife with her own agenda. Henry was too busy and self-absorbed; his wife Leila found it convenient to go along with the new regime, although she was supposed to be a great friend and admirer of both Lila and me before the "Queen Lear" script played itself out. I used to think that Shakespeare had exaggerated with *King Lear*.

After all that loving time with Lila, I was deeply affected emotionally. I believe I suffered from codependency. A psychiatrist recommended that I go for a long weekend at a rehab center in Pennsylvania to help remedy the problem. While there, I met a priest from Holy Cross Monastery on the Hudson River. I enrolled there in a special retreat program for further insight into my spiritual and emotional needs as a gay man in society. It was my second monastery experience. Lila and I had been for a week's stay at the Roman Catholic Benedictine Christ in the Desert Monastery above Abiquiu, New Mexico, a few years before. We thought it would be a great place to write and rest. I enjoyed monastic life and was open to additional investigation that would enrich me spiritually.

My longtime friend Sylvia van der Stegen, the "peanut (because she was so diminutive) countess" from Paris, had recently told me about a beneficial meeting with a Catholic priest in a Jesuit monastery near Palo Alto. He had been so effective in dealing with her that she learned to pray on a daily basis as a result. I wanted to meet him. If he could do for me what I discerned that he had done for Sylvia, I was in favor.

After "Sundays" finished another busy season, I went to California and New Mexico. It was with one of the Sons of Jesus, the same priest about whom Sylvia had expressed her enthusiasm, that I learned to pray for the health, wealth and prosperity of those who had injured me. For more than five years now, I have begun each day on my knees praying for Lila's comfort in her declining years; then, for the well-being of her family and keepers, if that is God's will. Today, she has withdrawn into herself, almost like a baby. Someone told me that she had been brainwashed into giving a diatribe against the young man who took advantage of her. When asked if she meant Eric, who for so many years had been a caring and loving friend, she got confused. Then, pointing to a portrait of Henry Robinson Luce, she said, with her eyes brightening and love in her voice, "That's Eric!"

I could not bear being geographically so close to Lila but unable to see her. The little greenhouse cottage that she and I had had such fun fixing up was contiguous to Lu Shan. Just up the hill was my beloved Lila, locked away. It was too painful. Despite the financial loss I would take in selling my home quickly, I wanted peace of mind, not a constant reminder of the maliciousness of my fellow humans. I sold the cottage and settled in Gladstone New Jersey. It is only a few miles away in actual distance but a world away emotionally.

Lila did not die as was expected a few years ago. Shortly after returning from the hospital, her sons officially bought Lu Shan for a mere one million dollars. This is a pittance, as it was worth many times that amount. Lila had suffered years of indoctrination from her overbearing mother, which colored her notions about politics, fashions and food. There is one thing that both women were correct about: money is corrupting! Just as fairy godmothers come in various guises and sexes, so do wicked stepsisters.

Today, I strive to function with an ever-enlarging heart, intended to accommodate more and more love. My new home is charmingly situated, with lovely views and gardens. Apollo Muses enjoys great success with sold out seasons and continual good press. It is only at this writing that long-time companion Fred ended his twilight years to go on to canine heaven.

It has been wisely stated that it isn't over until the fat lady sings. Those are terrific words of encouragement, not to give up but to persist. Thanks to my spirituality and growing sobriety, my hope is supported by faith. I know that I must be out in life available for the many unexpected possibilities and miracles that happen. The fairy godmother's gift of the slipper of true love will present itself. And, it will fit—both of us! Whenever he shall appear, I am prepared to stroll along the Boulevard of Enchantment with my Prince, happily ever after—not as in a fairy tale but anchored in the reality of sober living.

Happily Ever After

Life is no longer for me a fairy tale full of make-believe and illusion. For decades my existence was spent in pursuit of grandiose fantasy, motivated by alcohol. Today, I have exchanged the extravagant for the abundant. How much more comfortable I now feel, functioning as a sober, responsible individual in the world. Gone is the sensation of looking in at a feast in progress, as did the poor little match girl. I strive to take responsibility as an active participant in the world around me.

I wake up each day and pursue a daily exercise in focusing. Before sunrise each morning, after stretching, an hour is devoted to contemplation. The session ends with prayers of gratitude to God, asking divine direction in my life. There is a comfortable strength that comes with a centered spiritual life driven by love and an ever-growing faith in God's intentions for me. As stated in James 2: 26, "Faith without works is dead." Hence, I strive to achieve right action. The preparedness for any action is, first, to be available. Proper sleep in conjunction with a nutritious diet assures me greater availability to life as well as an increased ability to persevere when faced with life's many trials.

For so much of my life, my urge for drama, inherent in pursuing fantasies, was involved in continually trying to jam on the recalcitrant and unsuitable slipper. I have learned to wait patiently for the right mutual suitable fit. Being "Mr. Right" is better than looking for "Mr. Right." If Cinderella's prince will

341

come, it will be when I have achieved "Mr. Right" status. Living comfortably, knowing who I am and where I come from, helps me to reach that point. Although I was not a cinder-sweeper as a child, my origins are humble. That contrasts sharply with many of the circumstances in which I have spent most of my adult life. Bill Moyers states that it is necessary to use a rear-view mirror to get where you want to go. Without knowing where you came from, it is hard to determine where you are going. Acknowledging my path makes for a safe highway to the future. Part of the process is to absorb the healthy, even godly aspects of androgyny into my life with openness. Acceptance of the dual nature of my makeup, like everyone's, permits me to live with dignity and strength.

My love of the retreat experience led me to visit Nada Hermitage, a Carmelite retreat in southern Colorado. Each retreat-ant lives independently in a small hermitage in the high desert, surrounded by high mountains on two sides and a broad, beautiful valley below. Warm during the day, the temperatures at night are very cold. I went to bed with my Franklin stove ready for lighting at 4:00 a.m., when I rose to begin meditations. With the fire warming my cabin, I stared out at the starry heavens. What joy to behold the meteor showers that were a phenomenon at that precise time. With no light to detract from them, I was blessed with an amazing sight. It was appropriate and I expressed gratitude for this divine gift. Another gift was my next-door neighbor. In a barely perceptible hole about fifteen feet from my door lived an adorable shy ermine. Big black saucer eyes and a black tip on the tail contrasted with the sleek white fur. Another thrill and possibly a talisman.

Oscar Wilde wrote, "God's law is only love." I believe love to be holy, just as beauty is holy. Art is our avenue to divinity. Music was a great comfort to me in my teens when I struggled with loneliness. Now, I write a column in the Gannett publications about classical music, and I have continual access to great music. It has enriched my life immeasurably. Likewise, my close association

Retreatants Phyllis Babbitt Nugent and I at Mount Calvary Monastery, high above Santa Barbara.

with the fine arts through my gallery and museum work has expanded my spiritual world and nourished my soul with beauty. Unlike myopic politicians, who like to trim budgets for the arts because they are considered frills, I know the arts to be a basic necessity to healthy living.

The creation of Apollo Muses brought my various skills and talents in the arts together for the enjoyment and enrichment of the community at large. At first, I thought I was doing the grueling work of operating an arts festival for the benefit of the young professional talents so desperately in need of a showcase. After years of producing the programs, I realized that it was the community that benefited the most. Arousing their cultural awareness by making music and its allied disciplines accessible in a comfortable surrounding encourages a reawakening interest in the nourishing springs that feed the soul. This is vital because the veneer of functional society gets constantly thinner.

Much of my life was spent in confusion and self-doubt. I used alcohol to overcome, albeit for only a moment at a time, shyness, alienation and deep-seated insecurity. Now that I perceive that I am on a lifelong road to recovery and constant challenge, I can pray for guidance and courage in the struggle. My intent is to travel the open road of what is spiritually beautiful. My goal is to live in harmony with the world, even with the universe, so that my sense of being may be attuned to the Music of the Spheres.

INDEX

Spiesman, Dr. Margaret 29
Spilman, Jamie 77, 81
Stack, Robert and Rosemary 236
Stade, Frederica von "Flicka" 173, 332
Stamp, Terence 157
Stane, Walter 164
Stark, Ray 213
Stavropoulos, George 268, 284
Stead, Richard 270
Steber, Eleanor 241, 242
Steele, Barbara 108
Stein, Gertrude 42
Steinbrecker, Edward 232
Stern, Dr. Fred 59, 60
Stevens, Risë 16
Stewart, Tom 268
Stielle, Josette 198, 204, 206, 209, 210
Stiga, Paul 146, 283, 300
Stoffreagen, Dr. 24
Stooshnof, Christine 153
Stooshnof, Paul 153
Streisand, Barbra 213
Suskind, Jean 68, 70
Sutherland, Joan 106, 107, 285, 286, 289, 290, 291, 296, 297, 300
Swenson, Inga 66
Swope, Herbert Bayard 216

T

Taittinger, Baroness 104
Takaezu, Toshiko 332
Taylor, Allegra Kent 134, 156, 165, 186, 207, 213, 223, 235, 236, 238, 293
Taylor, Bertrand, III "Bert" 240, 284
Taylor, Elizabeth x, 40, 106, 107, 113, 261, 316, 327
Taylor, Lisa 239, 268, 283, 284
Taylor, Lisa and Bert 265
Taylor, Nancy Thomson 246

Tebaldi, Renata 213
Temple, Shirley 1
Ter-Arutunian, Rouben 170
Thomson, Virgil 268
Tobin, Robert Lynn Batts 268
Toklas, Alice B. 42, 214
Toscanini, Arturo 16
Toulouse-Lautrec 43
Tourel, Jennie 59, 68, 69
Trapp, Maria von 119
Trash, Glorietta 175
Treaster, Byron 328
Troyanos, Tatiana 187
Truman, Bess Wallace 97, 99, 100, 102
  brother 97
Truman, Harry S 99, 100, 102, 103
Trumans, the 99
Tschelitchew, Pavel 148
Turkkan, Zeynep 243
Tyng, Lila Hotz Luce 257, 258, 261, 264, 277, 278, 284, 291, 294, 296, 302, 303, 304, 305, 306, 311, 312, 318, 332, 333, 334, 335, 336, 337, 339
Tysik, Sylvia 60, 85, 186
  See also van der Stegen

U

Ulfung, Ragnar 253
Uncle Monkey (a.k.a. Osborne Maitland Miller) 213, 219, 220, 222, 223, 234, 242, 244, 255, 279

V

Valentino, Rudolph 239
Valli 44
Valli, Ramolo 164
van der Stegen, Hughes 186
van der Stegen, Serge 186
van der Stegen, Sylvia 338
  See also Tysik, Sylvia
van Fleet, Jo 44
van Rensselaer, Charles 143

ABOUT THE AUTHOR

R. Eric Gustafson has worn various hats in the arts for more than four decades. A graduate of Stuyvesant High School in lower Manhattan, he went on to Queens College where he received his Bachelor of Arts degree in January 1957. After a tour of Europe, he was one of ten students accepted in the graduate program of theater arts at Carnegie Institute (now Carnegie Mellon). His Master of Fine Arts thesis was on the Japanese medieval Noh drama (1959).

Many trips to Europe, north Africa, Central and South America have afforded him a networking of extraordinary people and an expanded view of the world.

Several years during the 1960s at prestigious Parke-Bernet auction house (now Sotheby's) and later under his directorship of art galleries in New York, Santa Fe, and at the Festival of Two Worlds in Spoleto, Italy, several opportunities to develop impressive innovations in the art world sparked his budding career.

Museum curatorship followed with exhibitions at the Cooper-Hewitt Museum (1978), Lincoln Center Library & Museum for the Performing Arts (1980) and others.

Author of *The Court Theaters of Europe* (1982), he has lectured internationally on the subject. For the

Eric Gustafson at the film festival in Deauville.

past five years, his column, "Classical Notes," has appeared in Gannett's *Courier-News*.

His brainchild, Apollo Muses, was created fifteen years ago by Gustafson as a means of providing showcases for young professional talents in the fine and performing arts. In addition, seasoned artists of note have been invited to participate in the conversation among the arts, usually on Sunday afternoons at exceptional sites in June or July.

When not travelling or creating beautiful environments, the author has appeared on stage, television and cinema in cameo performances. He resides in New Jersey and Florida.